MW00987821

Saints vs. Scoundrels

Benjamin Wiker

SAINTS

vs.

SCOUNDRELS

Debating Life's Greatest Questions

EWTN PUBLISHING, INC.
Irondale, Alabama

Copyright © 2017 by Benjamin Wiker

Printed in the United States of America.

All rights reserved.

Cover design by Coronation Media.

On the cover: Sir Thomas More (DR3JXR), GL Archive/Alamy Stock
Photo; Edith Stein (B3YNM1), INTERFOTO/Alamy Stock Photo; Friedrich
Nietzsche (H28HBE), GL Archive/Alamy Stock Photo; Henry VIII, by Hans
Holbein (D8TFRH), Glasshouse Images/Alamy Stock Photo.

No part of this book may be reproduced, stored in a retrieval system, or trans-
mitted in any form, or by any means, electronic, mechanical, photocopying, or
otherwise, without the prior written permission of the publisher, except by a
reviewer, who may quote brief passages in a review.

EWTN Publishing, Inc.
5817 Old Leeds Road, Irondale, AL 35210

Distributed by Sophia Institute Press, Box 5284, Manchester, NH 03108.

Library of Congress Cataloging-in-Publication Data
Names: Wiker, Benjamin, 1960- author.
Title: Saints vs. scoundrels : debating life's greatest questions / Benjamin
  Wiker.
Description: Irondale, Alabama : EWTN Publishing, Inc., 2017.
Identifiers: LCCN 2017045637 ISBN 9781682780282 (pbk. : alk. paper)
Subjects: LCSH: Christian saints. Authors. Life. Philosophy.
Classification: LCC BX4655.3 .W54 2017 DDC 128—dc23 LC record avail-
able at https://lccn.loc.gov/2017045637

First printing

To Mike Masny, *a producer and director of infinite patience and good cheer, and to all of the wonderful crew at EWTN who make the series happen. And a special thanks to Doug Keck for saying yes.*

Contents

St. Thomas More and Henry VIII

Edith Stein (St. Teresa Benedicta of the Cross) and Friedrich Nietzsche

Introduction

I don't expect you'll believe that people long dead have been visiting my house. You don't really need to believe it to read this book. Just pretend that it's a work of enlightening fiction, or a clever way to talk about the great questions, debates, and answers. Those things are the real focus anyway, I suppose.

I say that half-convinced, I admit. "Is there life after death?" "Do we have an immortal soul?" These are certainly two of the greatest questions—or really one question from two different angles. But if two men who died centuries ago—say, Jean-Jacques Rousseau and St. Augustine—were arguing about it in your living room and drinking your coffee, then the question itself is, in a strange but obvious way, answered. The dead speak, and even stranger, they both take cream in their coffee.

That's the way it is with a lot of the great questions we wrestle with, isn't it? A single, significant experience would settle the issue, and there would be no need for further debate. "Does a human being have an immortal soul?" is no longer a question if you're visited by the dead, in the same way that "Will my lonely cousin ever get married?" is resolved by his showing up for lunch with his new bride.

If all our great questions were settled with experiential evidence, we wouldn't have our great debates, would we? Imagine that. No sooner does someone ask, "Is there a God?" and then, poof, the answer Himself shows up. "Here I am!" End of debate.

But that's not how things work, and—so I'm not misleading the reader—it wasn't that way with what I experienced, and continue to experience. I'm not visited by ghosts. Ghosts don't drink coffee. They don't try to shoot each other. They don't ask for more sandwiches. And, one thinks, since ghosts are traditionally understood to be disembodied spirits—that is, immaterial souls—they wouldn't argue about whether human beings had immaterial souls.

So, this isn't a ghost story—or stories. I need to be clear about that. These men and women don't know they're dead. They show up in pairs, acting and arguing just as they did when they were alive, except that they're in my living room, or office, I guess you should call it, since that's where all my books are and where I do all my best thinking and writing. All this happens, that is, when I am reading their books, or sometimes just after.

Forgive me, I'm starting in the middle of things. I should make clear that I am a college professor, and that's why I read books that contain the greatest debates about the most important questions. Or perhaps the better way to say it is that I love to read the greatest books written by the greatest thinkers, and that is why I became a college professor. I would do it even if no one paid me, though much less than I'd like.

This isn't some kind of hobby. How we answer the great questions determines how we live and what we consider good or evil, just or unjust. History is made, for good or ill, by the answers we give to life's greatest questions: What is a human being? Do we have an immortal soul, or are we merely a body? Does God exist? What is justice? Is the universe the result of a divine creator's wise ordering, or is it all produced by mere chance? It was through sorting out these great debates that I became a *Catholic* college professor. Reason led to faith.

Introduction

We tend to think that we are each giving our own answers to these great questions. If we study history, however, we find out that almost all of us are the disciples of this or that thinker, whose arguments were immensely influential, and so were passed down to us, sometimes directly through education, sometimes indirectly through culture. But as I've found through years of study, we generally have little idea of the real depth of the possible answers to the great questions. To discover that depth, we need to return to those few thinkers who have plumbed it — who have really thought about it, long and hard.

The obvious problem is that they are all dead. Actually, there are two problems: They are all dead, and the greatest minds do not agree on the answers to the greatest questions.

So, since we cannot raise the dead, so to speak, we are left with one option, and that is to read the greatest books and to try to sort out the most profound answers to the most profound questions written by the most profound thinkers.

And so I read their books; I read about their lives; I imagine what it would be like if I could bring them before me and hear what they had to say — not just what each has to say for himself, but what each would say if suddenly confronted by an equally profound opposite. What would the great St. Francis say to the great teacher of evil Machiavelli, if they could meet? In life, this wasn't possible. St. Francis was long dead by the time Machiavelli arrived on the scene in Italy. And the great atheist Machiavelli so despised Franciscans — because he despised Christianity — that I'm not sure he would have deigned to talk to the saint if they had been contemporaries.

I was, in fact, reading about them both and thinking, "How *would* it have changed Machiavelli *if* he could have experienced a meeting with St. Francis, a man who was a walking icon of Christ crucified?" (If you are not aware of this wonderful fact, St. Francis had the stigmata—the wounds of Christ—so that his hands and feet were continually bleeding.)

So, I was pondering all this, and then it happened. They both actually showed up—St. Francis first, then Machiavelli banging on my door a bit after. I'll tell you what happened later on, but the point here is that neither was a ghost, but a visitor stepping out of his life and into mine—not into my feverish mind or into my dreams or into my imagination, but into my home. I have proof —Machiavelli spit his cola all over my bookshelf and soiled my paperback copy of Plato's *Republic*. Stinker.

I use this pair as an example; they weren't the first. That point is, that's the way it is with each pair—each Saint and Scoundrel, as I call them, squaring off about how to answer the greatest questions. But I repeat: You don't have to believe it happens that way. Feel free to think it's just a clever literary device or something like that. It's all the same to me, as long as you take *what* they all had to say with the utmost seriousness.

You may have some questions about this very odd situation, and so I'll answer some of the most obvious ones now, before we begin.

First, my guests do experience a kind of shock at suddenly being in a house with electric lights and so on. Modern technology amazes them, so I'm not including that aspect of every encounter, because it's pretty repetitious. They all turn the lights on and off, like little children discovering a new toy. But then they get down to greater things. I avoid distracting them with other devices, unless it proves helpful (such as a telescope for Henry VIII and St. Thomas More).

Second, they're all able to speak with me and with each other, and yes, it's in English. I don't know how this occurs. And for some even more mysterious reason, they don't express any surprise at it, as if the barrier to communication presented by languages were a thin veneer that could be easily cast away.

Introduction

This makes no sense to me, and I will not tire the reader with conjectures. All I can say is that the more I thought about it, the more miraculous it was to me that language works at all—that we human beings have immensely complex thoughts we can communicate by moving our lips and tongues as we push air from our lungs, or by the use of strange symbols (such as these) written on wood pulp or with pixels on a screen. Solve *that* mystery, and the other one seems, by comparison, a rather small thing.

Third, I do seem to have some control over who shows up, or at least I have learned to exercise a bit of control by what I read. No, that's not quite it. It's more like this: I feel as if I *should* read particular books, *should* connect a particular pair—not some kind of exterior compulsion, but a feeling of "herein lies treasure!" Something like that. Then, of course, I read their books *and* I read about their lives, since there is always a connection between the kinds of answers they give to the greatest questions, and the way that they lived. To be all too quick about it, bad ideas produce bad lives, almost invariably.

Finally, as I said above, they aren't dead. They don't show up, like Jacob Marley, knowing what's on the other side. They show up as if they walked from the middle of their lives into the middle of mine. Sometimes the effect one has on the other is dramatic, even life changing, it would seem. But then I know, because the past is past, that all the effects of their *not* changing have already played out. I was there when Flannery O'Connor pulled a pistol on Ayn Rand (for her own good, mind you). I can't imagine the experience wasn't life changing for Rand. It certainly seemed so at the time. But I also know that Rand died an unrepentant, self-centered, miserable wretch.

How can this be? I'm not hallucinating. I have these various visitations on film (and you can see them on EWTN). I did miss a few at the beginning because I stupidly didn't think of the obvious:

If you have dead people show up who aren't ghosts, it might be a good idea to record the events, if only to verify your sanity.

I am sane, mind you, at least as sane as many scientists. Physicists today tell us all kinds of amazing fables about the universe, such as the idea that all the possible choices of all the possible people are played out in an infinite number of possible but radically different universes, all running parallel. So, I guess these physicists would say that all I was experiencing was an irruption from one or two parallel universes into the one I happen to inhabit, and that in some other universe it's possible for, say, Ayn Rand to have a soul-crashing experience that turns her life in an entirely new direction, a direction she didn't take in our universe.

I don't say that because I believe all these conjectures by people who call themselves scientists, but only to show that physicists nowadays will believe *anything,* so science can't really say that what happened to me isn't possible.

But rather than get into spats with physicists, I prefer to tell it as it was and let the mystery remain mysterious, rather than suffer it to be smothered by an explanation that's more unlikely than the event it's trying to explain.

What I can tell you from my experiences is this: What we believe, how we live, and the effects we have on how other people think and live is immeasurably great, for better or for worse. Lives are salvaged and lives are destroyed. We know from history the enormous effects that people such as St. Francis have had for good and people such as Machiavelli have had for evil. The great debates are deadly serious because different answers given by the different towering figures form later generations for good or ill. If the scoundrels could have met saints, their lives and the lives of countless others they've influenced might have been radically different.

That lesson applies to each of us, all of us, whether we are famous or not. The little things in unknown lives can change history, for better or for worse. I don't imagine Isaac Rousseau knew he was shaking the earth when he decided to hunt on someone else's property on a particular eighteenth-century day. He couldn't have known that he'd be caught, then *choose* to flee from the law, and then abandon his ten-year-old son. In many ways, the monstrous beliefs and dissolute life of his son, Jean-Jacques, are the unhappy result of this series of choices (as we shall soon see).

Think on this, often, as you read what follows. It matters greatly what we think and do. Whatever the ultimate explanation for the strange goings-on in my house, that lesson is the real core of what I'd like to share with readers of these accounts.

Saints vs. Scoundrels

St. Augustine and Jean-Jacques Rousseau

Part 1

One of the strangest things in actually meeting people you've read about — especially if they lived long before the age of photography — is that they don't look as you've been picturing them for so long. It's very disorienting.

I think I'm fairly normal in that when I'm reading about someone — say, a character in a book of fiction or a real-life person such as St. Augustine who lived before photography and escaped the portrait painters of his time — I have to imagine that person in a certain way. I can't just read about a disembodied spirit or a generalized human being. So, as I read, the image or picture I've decided on becomes, in my mind, the actual person.

I'm not the only person who supplies such imaginary portraits. Do an Internet search for images of St. Augustine, and you'll get all kinds of austere, bearded white men, many of whom are decked out in elaborate clerical regalia. I remember a good-intentioned prayer card in which St. Augustine was pictured as a delicate European, a luxuriously adorned bishop with rings on his silken-gloved fingers!

Now I didn't think any of those were accurate. Moreover, I did know that St. Augustine was born in Northern Africa — Thagaste, to be precise, which is now Souk Ahras in northeast Algeria, near the coast of the Mediterranean Sea. But knowing that fact in an abstract way is different from *seeing* the great saint in person, and he was nothing like what I'd imagined. The good saint was a moderately sized man of dark complexion, with a somewhat pockmarked face, a dirty-gray beard, and wavy-kinky black and gray hair, dressed not in ecclesiastical finery but in a rough, worn black robe. As for his face, we imagine famous but never-seen people as somehow not having particular features, and especially defects, as if they were living models of ancient Greek statues. But St. Augustine had a real face, and you can't have a real face without its peculiarities, good and bad. His face was pretty wrinkled from being in the sun, I guess, or from being scoured by wind-blown sand. His brown eyes were a bit droopy and bloodshot but, as I said, cheerful and serene. (The eyes are, as they say, the windows of the soul.) Needless to say, there were no rings on his fingers, but there was a bit of dirt under his fingernails. He's quite an amusing man, too — or better, serenely cheerful.

All this was very startling to me. I had been reading St. Augustine, off and on, since graduate school over thirty years ago, and I've regularly assigned his *Confessions* to my students over the years. I had a pretty good embedded idea of what he *should* look like, given how I had imagined him. So, it took me a while to get used to him, but soon enough, having met the real man, I couldn't imagine him otherwise.

The same was true for Jean-Jacques Rousseau. Of course, we do have paintings of him, so it wasn't a complete shock. You can look them up, and you'll see the same boyish face, brown eyes, and brown hair (unless he's wearing a wig). But still, a painting is not a person. Plus, paintings don't smell, and I'm somewhat embarrassed to say that Rousseau was a bit, shall we say, sniffy. There was some weird idea in France at the time that bathing was unhealthy. The eighteenth was a very malodorous century, at least in Paris.

To be clear, Rousseau was not born in France, but in Geneva in 1712, the son of Isaac and Suzanne Rousseau. He did not start out well. Three days after his baptism his mother died, and Jean-Jacques never got over the guilt of feeling that, somehow, he had killed her. This awful guilt was made worse by his father's frequent tearful laments over his deceased wife, and the fact that Jean-Jacques looked a good bit like her (a fact that the father pointed out to the son on too many occasions). Isaac was no prize. He abandoned Jean-Jacques when he was just a very young boy, as I mentioned earlier.

But we'll pick up that thread later. It's best to get on to the meeting. St. Augustine showed up first, in the morning—what was it, a Thursday, I think? Again, I was quite surprised to find out what he looked like, and even more by how gracious he was. That's the only word I can think to use. He was both graceful in his manner and also filled with grace, filled with a deep peace, a reservoir of experience of suffering and great joy, all distilled by divine wisdom.

Rousseau showed up much later on, near dusk. (At the time, St. Augustine was resting in my spare room, or more likely reading, since I had given him a copy of Rousseau's *Confessions*.) Some people knock on the door. Some people just appear in the room. Rousseau was one of the latter. He showed up wearing a nondescript light-brown coat over his white ruffled shirt. He had the typical pants of the eighteenth century, with the cuffs hitting just below the knee so a man could show off his calf muscles to admiring ladies! He wasn't wearing a wig.

I had bought the best coffee I could get, since I knew Rousseau was so fond of the revolutionary beverage. Coffee houses were all the thing in eighteenth-century Enlightenment France, the place where radicals quaffed and plotted. St. Augustine, of course, had never heard of coffee, but he was amazed at its enlivening properties.

After some formalities, I ushered the Frenchman into a chair by my chess table, and we sat down. He loves chess, as I found out with a little research, so I was glad to have it all set up for him.

"I have been reading your *Confessions*, Mr. Rousseau. Quite . . ." I searched for the right word, ". . . revealing."

He smiled a bit, "As they were meant to be, yes, as they were meant to be. I was pushed by some of my friends to write a memoir of my life," he explained, as he picked up the black king on his side of the board and looked at it carefully. "I accepted the challenge! Whatever may be said of my life, in writing it all down, I resolved to make it a unique work, to be *entirely* truthful, leaving nothing hidden or in the shadows. That way, at least *one* man could be seen as he is on the inside. I call it my 'confessions' because I confess everything, so that readers may know me as I truly am, not as others would imagine me to be."

"I certainly felt as if nothing was hidden," I said, with a bit of a blush, "as if I were a priest hearing your confession, and a rather long one at that."

"I was not confessing my sins, but confessing who I, Jean-Jacques Rousseau, am," he said, putting the king carefully back on the table. "Do you play?"

"If what I've heard about your skill as a chess player is true, then, yes, I play, but I don't stand much of a chance." He liked that little tip of the hat. He clearly was not immune from flattery.

As if reading the line of my thinking, he said, somewhat impishly, "You must know that it is part of my character that once I am introduced to something new, if it sparks my interest, I throw myself into it entirely, body and soul. A real scoundrel, a parasite of a man, Gabriel Bagueret, taught chess to me, and I can tell you, it was the only good thing he had ever done! But I was seized by a passion for the game, and studied and played it night and day, to the point of madness and exhaustion. But I mastered it." He leaned toward me and said in a smiling whisper, "I used to destroy the great Denis Diderot at every opportunity!" He sat back in his chair looking quite self-satisfied. "Well, then, shall we?" he asked, waving his hand toward the chessboard. "I give you the first move!"

I'm not a good chess player; in that, I wasn't lying. For me, it's just a game, so I can't get very serious about it. I moved out one of my knights just to make him think I might have some deeply clever plan.

"To get back to your *Confessions*, it's no secret, is it, that you wrote your book as a kind of answer to St. Augustine's *Confessions*?"

"An 'antidote' might be a better word," he replied, moving his queen's pawn out two spaces. "I assume that we want to be as honest with each other as I am about myself in my book."

"Then let's make honesty our policy, shall we? To get to the point, you believe that Christianity was, and is, a dreadful mistake, and that it should be replaced by *your* philosophy. And your philosophy, so you tell us, isn't really something new, but a kind of return to the truths of the pre-Christian pagan world, a world free of Christian faith." I moved one of my rook's pawns out two spaces—an entirely arbitrary move on my part.

He looked at me a bit quizzically, even less sure of what my strategy might be.

"We are confessing two things, then, are we not, Augustine and I? He believed in the Christian God who judges sins, and so he spends his account of his life confessing his sins. But I ..."

"But *you* inform the reader, or perhaps challenge him, at the very beginning of your *Confessions*—how did you say it? 'Let anyone dare say, after reading my confessions, that I was better than that man.' But then you go on to confess—and forgive me, I assume we are going to be frank—that you had *multiple* affairs with *many* women, some of whom were married, and engaged in a number of other private sexual sins I'd rather not repeat. Living for years with a woman whom you refused to marry, lying, stealing, and so on. What is obvious, to anyone who has also read St.

Augustine, is that many of these are the very same things that St. Augustine confessed in his *Confessions*. The difference—and it is a great one, the greatest—is that *you* don't confess them as sins at all! That's a bit hard to understand, given that you claim, at the beginning, that no one should dare to say that he was a better man than you!"

Rather than taking offense, Rousseau seemed quite pleased. "And that claim is true, very true, precisely because I was—I am —brave enough to proclaim the truth about my life, of human life, as it really is, *with the confusions of Christianity removed*. Especially the confusion that there is such a thing as sin, that we are marked by some awful taint deep in our nature that works evil in us, a thing called 'original sin,' that we inherit just by being born a man. This is St. Augustine's great contribution, no? I reject the Christian condemnation of my innocent nature. That is why I thought that we needed another *Confessions*."

"Well, then, what are you confessing in yours, if it isn't your sins?"

"I am confessing what I saw, deep down, when I looked past the veneer of Christianity that hides us from our true selves. I saw man as he is by seeing man as he was, with no religious creeds spoiling his view. I saw man in his original condition, his natural condition—simple, free, with no artificial yokes burdening his shoulders and weighing him down. There, in that vision, I beheld his true natural heart, the heart nature has given him, an innocent heart, one meant for the simplest pleasures nature had to offer. I see no sin in that original condition. And that condition is where we find our happiness, our lost happiness, our natural happiness. That is where our heart was truly fulfilled—our restless heart, if I may borrow from your Augustine! That is what our restless heart truly longs for, that state of natural animal innocence. Not for God, but for the natural and pure condition that prevailed before all of

the artificialities of so-called civilization developed, including the
artificiality of religion."

"Your 'state of nature,' as you call it, is a kind of Eden that
existed before human beings developed their reason, developed
culture, the arts, language, morality—and religion, as you've just
emphasized?"

"Yes, you have read my works, I see." He settled back in his
chair, rather smugly awaiting my admiration. "'Developed' is not
the right word. What you call 'development' is really a malforma-
tion, a fall from the original goodness of the state of nature."

"And to make sure I'm getting things straight, you believe that
this primitive creature, this entirely undeveloped animal, whose
only cares are simple ones—some leaves to sleep on when he tires,
some roots or nuts to eat when he gets hungry, a woman who happens by when another desire strikes him—he's the real Adam."

"Yes, he is the real Adam, the only Adam," he agreed. "And
that is the real Eden. That was man's true, unspoiled beginning,
and hence his lost happiness, free of all the burdens and artificial
cares of society. Unspoiled man in unspoiled nature!" He sighed.
"There, and only there, can his heart be happy. I looked into the
depths of history, into the original depths of man, and that is what
I saw. Our lost happiness."

Rousseau looked down at his folded hands and thoughtfully
rubbed his thumbs together. "And then I looked at the heart that
had replaced this happy heart, and I saw a heart twisted, torn,
and tortured by artificial chains, ridiculous desires, and misplaced
guilt, all of which came from the 'developments' of society, as you
call them. As man advances, as he becomes more civilized, as the
chains of society ever more tightly bind him, he thereby becomes
both more unnatural and so, more miserable."

I let him stay lost in thought for a half minute. He shook his
head a bit, sat up, and said, "But we are forgetting our game!"

SAINTS VS. SCOUNDRELS

We had each made several moves during our conversation. It was clear to him by now that I was, in fact, a poor chess player, to which the lineup of my captured white figures attested.

"You are not much for strategy, if I might not be considered rude in saying," Rousseau said, lifting one eyebrow at me.

"I confessed my lack of skill quite honestly!"

Actually, playing chess badly was part of my strategy. I thought it would deflect him from noticing that I was playing a different game, with a different strategy, one focused on getting to the real root of Rousseau.

"You are like St. Augustine in this: You confess to having great love, in fact, a great many loves. Refresh my mind, would you? My copy of your *Confessions* is, uh, elsewhere at the moment. I can't quite keep track of the women. You're quite an amorous man, skipping from one romance to another, like a bee from flower to flower."

Rousseau laughed. "You are seeing the real man now," he said, tapping his chest with his fist. "The least little pleasure that offers itself at my door, my friend, I cannot resist it. It tempts me more than the joys of Paradise!" He gave a knowing smirk. "But I am making light of a serious thing," he continued, "a very serious thing. I was meant for love." He looked off wistfully. "I have a heart made for love, quite literally, to be devoured by love." His eyes widened with passion, but then he slouched back in resignation. "And yet, I was destined never to find an object, a proper object, for this great heart of mine."

"Not for want of looking," I replied. "There was, of course, Madame de Warens. You called her Mamma, perhaps because she was some twelve years older than you. A rich Catholic woman who protected you and acted as your patroness. But you ended up her lover."

He smiled, as he recalled her. "She was the great love of my life!"

12

"And there was Madame Basile …"

"Ah yes, never has love been so pure or passions so lively as mine were then! Was I yet even sixteen? It has been so long! I was in Turin, that I know, wandering as I did in my young life — as I have all my life. She took me in, the pretty little wife of a shop-keeper. Her husband was away at the time. I followed her everywhere. Devoured her with my eyes. And then one day in the back room of the shop, I grasped her hand with all of my passion, my love, and kissed it twice. I felt her hand press upon my lips, a sign of similar devotion."

"Dabbling in adultery?"

"I only kissed her hand! And anyway, her husband came back and found out about young Jean-Jacques, found me there in his home, and showed me the door. That was the end of the romance. He chased me with a stick when I showed up again!"

"Madame de Larnage — what about her? Again, a woman quite a bit older than you were. She was your seducer, was she not?"

"Ah, Madame de Larnage! If I live a hundred years, I will never forget that pleasure, her charm, those few days when I threw off all feelings of guilt, of social disapprobation, of prying eyes, and gave myself to those most natural of passions!"

"And Madame Dupin — she spurned your advances, didn't she?"

"I must admit, that one did not go very well. I was filled with love, as is my wont, love that I dared not speak. I wrote her a letter instead, unburdening my swollen heart. But my letter was received coldly and without comment. I was crushed."

"The two prostitutes, La Padoana and Zulietta?"

He blushed, and murmured something inaudible.

"Let's skip those and go to Anzoletta," I said. "If I remember from your *Confessions*, she was a little girl in Venice, of eleven or twelve years old. You and a friend got together and *bought* her from her 'worthless mother,' as you call her. You *purchased* her for your future sexual pleasure, in exchange for raising her. Did you really do that?" As he read from my face, I could not withhold my contempt.

"But here you are misjudging me!" he protested. "This was a very common arrangement in Venice. But even more to my credit —along with Carrio, with whom I bought her—soon enough we became attached to her, and I could no longer conceive of doing such a deed. It would be incest—or so it felt to me! We let her out of the bargain we had made."

Rousseau uttered the last sentence as if he had done something noble, as if this were a sign of his great heart. Needless to say, I was unmoved by his magnanimity. I wanted to say something about millstones as an appropriate necklace, but withheld any comment, as I wanted to press further into his philosophy.

Icily, I continued, "Let's go on to Thérèse Levasseur."

"Yes, yes, my sweet, my darling. I lived with my Thérèse as pleasantly as with the very finest genius in the universe."

"You mean that as a compliment, I take it, because of her low social station. She was a laundress you met in a place you were lodging, an unmarried woman of twenty-two, and she stayed that way afterward, unmarried."

"But I did marry her!" he protested.

"Yes, after twenty-five years of enjoying her company, an arrangement that allowed you to throw yourself at other women, married women, such as Madame d'Houdetot. You recall her, no doubt."

"Ah, yes, Madame d'Houdetot! It was love this time, love in all its energy, with all the fury of its passion. But her husband did not mind! She had an arrangement with him, as he did with many others. He could enjoy the fruits of trees in other orchards, as could she—although he would have considered me below someone worthy of making his wife a mistress. But I never consummated this greatest of passions, even though I—"

"Please, I've read all about it! But you were living with your darling Thérèse at the time. Did you really *use* her to run your love letters to Madame d'Houdetot? Didn't that seem a bit cruel?"

"Well, I . . . let us say that Thérèse soon tired of the arrangement."

I chose not to press Rousseau on his treatment of Thérèse, a woman of whom he took every advantage, treating her with the contempt of a female servant kept for sexual convenience as well as the usual services of a maid. At the same time, in some respects, he treated her as someone *just shy* of being a wife.

"You had five children with her, Thérèse?" I asked. "She was the mother of your children—the children you abandoned, every one of them. How did Thérèse feel about *that* arrangement?"

"I did not abandon them!" shouted Rousseau, standing up, obviously flustered. "I placed them in a foundling hospital for their own good! It was best for them."

"For them. Or for you?"

I could see his jaw set, and he walked away from the chess table and toward the second-story window looking out on my garden.

"Enough! Do you think Jean-Jacques has a heart of stone? I freely confessed in my *Confessions* that my heart was indeed hardened, but it was a kind heart nonetheless. If I happened to be some kind of low-born man, a scoundrel, a man deaf to nature's gentle, pleading voice, a man devoid of feelings of justice and profound humanity, then my hard heart would need no explanation. But I am not such a man. My true heart is warm, not cold, marked by a very lively sensitivity, a heart made to form deep attachments that can be broken only with the greatest, wrenching pain."

He turned halfway toward me, so he could just catch my eye, as he continued numbering his admirable traits. "I have an inborn goodwill toward my fellow man, a burning love of what is great, what is beautiful, and what is just. And, my friend, I recoil at evil; I cannot hate or harm. All that is virtuous, all that is generous and truly lovable summons the sweetest emotion in my breast. All that is suffering and frail, the greatest pity."

Rousseau turned around fully, facing me now that he had revealed what he believed was his true and natural heart, the one somehow hardened when faced with the difficulties and inconveniences of fatherhood. I must admit, I was both moved by his rhetoric yet uneasy at the odor of self-justification.

I think he caught a whiff of the same odor, since he then said, "How can all this—which is truly in my heart—how can it be reconciled in the very same soul with the depravity that caused what should be the sweetest of duties to be trampled underfoot with no scruples? I say to you, to everyone who may care to hear, this is not possible! To be a father stripped of the sweet emotions of fatherhood. How could Jean-Jacques not feel something? I may have *deceived myself*; I may have talked myself into what my heart could not allow, but *that heart was not hardened*."

I hardly knew what to say to this roundabout confession. What was it a confession of—guilt or innocence? I'm not sure Rousseau himself knew. He seemed to be dipping into an admission of guilt as a way to show me he was to be pitied, even admired for his honesty, rather than scorned for his immorality.

"I had reasons at the time for giving up my children, reasons that were able to seduce me, and would surely seduce others as well. Jean-Jacques is not alone in this. I could not take care of them with my irregular life and income, so I told myself. They would only end up as vagabonds or thieves. In the foundling home, they would receive an education that would prepare them to become good, solid citizens. That's what I told myself, what I spoke to my heart."

He walked back toward his chair and leaned on it, looking down. Then he said more softly, "But more than once, many times, since then, I have felt keen regrets in my heart, teaching me that I have only deceived myself."

Then, perhaps a little too quickly, he adopted a satisfied air as he straightened up. "Yet, I also thank Heaven, again and again, that they were thereby put in a better situation than they would have been if I had tried to raise them. The arrangement with the foundling hospital appeared good to me because I did not see any evil in it. Putting all in the balance, I did what was best for my children. Indeed, I would have wished, indeed still wish, that I myself could have been brought up, nurtured, and cared for as my children have been."

After all the rhetorical posturing, some of which had momentarily taken me in, this last bit fell like a brick. I knew he was trying to elicit sympathy from me, and make it seem as if, on the whole, he had done the right thing. I also knew of the scars he must carry because his mother had died a few days after his birth and his father had abandoned him without any regrets at a very early age. But to use any of this as an excuse for abandoning his own children—which, as he admits in his *Confessions*, really did break Thérèse's heart as he coldly demanded she give them up, one after the other—well, I didn't know what to say.

So I said what rushed into my mind. "Cared for as your children have been? Surely you know, surely you were aware, that most of the children deposited at the Hôpital des Enfants-Trouvés died! Somewhere around 70 percent of them. You were giving them up to almost certain death! Abandoning them as the pagan Romans used to abandon their children, exposing them on the hillsides for the wild beasts to devour! How are you any better than they were?"

I got up from the chess table, obviously upset at his attempt to manipulate me, or himself, or both of us. I had vowed to keep calm and dispassionate when talking with Rousseau. So much for that.

"Forgive me for being so blunt, Monsieur Rousseau," I said quite insincerely, meaning instead something like, "Perhaps I might knock some moral sense into you with a righteous cudgel." The latter didn't seem to be a good way to keep the conversation going, however, and only revealed one of my own moral soft spots—a quick temper.

"Forgive me for being so blunt," I repeated, trying to cool myself down, "but this all seems like an elaborate exercise in self-justification, both a confession and an all-too-easy absolution."

"I am confessing my true self, my innate goodness, my love of humanity, my love of justice, but also my faults."

"But how are the two sides connected—goodness and love on the one side and faults on the other?" I asked as I walked toward my disheveled desk. "St. Augustine would say that your love was disordered by sin, and with sin comes weakness of will, and with weakness of the will comes the desire to deceive ourselves, to justify our actions, to excuse ourselves when we should be condemning ourselves. But you still are not confessing guilt, even while you're confessing faults—*sins*, I would call them. Tell me how that fits together."

Rather than looking dismayed, he smiled. "Let me tell you, for that will bring us to the heart of my philosophy, wherein I uncover the real and original nature of man—that is what you were asking me to reveal earlier, was it not?"

"Please, in your own words. You have the stage!" I sat down in my chair, ready to hear him display his wisdom.

"The notion of sin that Christianity gives us, as I noted before, obscures rather than illuminates our true nature," he said, warming to the task. "We must go back to the beginning, the real beginning, the state of nature. There, there is the real revelation, not in the Bible. And what do we see there, at our origin? When I look at man in his natural condition, his original condition, I do not see the Garden of Eden, but a great primeval forest. And there among the leaves, I see an animal," he said, dramatically pushing away imaginative branches to reveal the "manimal" of his vision.

"That animal is not as strong as others, certainly less agile, but looked at on the whole, most advantageously organized."

He continued the pantomime, pointing to several spots around the room. "There, I see him satisfying his hunger under an ancient oak, eating acorns that have fallen in abundance. There, I see him quenching his thirst at the first stream, crystal pure. And there, he finds a ready bed of leaves, under the very same oak that filled him with a meal. All his needs are met, with no labor, no language, no laws, no rules, and no social entanglements. That man is truly happy, and good, and innocent, and free. That is our true, original happiness. There is no sin in that blessed natural condition, and no God who condemns."

"What of the family? I assume that this 'manimal' doesn't just pop into existence."

"As you see, in this original condition, man's first care is his self-preservation, but he desires very little, since his desires have not been inflamed by the luxuries of so-called civilization. He does not farm, because the oak provides his meals. He has no property, so he has nothing to steal. He does not worry himself about a house, because the leaves overhead are his roof. All his desires are met by nature's outstretched hand."

The corner of his mouth drew up in a smile. "And there was another desire, one that arises to perpetuate the species, but this was a blind inclination, no different from hunger, an inclination entirely free from any sentiment of the heart. This inclination produced only an animal act when a woman happened to pass by. But once this need was satisfied, the two sexes dispersed. No longer even recognizing each other, they went off into the dense forest, going their separate ways. The child was born months later. There was no longer any connection in that animal mind to the original act of reproduction, or to the actor. There was no notion of romantic mine and thine, husband and wife. A female gave birth amidst the trees on a bed of leaves and nursed the child as a brute instinct, in great part just to relieve the pressure on her breasts. When the child no longer needed this nourishment—and do understand how much stronger and more independent such an animal would be, quite unlike our soft and dependent youths today—when that child could wander off, it did so, never to see again the woman from whose womb it arrived. Nor did she care, for there was no tie of sentiment to her offspring."

"Not very … romantic, was it?" I chided him.

"No," he smiled again. "Males and females united fortuitously; by mere chance an occasion arose and a fleeting desire with it, and then," he paused for effect, "they left each other with the same ease. There was no swooning with love, no poetry, no jealousy, no self-conscious hesitation. Any woman who happens by is good for him, and she wanders off afterward, leaving him with no regrets."

I looked him hard in the eye. "This all seems rather familiar, Jean-Jacques. This 'manimal' appears to be a lot like you, flitting from one woman to another, abandoning your children with the same ease as the satisfied male dreamily walking back into the forest after an encounter. That makes me rather suspicious of your philosophy. I think that, in all this 'romancing,' you believed that you were acting with a kind of natural innocence. Doing what was condemned by society, condemned by Christianity, you'd like to believe your own philosophy because it gets you off the hook morally. Your own philosophy all too conveniently makes you innocent rather than evil, a saint rather than a scoundrel."

"You have it all upside down, my friend! Morality is a product of society, of human beings who have come out of that blessed natural state I've described and bound themselves together with artificial chains. Society is the source of evil—not Jean-Jacques!"

"Really?"

"Yes! Think of this, my friend: Could there be jealousy—certainly a great evil that gnaws at the hearts of men and women, that brings one man to murder another in rage—if there were no marriage, if there were no notion of sexual ownership? The great evil of jealousy is not in our original condition! It is not natural. And adultery? How can there be adultery if there is no marriage? And there was no marriage in our natural state. Can there be the infamy of abandoning one's child, the very evil you charge me with, if, like other animals, human males simply mated and disappeared, leaving the female to deal with the offspring until it is strong enough to wander off on its own?"

He was now worked up into a real froth, pacing back and forth, and gesturing. "No, no, it is society—the so-called *development* away from this primitive condition—that brings us both what we call wickedness and real misery. Think of it, monsieur! In this natural condition, we ate the simplest foods. With society, we develop every kind of delicacy that not only makes us gluttons but destroys our natural bodily health! With society comes property—the notion that we own pieces of the earth and the fruit of that earth, and with that comes both oppression by the rich landowners and theft by the desperate poor deprived unnaturally of the natural plenty the earth provides."

Rousseau then rounded on me, as if I were sitting in the trial dock. "Tell me, if you can, if no one owned anything, could there be such a thing as theft? Thou shalt not commit adultery! Thou shalt not steal! What could these 'Thou shalt nots' mean to natural man? He owns nothing, not even a wife!"

I tried to insert myself in this rather one-sided conversation, but Rousseau was hurtling forward under his own philosophical momentum. "And think about this: Could there be the 'sin' of avarice if there was no money? The sin of envy, if all our wants were so simple as to be easily satisfied? Wrath, if there was only the experience of satisfaction, and no desire to go beyond that? Sloth a sin? But our entire life would be defined by leisure! The unceasing demand for toil only comes when we are not happy with the pure pleasures that nature provides us on her own. Lust! A sin! Lust is the result of the natural sexual desire remaining unsatisfied, but in the state of nature, the desire is immediately met with its consummation! Without toil! Without jealousy! Without the constricting and artificial bonds of marriage! Could there be the pride of the tyrant, if there were no cities to rule? Could there be wars, if there were no territories to defend or conquer, no riches to be gained?"

Again I tried to wedge in a few objections, but he was in a real lather. "No, monsieur, I think you will admit that all these 'vices' disappear when we go back to man in his original condition. Both the need for virtue and the reality of vice and wickedness arise only as human beings fall away from this original, simple, good, natural condition. *That* is where our true happiness was. *That* is what our hearts long for. *That* is why we are plagued with such restless hearts—not a desire for God. That is not what our hearts long for—as your St. Augustine maintains. Religion itself is, I tell you, one of the artificialities that develops along with society, one of the chains that binds us. Man in his original condition was blissfully free of any fear of death and, just as with any other animal, was free of any notion of an invisible deity brooding over him, meting out his punishments and rewards."

He paused, and I saw my opportunity to speak when behind me I heard St. Augustine call out, as he clapped his hands, "Splendid display! As good as any student in my rhetoric classes! Fine pausing for effect, nice arch of the eyebrows at just the right place, well-timed raspy whispering and triumphant bellowing as well! Yes, yes, very fine display."

He then stroked his chin and looked off toward the bookcase, "Whether it's true is another thing, of course, but please, Master

Rousseau—have I pronounced that correctly?" He looked back with a smile, "I was hoping you would teach me how to play this chess game. I've heard of your formidable powers!"

"Why, I would be delighted," replied Rousseau, quite open to flattery, and to the opportunity to give a good drubbing to the saint.

Part 2

This was an interesting move on St. Augustine's part, a kind of double flattery, applauding Rousseau's torrent of rhetoric and then asking the cad to teach him how to play chess. It wasn't clear to me whether Rousseau understood the double meaning of the accolades he was getting from Augustine. The saint was first of all a sinner himself, not quite as bad as Rousseau, but certainly bad enough. He didn't begin his life aiming for God, but for fame as a rhetorician.

In the ancient world, both Greece and Rome, learning the art of effective public speaking—the power of persuasion, the polished ability to lift up and carry the masses by one's eloquence—was one of the most esteemed vocations one could pursue. It brought success in the law courts and in political life, leading to both great honors and great riches. Some things, it seems, never change.

And Augustine did succeed, for he had a deep natural talent for words. After studying rhetoric under accomplished masters, he became a teacher of rhetoric himself, first at Thagaste and then at Carthage. He soon landed a much more prestigious professorship in Milan, a center of scholarship in the world of late antiquity.

But gradually, as God kept working on Augustine, the talented rhetorician began to realize that earthly fame and fortune were so much smoke that one tried to hoard only to have it escape, if not now then at death. He became ashamed at having used his gifts simply for getting whatever he or his clients desired. The art of rhetoric, as he used it, was about triumphing over his opponent with words. It aimed at victory, not at truth, and did so by cleverly manipulating the passions and prejudices of the listeners.

That's why he was applauding Rousseau for giving a good "performance." It was St. Augustine's way of saying, "Very clever, Jean-Jacques, a fine display of hot air and passion, but that doesn't tell us whether what you say is true, well said though it may be."

It's not just about deceiving others on the surface of things. Rhetoricians learn how people think, how their passions work, how ideas can be subtly implanted and uprooted—all so that they may more effectively play their listeners for their own purposes. But if they can do it to others, then they can do it to themselves, persuading themselves of just what they want to hear in the inner dialogue of the soul.

I'm sure Rousseau had given that last speech to himself on many occasions to calm his conscience about abandoning his children and to convince himself that he was a good man. In doing so, he was a willing victim of his own eloquence. St. Augustine had spent too much time as a professional rhetorician, and even more as a shepherd of souls, to be fooled. The saint's *Confessions* is, in great part, an account of how God, by the Word made flesh, interrupted the self-serving eloquence by which he tried to excuse his soul for its sins. The Truth is not fooled.

That's a painful lesson for all of us, isn't it? How sweetly and gently I speak to my own soul, lightly confessing faults that I've already "forgiven," overlooking other sins, excusing myself rather than letting God be the judge, altering the truth to fit my desires. We're all a bit like Rousseau here, except for this, of course: He set out an entire philosophy that excused his sins by *eliminating* both sin and the Judge, a system designed to eliminate his guilt, a world built around his malformed desires—and that philosophy has shaped a large part of the modern world.

As a result, we are in no small part Rousseau's children, not Augustine's. We've given up on God and embraced a universe in which we are, at bottom, just one more animal whose every passion, especially sexual passion, is natural and good. We shun fatherhood and motherhood for worldly success and frivolity, abandoning or aborting our children with the same callousness as Rousseau treated his. We've thereby destroyed marriage. Today, our males and females meet by happenstance, just as Rousseau's did in his primordial forest, yield to blind inclination freed from any sentiment of the heart, and, once the desires are satisfied, disperse, no longer even recognizing each other. But I suppose even this sounds old-fashioned these days. Rousseau would probably be accused of "heteronormativity" today, daring to describe his primitive sexual Eden only in terms of male and female!

But this is enough digression. I saw immediately that St. Augustine had something in mind, some clever scheme to get to the bottom of Rousseau's soul and to see if he could awaken it. So, he applauded his rhetorical skill even while calling into question his philosophical acumen, and also flattered Jean-Jacques's considerable pride in his mastery of chess. The two were related in one strategy, as I soon enough found out.

The interesting thing that happened, which I assume was not part of the plan, was that St. Augustine became genuinely and intensely fascinated by the game, falling into his own trap, we might say. Or at least that's how it seemed to me, since they played for hours and hours, from that afternoon until late at night, aided by the magic of coffee, a drink whose powers Augustine found much to his liking. I fell asleep in my chair, my blue comfy chair by the bookcase, sometime around ten. When I woke up near midnight, they were still at it, Augustine apparently getting better and better with each game, thereby spurring on Rousseau. They were becoming friends, something I hadn't anticipated, but I suspect the good bishop had.

I believe I failed to mention that St. Augustine was a bishop — to be exact, the bishop of Hippo Regius in Northern Africa, from 395 to 430. He died with his episcopal boots on, so to speak. In the year 430 Vandal Barbarians swept down upon the coast of Africa, sacking cities and despoiling churches. The Vandals besieged the city of Hippo, but Bishop Augustine would not attempt to escape. He knew that his place was to be by his flock. "Let no one dream of holding our ship so cheaply," he wrote, "that not just the sailors, but the captain himself, should desert her in time of peril."[1] And so he died as the Vandals overran Hippo.

This was the beginning of a great darkness that would descend upon Europe for centuries to come, until the mid-900s or so. The pagan Roman Empire fell into ruin from its own excesses, with waves of Germanic tribes breaking apart nearly all political and social order. The West looked doomed, but Christianity spread its light during these Dark Ages, and a significant part of that light was carried in the prolific writings of St. Augustine. There was a saying in the Middle Ages that went something like, "He who says he has read all of St. Augustine is a liar." And just so I won't be accused of any such fibbery, I've barely made a dent, relatively speaking.

Who knows how much of Augustine Rousseau had read, but he had certainly gotten to Augustine's *Confessions*, because it's very clear that his own *Confessions* was a refutation of the saint's. He was making a bold bid to replace the immense influence of St. Augustine, swapping a God-filled for God-less self-revelation.

---

[1] Peter Brown, *Augustine of Hippo* (Berkeley, CA: University of California Press, 1969), p. 425.

St. Augustine and Jean-Jacques Rousseau: Part 2

Well, there they both were, playing yet another game of chess, but Rousseau looked as if he was flagging. "Master Rousseau," I said, "it seems to me that you're about to slip under the table. How about a bit of rest? I have a spare bedroom, if you'd like. And you, St. Augustine?"

Rousseau stretched his legs straight out and shook his head a bit. "I believe you are right; a small nap might be just the thing to resharpen my mind." He stood up. "May I just rest in that chair over by the bookcase?"

"Please!" I motioned toward it. "Be my guest, if you prefer a chair to a bed; consider it yours for the taking." He settled in and was softly snoring almost immediately.

St. Augustine, on the other hand, was wide awake. "I do not sleep much," he explained. "My days are entirely taken up in the duties of a bishop. I have time to write only after the sun has set, and I have trained myself to take advantage of the only hours when I am not being pressed from all sides." Then he looked at his cup. "And then there is this … this … extraordinary drink."

"Coffee."

"Yes, coffee. Amazing properties of reviving the intellect! Almost too amazing," he added, thoughtfully. "I could too easily talk myself into falling under its spell!"

"Not going to take me up on the offer of a bed then?"

He laughed gently. "Yes, but I do not think I will need it until tomorrow night!"

"Well, I've had enough of a nap, so perhaps you won't mind having a little talk?"

"My pleasure," he replied, motioning toward the empty chair. "We can speak together, just loud enough for us to hear, but not loud enough to awaken Rousseau."

I settled in, struck by how strange it was that I, of all people, was about to speak to one of the greatest theologians of the Catholic

Church, a man whose writings did more to form the Roman Catholic Church's understanding of Christ and the world than any other mere mortal, aside from the Evangelists and St. Paul. What would it feel like to be that man? Did he know, toiling away night after night by a dim oil lantern, that the words flowing from his pen at such an astounding rate would transform a pagan empire into Christendom? This made me a tad nervous as it flashed through my mind.

"So, St. Augustine, I must say what an honor this is ..."

"Saint! Saint! Why do you keep calling me a saint!" He leaned toward me, pretending to be offended, a very thin disguise given the smile lines around his eyes. "I thought you were supposed to have read my *Confessions*! I'd rather be called Sinner Augustine. Now there's a worthy title!"

"Yes, I mean, I'm just used to using it before your name, sort of like 'Mister.' Plus, I know you through all your writings. Not all of them, of course, but most of them, or many of them ..." I was becoming an even more self-conscious, tongue-tied bungler.

"You should call me Bishop Augustine, eh?" he cheerfully interrupted. "That is the duty that defines my life, how I have served God for so many, many years."

His eyes were elsewhere for a moment, his mind presumably glancing over his decades as pastor of Hippo, but he came back just as quickly. "You think with all these writings of mine that I am just sitting around all the time, scratching my beard and scratching down books, but I'm not. I tend my flock. Births, deaths, baptisms, marriages, breaking up fights, mending family feuds."

He shook his head, as he settled back into his chair. "As bishop I am also a judge. People expect me to settle everything, so every morning I wake up to a long line of quarreling people outside my door, and I have to figure out who's right and who's wrong. Takes me until the late afternoon. If I'm not doing that, I'm sitting in the law courts all day or outside the offices of the 'great men,' because my sheep expect me to defend them against the grasping hands of the rulers. I confess one thing to you right now, and to God above," he pointed a finger heavenward. "I *hate* waiting and waiting to see the 'great men,' the governors, in their waiting rooms! Big waste of my time. But what else can I do? So, I'm busy all day and end up writing at night — including my *Confessions*. I wrote that just after I became bishop of Hippo. A very painful exercise, one I would never have undertaken if God had not pressed it upon me."

He folded his hands over his black woolen cloak. "So, enough of the 'Saint' Augustine. Augustine, he is first and foremost a bishop. That is what God called me to do — and when God, the Creator and Author of all that exists, calls on you, you are much better off answering the door than ignoring the knock, as I did for so long!"

"Bishop Augustine it is, then," I conceded.

"And don't think being bishop was something I sought out as a great honor! Let me tell you the truth: After my conversion to Christianity I wanted to withdraw from the world, to settle in a community of holy brethren living a life a solitude, poverty, prayer, and quiet study. But, see, my reputation as a servant of God grew — despite the fact that I was a repentant sinner being continually re-formed by God!"

He got up from the chess table, stretched his legs, and rubbed his neck. "In those days — I don't know how it is now for you — a man could walk into a church, and the people could snatch him up and force him to become their bishop! I didn't want that! Just leave me alone! I was so frightened of the possibility — I had heard some rumors that I might be next — that for some time I avoided going to anyplace, to any town, where I knew they didn't have a bishop! Didn't want them to grab me, you see." Augustine laughed softly.

He'd been acting this all out, pretending to be first the snatcher and then the snatchee, quite enjoying himself.

"I wasn't even a priest at the time. What happened? Well, I think the Good God tricked me! I went to Hippo to see a friend —that was *my* intention. I had a plan to try to convince him to join our monastic community. I thought I would be safe because they already had a bishop there, Bishop Valerius. How could my plan go wrong?" he asked, wide-eyed, shrugging his shoulders.

"Bishop Valerius! What a character!" he continued. "He was Greek, a holy man, but couldn't speak Latin very well, and he didn't understand the local Punic dialect at all. Well, here comes Augustine," he said as he strutted into an imaginary church door, "and they seize me and make me a priest! And then a bishop, along *with* Valerius. Two bishops in one place! That was a first in the Church, so how could I have known? My perfect plan shattered! It was Valerius's idea too!"

He realized his voice had gotten a bit too loud, and he looked over at Rousseau, checking to see if he was still asleep.

"I think it would take something a bit louder to stir him from those depths," I said, glancing at him snoozing away. "You really wore him out."

"I think you are right. Back to my story," he said, in a lowered voice. "There I was—God caught me in a trap! But that is the way of Providence, is it not?"

"It's rather difficult to outsmart the Omniscient One."

He nodded. "And they did need me there. The Catholic Church in Hippo was small and surrounded by more-powerful heretical sects, the Donatists and the Manicheans. You know of them?"

"Yes, the Donatists believed that the Church was only a college of saints and that the clergy had to be sinless in order to be ministers of sacraments, and the Manicheans believed in two gods, one good and one evil."

That was the gist of it, just to let him knew I understood. The actual heresies were much more complex, but I had no reason to lecture a man who lived amidst the turmoil caused by both.

"Exactly. They had their own bishops, very powerful, and they used their power to harass the true Catholics continually. The people need a voice, and they needed protection. That's why I wrote so much against these heresies." He paused. "Of course, as you know from reading my *Confessions*, I was, for all too long, a heretic myself! A Manichean! But God brought me to see the error of my ways. That's why I must be patient with other lost sheep," he nodded toward Rousseau. "God was very, very patient with me."

"And speaking of which, how did you … like the *Confessions* of Jean-Jacques? I thought you might be glancing through it instead of sleeping in my spare room."

"He does not understand the demons he courts," Augustine shook his head sadly.

"Quite a different aim from yours," I said, as I got up to get some notes from my desk. "But I noticed in going back through these two *Confessions* that there are a few interesting similarities as well. In fact, I've made a list here. Both of you were born of what we might call the lower middle class, and you both spent your youth seeking to rise through society, to get honor and worldly fame. Both of you were — if I might borrow a phrase from your *Confessions* — in love with love. You both loved romance, the romance of literature and actual romance. And you both confessed to having a concubine, Rousseau for twenty-five years, and you for fifteen. Both of you had children with your concubine — Rousseau five and you one, a son, Adeodatus."

"Yes, my dear Adeodatus," he said, the love for his son clearly written on his face.

"And this I thought was quite interesting," I continued, "both of you confessed to stealing — and I'm very sure Rousseau confessed his crime with yours in mind. In fact, each of you confessed a whole number of personal weaknesses and failures. And the list of similarities goes on. Both of you, after seeking honor and renown in high society, became entirely disillusioned with fame, luxury, the court, and power, and threw away the trappings of sophisticated society, going into a kind of seclusion, away from the allure and bustle of the city. Both of you confessed to be searching for true human happiness, and both of you ended up as pilgrims, wanderers, deeply dissatisfied with the ways of the world, rather than at home in the world."

Augustine was nodding in agreement, arms folded on his chest while he listened to my inventory. "But there is the greatest of differences," he said as he leaned forward and drummed his index finger on the back of the chair, "and that is *why* we were confessing. I was confessing my own ignorance and God's wisdom, and Rousseau, *his own* alleged wisdom. His 'wisdom' is familiar to me. All too familiar."

He moved around the chair and sat down again. "You see, I recognize this Rousseau well. As I read his *Confessions* I said to myself, 'There is nothing new under the sun, and here is one more example of it.' There were Rousseaus all over Rome's empire, men and boys devoted to the liberation of their passions from all restraint, always ready to give great speeches in support of their degraded actions."

I sat down with him as he slipped into his memories. Then he looked up once I had settled in. "In my youth, I too was Rousseau, a man inflamed by the desire for truth—as Rousseau proclaims that he was—but also by the desire for love, or what I *thought* was love. I know all about this. So do you, because I confessed it in my book. It was a very painful task God made for me, to speak of such things. As a young man, I went off to the big city, to Carthage, at seventeen. I had already engaged in many shameful acts, wallowed in the pleasures of the flesh driven by the bubbling impulses of youth. I went to Carthage already soiled in such muck. It was there that I planned to find true love, fame, and happiness! Well, Carthage was a sputtering cauldron of disgraceful loves, and into that cauldron I gladly leapt. Searching for love in a boiling stew of lust. I had never been in love, but believe me, I was in love with love! Yes, you know that phrase—you just used it!"

He got up again and crossed over to the window, obviously agitated by bringing to mind what was, to him, so painfully shameful a memory. But to Rousseau, such things were not painful at all—or at least he never let on that they were. His goal was to remove all shame and indeed to make shamelessness a kind of virtue. And it is just this way for us today, we sons of Rousseau.

"But actually, my soul was in rotten health! God knew it. I did not. What I confess now, I could not confess then, because I had willfully embraced ignorance so that I could serve pleasure. I didn't want real love. I *wanted* the disgraceful loves." He turned toward me. "I wanted only to have my itches scratched by the world of the senses. Oh yes, in love with love," he declared dramatically, "such a sweet thing, all the more so if I could enjoy the body of my beloved."

I looked down to avert his eyes, feeling a bit as if I'd stepped into a confessional. But he continued, relentless in his honest appraisal. I am afraid of this kind of honesty in other people. I think we all are. It reminds us of what we, too, might have to confess if God called on us to write our own books about our own lives.

"I thus muddied the stream of true friendship, of true love, by the corruption of lust, and yet, befouled as I was, I used to carry myself about, elegant and urbane," he took a few haughty mincing steps. "Well, it wasn't long after that I took a concubine, the one you mentioned. Oh yes, I know Rousseau's hardened heart very well, enflamed by passion, by impure love, and hence burned to a hard crust. And a mind to go with it, shutting out the truth and creating its own 'truth' instead."

"The world according to Rousseau?" I offered.

"The passion to be godlike, to be a creator of our world — that's a sin that drives many a philosopher, isn't it? Not truth, as they pretend, but the love of one's own ideas, the love of one's own loves."

He stopped by my bookcase and ran his fingers over the spines of a few books. "And the lesson that I finally learned?" he said, turning to look me in the eye. "What happens when your desire for love isn't pure? What happens when it is not love but lust? I can tell you from my experience! It *bends* your desire for truth! It makes you desire the truth you *want* to be true, not the real truth. Truth then becomes defined by disordered love, an all-too-human condition. And I can tell you what comes next," and here his voice started to rise, as his eyes flicked over toward Rousseau. "I can tell you what has happened to our friend Jean-Jacques over there, because it happened to me. You hate the actual truth for the sake of what you happen to love. *That* is why he hates Christianity. *That* is why he turns against Jesus Christ, although Jesus Christ has not turned against him."

He had walked closer to Rousseau as he talked, and now said just a little louder. "To say it in another way, this Rousseau, in his philosophy, is painting man in *his* image, Rousseau's image according to what Rousseau loves. His 'natural man' is none other than," and here he made a flourish with his hand toward the man, "Rousseau himself!"

I had a quick image of Rousseau, sans culottes, capering through the woods, looking for acorns, and had to suppress a laugh.

"So, what we have in Rousseau's *Confessions* is not the real picture of man, not the truth about mankind, as he claims," I added, "but simply a description of a particular fallen man, Jean-Jacques Rousseau himself, put forward as if it were the real, natural, original, good man. A kind of autobiography masquerading as philosophy?"

"Yes, yes, and please believe me, I have seen it often. Most philosophy is autobiography, a way of praising oneself indirectly by creating a world in one's own image. To be truly a philosopher, to love wisdom faithfully, is much too painful for most people, because — as Socrates noted — if we really seek truth and wisdom, we soon find out how little we know, how very small our largest thoughts are, how very partial in every sense our judgments. True philosophy, the true love of wisdom, brings great humility and an ever-growing desire for divine aid, for help from Wisdom above. If we love God, we are loving wisdom. That is the love we should seek above all, not the love of our own hapless selves or our own meager thoughts."

The good bishop was very close to Rousseau now, but had turned his back to him as he was speaking with me — and speaking much louder all the time. "Jean-Jacques Rousseau, he is a man whose disordered loves defined his truth, and so he looks in the mirror, and says, 'Ecce homo!' 'Behold the Man!'"

"The very words spoken by Pontius Pilate about Jesus," I said, realizing where he was headed. I saw Rousseau stirring behind the saint.

"Yes, so this Rousseau, he thinks he's the new savior, the new Christ, the key to our understanding our true nature and true happiness! What is his truth? What is it that he is really declaring if we cut through all the rhetoric, the rhetoric that even Rousseau himself didn't recognize as misleading and corrupted?"

St. Augustine slapped the desk. "He loved the women, but he didn't want to be a real husband and father, and so he wanted to recreate the world to fit these desires. He thus bends his mind to the task of recreating human beings in his own image. Rousseau's male and female — they are what? They are what Rousseau, with his twisted loves, wished male and female to be: animals governed merely by sensual passions, mythical creatures of his own lust-besotted imagination! These creatures have no natural desire for anything but the pleasures of the flesh, nothing above the satisfaction of the moment! To get the itch scratched! No family to care for, no moral duties, no pangs of conscience, no work, no labor—a life of ease! Rousseau's man? He is no better than a dog! He has his way with the female, and he's off! So that is the picture of human beings Rousseau paints in his imagination, and he passes it off as if he had found the truth! That is the truth he wants to be true! That is the Jean-Jacques Rousseau that I find in his *Confessions*!"

St. Augustine picked up the offending book, which I hadn't noticed he had set on my desk when he'd returned much earlier in the day. "Rousseau's *Confessions*? The blind leading the blind. Sinfulness can see nothing clearly, but only its own mud, a mud that it calls clean! When we finally see our sinfulness and can confess that what we love is mud and lies, only then can we finally begin to see ourselves and everything else ever more clearly. By the light of Christ, we finally see what is real, what is true—especially about ourselves. So I repeat," he said much louder, "because sin makes us hard of hearing too, as well as blind, the beginning of truly seeing is seeing our real sinfulness, seeing ourselves as we really are. That is where Christ shines His light first—on our sins. The gate to truth is the confession of our sins. I say this because I have experienced it. I know it from my own life. That is the substance of my *Confessions*."

Thick as I am sometimes, it was only now that I realized the good bishop was *trying* to wake Rousseau, in more ways than one. Now I played along. "And you are aware, after reading Rousseau's *Confessions*, that he rejects the Christian understanding of sin. For Rousseau, we are naturally good and all our instinctual desires are naturally good. It's society that's the source of evil."

"A song as old as the sophists, sung to the tune of the devil, played on the pipes of Pelagius! Quite unoriginal — in fact, quite close to the original sin," St. Augustine chimed in.

Rousseau was clearly awake now, and even more clearly annoyed, but St. Augustine pretended not to notice, and I followed his lead. "The original sin — that of thinking oneself wiser than God, and recreating good and evil?"

"The old sickness of sin, sold to us by Satan himself. And here we have another example of a very sick man declaring what's healthy and good! So it is with the multitude of man-made philosophies. Philosophers are almost always brilliant men, men gifted with powerful minds, but also sinful men, so their powerful minds are yoked to their impure hearts. They end up creating truth in their own image, *drunk* with the wine of their own imagination! I have seen it many times."

As he said these last words, he casually turned to see Rousseau sitting up bolt straight in his chair and very, very angry. Augustine said in the most innocent voice, "Oh, Jean-Jacques, did I wake you?"

I pretended to cough and clear my throat to keep from laughing. Rousseau stood up, drawing himself up to his full height, which was not very tall. But his feathers were definitely ruffled. "Drunk! I will tell you who is drunk," he rasped, "who is seeing what is really there, and who is blinded, Monsieur Augustine!"

"Do you feel rested?" I asked, at a bit of a loss as to where to steer things at this point.

"Rested! Who cares about rest!" He breezed haughtily around the front of my desk. "Yes, I will tell you who is blind and drunk. It is this bishop!" He spun around near the chess table and pointed a finger accusingly at Augustine, while he spoke to me. "He does not see natural man, man as he really is. *That* is what I show to everyone who has eyes to see! *He* puts on the bishop's hat, and it goes over his eyes, so that he can see the world only as a Christian, not as it really is." He slammed himself down in a chair by the chess table. "The pagan Romans had much clearer eyes, my friend—that I can tell you—much clearer eyes than the Christians."

Augustine had walked casually over to the chess table himself, and I, wanting to keep a safe distance from whatever storm was to come, sat in the chair by my desk. He gave Rousseau a mind-if-I-sit-down look, gesturing with his hand at the empty chair, and Jean-Jacques nodded grumpily, his arms crossed tightly against his chest.

Augustine sat down and pulled his chair closer to the table. "So, you're saying that being a bishop will ruin a man's reason," he said, as he picked up one of his bishops, "and wearing this hat will fill his mind with fantasies and fables about an imaginary world, a city of God, a fictitious heaven, so that he cannot truly see the real world before his eyes?"

Rousseau looked over at him. "I am being, perhaps, rather blunt, but you have aroused my passions by being unjust to my arguments, so I am forced to speak plainly to defend myself."

Augustine put his bishop down at another place on the board. "I thought we could continue our game?" He looked questioningly at Rousseau, who did not respond. "And the Christian understanding of sin—that's a great cause of blindness? On my part, that is." He sat back in his chair. "Your move."

"What? Ah, yes," he replied, looking over the board. "Sin! Yes, let's look at sin. Injustice is a sin, no? Stealing, no?" He leaned toward Augustine. "I believe that you stole some pears when you were young, no?"

"Exactly as I described in my *Confessions*."

"And the man who 'owned' the pears—why were they 'his'? Why was the land on which the pear trees grew 'his'? This land that existed long before we human beings arrived, this land that was common to all, that nature gave to all? And what does this

'his' mean? It means that if a poor man is caught taking a pear to fill his empty belly, the owner of the land may have that poor man whipped, for no crime other than hunger."

Rousseau moved a piece, a pawn, if I recall. "Or perhaps crucified! Was not your Christ Himself crucified next to two thieves? But why should a man be able to call a pear tree or the ground on which it grows 'his'? In our natural state, I tell you, anyone was free to eat the fruit of any tree he wished because there was no such thing as mine and thine. All was common, and since no one owned anything, there could not be a sin of stealing." He smirked a bit, "Surely you have seen the poor starve, while in plain sight the rich eat not just pears, but every delicacy! Your move, monsieur."

"As a bishop, I have seen the sufferings of the poor all too often. But in my own case, mind you, as a young thief? I wasn't hungry. I *wanted* to steal! I was filled with the thrill of taking what wasn't mine. And the pears? I had better ones in my own house."

Augustine made his move, I don't recall what. "My pleasure in stealing was not in eating, in satisfying my hunger, but in doing what was forbidden. I fed the pears to the pigs!"

"Ah, but even here, Augustine, even here, there would be no thrill in stealing if there were no property that you were forbidden to take!" He picked up one of his black bishops and held it aloft. "If the man didn't own the pears, if the pear trees were just sitting there in an open field, belonging to no one, would you even have the thrill of 'sinning'?"

He set his black knight down with a little flourish. "I believe that is check."

"After my king, eh? So, Christ the King, He died for nothing, because there is no sin to die for? You think that it would be much better if we were all just simple animals, roaming freely, taking of the common fruit of the earth, with no God looming over our heads as Creator or Judge or Redeemer? You would create a world in which there could be no thieves, especially no thieves on crosses, and hence no need of a cross for redeeming thieves?" Augustine moved his white bishop to block Rousseau's.

"Your mind is quick to see all that I am saying!" the Frenchman smiled and picked up one of his pawns. "Yes, I am after your king. It is chess, no? But I am out to get all kings, all queens, all noble knights, all the high-and-mighty bishops! They have taken what should be common to all, and hold it for themselves. Then they make the laws of society — the ones who have stolen all the lands for themselves — and they define 'justice' and the laws to protect what they have taken, and thus they *crush* the common man," he said, grasping the pawn, as if he were squeezing out its life. "And the Church gives its approval. It protects the 'justice' of the rich! And the poor man who is crushed? He is very often stronger, wiser, more talented, more intelligent than those 'nobles' whom society places above him! What could be more unjust? Yet, the Church gives its approval — the stamp of God!" He used the pawn to take one of Augustine's knights.

It was easy to see, given his emotion, that this was no abstract complaint by Rousseau. He was the son of a not-very-successful watchmaker. After his father abandoned him, he bounced among relatives to strangers, becoming an apprentice to an engraver for a while. After losing that job, he mostly wandered about, getting low-status jobs, such as being a lackey to a noble family, to keep body and soul together. He was always seeking a well-off patron but was keenly aware that the nobles who so disdained him and on whom he depended were far less intelligent and gifted than he was.

These experiences built up in Rousseau both envy and disdain for the upper-class property owners and great sympathy for the injustices that that class visited upon the poor, who had nothing but what the rich allowed them to have. All this became part of his larger philosophy, mainly in works other than the *Confessions*, such as the *Social Contract*. Rousseau's philosophy thereby became, after his death, the engine of the French Revolution, where the poor had their bloody revenge on the rich. Sadly, the great bishops and clerics of Rousseau's time, especially in France, were often less than holy; indeed, they tended to be self-serving members of the nobility who cared just as little for the poor. One can see why Rousseau hated bishops, whom he associated with hypocritical luxuriousness, and why the French revolutionaries took it upon themselves to murder the rich clergy of France.

Augustine moved his bishop from the other side of the board to take Rousseau's pawn—a bit of a provocative thing to do at this point, to say the least.

"Let's be straightforward here! I assume you mean to say that the Church and Her bishops, in preaching about the evils of sin, including stealing, are merely protecting the rich. You believe that there is no such thing as a bishop who would sacrifice himself, but only rich wolves in shepherds' clothing?"

"I admire your desire for openness and honesty. Yes, it is just as you say. I know it, because I have seen it. In France, the bishops themselves are rich! They go about dressing in the finest clothes—these bishops, with their golden-threaded stoles and chasubles, their silk gloves and ornate miters! Living in their episcopal palaces, and eating the finest dainty foods!" He took the bishop's bishop with his rook.

Augustine calmly stood up and pointed to his rough woolen robe. "What do you think of my episcopal finery? As bishop of Hippo, I wear this simple black cloak and demand the same from my priests. We eat only the simplest foods. I was once given a silk shirt, and I sent it back. I did not want people to think that Augustine, a poor man from Thagaste, became a bishop so he could get a silk shirt. No, I clothed myself in the poverty of Christ."

He sat down, having made his point, a point that Rousseau seemed to concede, at least judging by the subtle lift of his eyebrows in recognition of Augustine's garb. The saint looked over the board for a moment and moved his other bishop. Rousseau moved his rook again in response.

"And I agree with you, Jean-Jacques. Our earthly societies, the cities of man, are soiled by sin, and 'justice' in this fallen world is often a word that masks the lusts and crimes of the rich and powerful. But admitting that — we agree here on the degraded condition of all societies in *this* life, *this* world — isn't that only to admit what the Christian doctrine of sin declares? The world is fallen, corrupted by the vices of men. 'What is a kingdom but a great band of robbers, and what is a great band of robbers but a little kingdom?' I said that, you know, in my *City of God*. Have you read that?" he asked, moving another pawn.

Rousseau stared at the board for what seemed like a very long time. "Yes, yes, I know this. I have read it." He leaned forward and tapped his fist on the table. "But there is still the greatest of differences in the next steps we each take in our arguments, the very greatest of differences. Your next step is toward Heaven, a place beyond this world, a place of ... of fantasy, just like the biblical account of Adam and Eve in a supposed paradise existing in the misty past. An unreal future and an unreal past. But I take mankind back in real time to our real nature, our true original beginning in the state of nature, where we were still an unspoiled and happy animal. There I seek the key to our happiness, our lost happiness, in hopes that we can recover some small amount of that lost happiness now, here, in the only life we have."

He then moved one of his knights, which he seemed to do without the usual concentration. "I demonstrate the real 'fall,' the fall from our original condition into the artificial chains of society, if you would read my books with clear eyes."

"I wonder if you really believe all of what you say, Rousseau, really believe it in your heart?" the bishop asked as he moved one of his rooks.

"Of course I believe it! That is why I proclaim it!"

"Do you remember how outraged you were with my words, the words that awakened you from sleeping? I implied you were a kind of blind drunkard, a thoughtless man?"

"Indeed I do, monsieur," he snapped, picking up his queen and moving it across the board diagonally. "I must admit that that was quite unjust."

"So true, Rousseau. I knew you would feel that way. And it was unjust of me — that's why I said it." He continued the questioning, "And you are — rightly, I would say — inflamed at the ill treatment of the poor by the rich, at any injustice done to the innocent?"

"As I have made very clear, my heart burns with an ardent love of the great, the true, the beautiful, the just. And so any injustice always inflamed my heart as well with the greatest indignation and disgust!"

"And I believe it! For every human heart does long for justice. But according to your philosophy, justice itself doesn't really exist, does it? Didn't you tell us that natural man, man in his original and good condition, would be an animal with no sense of morality at all, and hence no natural inborn sense of justice? And did you not thereby claim that justice — what we call 'justice' — is really only a man-made thing, entirely artificial, an abstract word that, underneath it all, was invented to keep the poor man's hands off the property of the rich? Did you not say these things? Am I being unjust to what you have written?"

Rousseau was quiet for a moment, and then admitted, "I did say these things."

"Then you must choose, I'm afraid. If your philosophical arguments are true, and justice is merely a human-made artifact that has no real existence in our natural state, then why do you feel, deep in your heart, that there *is* justice, that justice is quite real? That it is unjust for the rich man to lord it over the poor? That it was unjust for you, Rousseau—yes, I read it in your *Confessions*—unjust for you to have to be a servant to men and women of the nobility who were inferior to you in every way, who were often little better than fools?"

He moved his queen several spaces diagonally. "So, which is it then? Is there or is there not justice, *natural* justice, *real* justice?" He paused, and then said, "Your move."

"What? Oh, yes, it is." Rousseau moved a knight within striking distance of Augustine's rook, but his mind was clearly elsewhere.

"I maintain that your heart is right even if your head is not," continued the bishop, "and that there is justice, true justice that exists *before* human beings ever existed, and that God implants in our souls that great desire—the great desire that you feel—for justice. But you have explained it away in your philosophy. You have explained away what you know in your heart is real."

He then moved an unassuming pawn forward to a square protected by a knight he had moved some three or four turns back and one space away from the black king. "That is what you call check, isn't it?"

"Ah, I was not paying attention," Rousseau mumbled and moved his king out of harm's way.

"Look at me, Jean-Jacques," Augustine implored. Rousseau lifted his lids and looked dejectedly at the bishop. "And that is why—look now more deeply into your heart—that is why you were never able to shake loose from the feeling that you were doing something unjust in abandoning your five children? Come now, you confessed it! You did not think that what you had done was good—shall I quote your own words to you?—even though you tell us elsewhere in your philosophy that man, naturally good man, would abandon his children without a care, without any concern, with no agony of conscience whatsoever? And that original 'man' was good and innocent? Were you trying to hide from your guilt *in that man?*"

Slowly, quietly, indeed painfully, he replied, "As I said, Jean-Jacques does not have a heart of stone. I might have deceived myself, but not hardened my heart."

"Precisely because your heart was not hardened you had to deceive yourself with your own words, a thing that happens quite often with philosophers unguided by truth, by true Wisdom. You could not forget those children, *your* children. You could not leave that unconfessed."

"I could not, monsieur. You know, the whole world knows; I have confessed it."

"As I confessed my sins, and still do."

Augustine had been going at him rather relentlessly, and it was somewhat difficult to watch, but now he seemed to soften. "We are not all that different, we sinners. I came to know that, most deeply, as a bishop."

He lifted his remaining bishop and spun it slowly between his fingers. "As one charged with the care of souls, I often have to be the bearer of hard truth to members of my flock." He looked from the face of his bishop to Rousseau. "Your children died, you know, all of them, in the foundling home, where you abandoned them. I know this; please don't ask how."

Rousseau's eyes were glistening slightly with tears. Augustine studied him for several moments and then placed the bishop seven steps diagonally from its original position. "I believe that is checkmate."

Jean-Jacques looked up, blinking, and studied the board for a few seconds. "I am afraid so, monsieur."

"Your father abandoned *you*, didn't he, Jean-Jacques? He left you to fend for yourself at quite an early age, a father you tried to love, but he did not love you in return? That is one of the greatest of injustices. You felt that—feel that, even now."

Rousseau remained silent, but obviously even more shaken.

"And to continue to speak the truth, however hard it is to hear, it was just as cruel for you to abandon your own children, all five. You understand, deep in your heart, that it is impossible for you or your father to undo these greatest of injustices—humanly impossible. He is now dead, and so are your children."

Rousseau was by this time weeping uncontrollably. "All too well, monsieur, all too well."

"Then let us hope there is a divine cure. And I confess, from the bottom of my heart, I know that there is."

I had unaccountably gotten some dust in my eyes just then, and took off my glasses so I could wipe it away with my handkerchief. But when I put them back on, they were both gone.

Reflections

If Rousseau had been fundamentally changed by meeting St. Augustine — if he, in fact, realized that his entire philosophy of "natural man" was all a fiction he invented to excuse his own treatment of women and the abandonment of his own children, and then changed it accordingly — then the world after Rousseau would have been much different.

But such is not the case. We are influenced by the unrepentant scoundrel. Rousseau was the intellectual father of all those in the 1960s who thought they were innovative in decrying marriage as an unnatural sham and social artifact to be cast aside by the sexually liberated, those who imagined that they were returning to their true, natural, original sexual selves. Thus liberated, the sexual revolutionaries needed a way to dispose of all those unwanted children, so they legalized abortion as a new way to abandon one's offspring to certain death.

Yet, I cannot help but wonder, having had the two in my office, how differently would human history have turned out if Rousseau, after meeting St. Augustine, had that deep change of heart and then wrote another *Confessions* declaring the errors he had embraced, just as St. Augustine declared his error in embracing the heresy of Manicheanism. Would there have been a sexual revolution?

But Rousseau is also the father of other revolutions: the French Revolution and even in some respects the later Marxist revolutions, the first claiming hundreds of thousands of lives and the rest tens of millions. Rousseau saw the injustice of the rich toward the poor, just as St. Augustine did, just as the Old Testament prophets did, just as Jesus Christ Himself did.

But Rousseau rejected their response. He didn't want to believe in God or sin. He thought he had a better solution, a solution exclusively of *this* world. He declared that private property itself was unjust, that in our original, natural, and good condition, human animals owned nothing. The implication was that we must return to this natural condition, which involved the destruction of private property through the elimination of the property owners. What was needed was a revolution, one that was merciless in its pursuit of the forced return to the "bliss" of our natural condition. You'd need to read not only Rousseau's *Second Discourse* but also his *Social Contract* to fill in all the philosophical details, but it's all implicit in his *Confessions*.

But in truth, St. Augustine was far more passionate about justice, which becomes clear especially in his *City of God*, where he chastises pagan Rome for its many brutish injustices perpetrated in pursuit of empire. As Augustine and the Church declare, justice is defined by God; it is, in fact, a virtue, one of the four cardinal virtues. In understanding injustice as a vice, the Church makes clear Her condemnation of the very injustices Rousseau decried.

Injustice is a violation of divine order. When Rousseau rejected the divine, he removed the main pillar supporting justice in this world. One can see how corrupt clergy in France would have soured Rousseau on religion, but he could see, at least in my office, what a holy bishop looked like. St. Augustine worked tirelessly for justice among his flock, an endless task he accepted as part of his office.

He is a model for all Catholic bishops and stands as living proof against Rousseau's philosophy.

After Rousseau's death, his philosophy inspired later generations who aimed to put his thought into action. The elimination of the rich nobility and the return of their lands to the poor in the French Revolution were conceived by many to be part of the return to nature; the elimination of Christianity went along with it, since Rousseau and his followers believed the Church to be only supporting the rich nobles. So these righteous revolutionaries, sons of Rousseau's philosophy, set about removing the heads of those who stood in the way of "progress," and thousands and thousands of clergy and Catholic laypeople were slaughtered.

Of all this and more, Rousseau was the father. An entire book could be written about his astounding influence in so many areas, from anthropology to psychology.

Think on the following irony, as an especially repugnant example of his influence. Due to his treatise *Emile*, Rousseau is one of the most influential modern thinkers in regard to *child raising and education*. Yes, the man who had no experience in raising or educating children because he abandoned all five of his own has become a modern "expert"! He was, as you might imagine, afraid that his readers would discover this inconvenient fact and call into question all of his wonderful wisdom.

But back to our previous question: What if Rousseau had met St. Augustine and realized that the "truth" he espoused came from a darkened heart, from his own deep resentment toward his father and his social superiors?

As you have seen — as I indeed did see with my own eyes — St. Augustine got to Rousseau's heart, to the sources of the wounds that became the inspirations for his philosophy. Conversions of the heart yield conversions of the mind, just as perversions and malformations of the heart yield subversions of the mind.

SAINTS VS. SCOUNDRELS

It always amazes me, in studying the history of philosophy, how immense is the effect ideas have on human history. As Richard Weaver famously stated, ideas have consequences. It isn't that we are what we think, as if we could change reality by our thoughts. It's that our thoughts either hide reality or guide us to it.

Rousseau was not better off for having intellectually justified the abandonment of his children. The world that followed him is even worse off for becoming Rousseau's disciples. I hope that, like Rousseau, we still have some faint recognition that our consciences have been all too easily calmed.

But here's the point I've been driving at, which continues to occupy my mind after all the meetings I've had: If Rousseau did have a deep change of heart, one that in turn demanded a deep change of mind, then there would have been an immense change in history since Rousseau. But when my two guests disappeared, nothing had, in fact, changed.

So, what to make of it? I wish I had a good, convincing answer about how it all fits together, but I'm sorry to disappoint you. The appearance of Rousseau and St. Augustine together in my office was as real as the *now* within which I exist and which has been formed by a Rousseau whose heart and philosophy remained hardened. There would seem to be two parallel realities, as I said earlier.

I confess, I cannot explain all of this. But it illuminates an important truth: Right now, in the things you choose to believe, to say, to do (or not to believe, or say, or do), you have the chance to produce totally distinct futures not just for yourself, but for your family, your community, and indeed the entire world.

In this way, the future of the universe does, in fact, depend on us — even if we don't have the extraordinarily powerful mind and rhetorical-literary capabilities of a Rousseau or an Augustine. Big things are built on little things, and sometimes seemingly obscure things.

St. Augustine and Jean-Jacques Rousseau: Reflections

Think on these things again: What if Isaac Rousseau had not reacted to his wife's death by implicitly but persistently blaming his son? What if he instead treated the boy as a gift from God who allowed the love he had for his wife to endure in the present? What if Isaac had then not abandoned little Jean-Jacques and wandered around Europe while his son became a vagabond, orphaned *by choice* by the man who should have been entirely devoted to him? Could Jean-Jacques ever have written of fatherhood as unnatural, and then abandoned his own children?

To come at it from another angle: Young Augustine was a sinner, but the ceaseless prayers of his mother, St. Monica, were wonderfully answered by God, and so he returned to the Church. What if Rousseau's father had been as devout and as devoted to his child as St. Monica was to hers?

But even with Isaac's failures, other things could have changed the young Rousseau's life. What if a rich and noble man had taken the young rebel under his protective wing and treated him with the love with which his own father should have treated him? What if this rich man devoted himself to the development of all the young man's great natural abilities, and had done so in the name of Jesus Christ, who demanded that we care for the orphaned? Would Jean-Jacques have still become the father of the French Revolution, or would he have become instead a good father to his five children, as St. Augustine was to his Adeodatus?

These questions weigh on me, given the strange things I have experienced in my office. I feel that same weight pressing down on my own *now*—on me and what I choose to say and to do, or not say and not do. None of us truly knows what might be the world-changing results of even our smallest actions or inactions.

Any scoundrel can become a great saint. If some kind and holy man had shown Rousseau the true face of Jesus Christ, he may have become a great saint and done as much for good as St. Augustine or St. Francis. Perhaps he would have transformed the hearts of the haughty nobles and luxurious bishops of France, turning their attention to the poor and the oppressed, as Christ commanded. Perhaps, in so doing, he could have cleared away, rather than igniting, the kindling of the French Revolution.

If, on the other hand, St. Monica—the mother of Augustine—had not prayed so fervently and faithfully for the conversion of her sinful son, Augustine would have been yet another scoundrel, perhaps spinning out a self-justifying philosophy along the line of Rousseau's, one as magnificently harmful as the saintly bishop's was for good. But she did, and so we have, by the grace of God, St. Augustine.

St. Francis of Assisi and Niccolò Machiavelli

Part 1

St. Francis is certainly one of the most misunderstood saints. Our ideas of him come from bad Hollywood representations as a proto-environmentalist or a quasi-hippie — or, more likely, from his omnipresence as a garden gnome making happy with the birds as he watches over our asters, peonies, irises, and yellow-faced daffodils.

That is not St. Francis. If the real one showed up in your garden — as he did in mine, about ten at night — you would probably run him out, thinking he was an invading tramp, or edge into the house politely while dialing your cell phone for the police. The real St. Francis looked like just what he was: a beggar who bathed only when it rained on him and whose cloak was a rag patched by rags. Even in the dim light of my garden, which came from the dining-room light shining through the bay window, this was all clear, and startlingly so.

He is certainly smaller than you'd imagine, especially since his posture was huddled over rather than standing straight and stately like the cement garden statue. But unlike the statue, who isn't bothersome and lets us go about our day without interference, the real St. Francis leaves no doubt that you are in the presence of a saint, someone whose soul is so filled with light that it's leaking through his body. It is both exhilarating and uncomfortable, like being too close to an immensely dense object of such concentrated mass that you want to escape lest you be drawn in, but also want to be drawn in lest you escape. The light is holiness, and its presence is like death, rearranging all your priorities simply by entering the room.

I have a St. Francis garden gnome, or had one. I took it over to the public park in town after midnight some three or four weeks after the saint's visit and set it among some black-eyed Susans along the path, a peculiar act of vandalism. I couldn't bear to look at it, such a pale imitation of the real thing. The statue is much safer, a kind of pet saint, cheerful, immobile, and well-behaved. Real saints are not tame. I suppose that's why we're satisfied with St. Francis statues. They ask nothing of us. Imagine the difference between a Jesus statue and meeting the real God-man.

What made the effect of the real St. Francis all the more disconcerting is that his intensity was encased in an even more striking levity, as if all the tragedy of the world had been devoured by a divine comedy—death swallowed by life, crucifixion by resurrection. Again, I do not think that this quality belonged to St. Francis himself, but rather it was a reflection of God's peace—a great favor, and yet no one could be humbler than this saint.

The last thing I thought he would ask for turned out to be the first—something to eat and drink. But of course, I thought immediately, the Franciscans were organized to be mendicants, holy beggars. So I assumed I would just put a meal before him, some basic saint food—bread, lentil soup, raw carrots or turnips, that kind of thing—since we imagine that holy men and women eat like rabbits or contemplative brown-eyed cows.

Unfortunately, I had none of that on hand, not even bread—I was planning to go to the store with my wife in the morning—and it was late at night. Even more confusing for me was that he refused to eat anything anyway, unless he worked for it. The saint wouldn't budge on that point. He said it was part of his rule, and he would not allow for himself what he would not permit for the brothers under his care.

So we went up to my office, which, to be little more honest than I'd like, needed a bit of spiffing here and there. It's my thinkery, so to speak, to remain undisturbed by disconcerting invasions from vacuum cleaners, people of the anti-dust party, those who wish books to be put back on shelves and wadded papers into wastebaskets. But it was just what St. Francis was looking for — a chance to roll up what remained of his sleeves and bring order to my chaos. He had me bring him a bucket, a brush, and a broom, and shooed me out the door to pick up some late-night fast food.

Now, the only thing that was open other than a pizza parlor across town was Smokin' Joes, a local eatery run — *mirabile dictu* — by a man named Joe, who indeed was generally smoking when not on the grill and who sincerely believed that vegetables, other than ketchup and a thin piece of iceberg lettuce, were meant to be eaten only by creatures lower on the food chain. Since it was nearly closing time, the only things available were two Mega-Monster burgers and some heat-lamped fries.

"Sorry, I already cleaned the grill," Joe apologized, with a modicum of sincerity.

"It'll have to do," I replied. I thought St. Francis could take the meat off and eat the rest, along with the fries.

When I returned to my office with the grease-stained bag, St. Francis was down on his knees scrubbing the floor and singing in French. I lifted the bag. "Your feast — and my apologies. All they had, at this hour, were hamburgers." I set his meal on the desk and gestured for him to dig in.

Instead, he looked at me with a kind of serene incomprehension. "What is a . . . ham burglar?"

"Hamburger. A round piece of ground up beef, uh, 'sister cow,' on bread with lettuce, and kind of, well, tomato sauce. I know you won't want the meat, but I thought you could eat the rest, along with the French fries."

"Ah, I do like French food. And you are wrong about meat, wrong in two ways." He sat back on his haunches. "We brothers are bound, in obedience, by the words of our most gracious Lord, Jesus Christ, to eat whatever is put before us, meat or not meat. My little brothers, they get this idea too about forbidding meat, and I constantly have to correct them."

He smiled and looked off into the distance of his memory. "Do you know, when I was away once from my brothers—for too long apparently—way over near the Holy Land, what do you think? Two of them came running to me from Assisi with news that certain brothers had taken it upon themselves to write up new ordinances—much stricter ones, as the other religious orders had!" He shook his head. "So I find they have burdened themselves with commands to fast that never came from our Lord, or from Holy Mother Church. I follow the Church: no meat on Fridays, and I add Saturdays, and, of course, no meat in Lent. But these brothers had forbidden meat on Mondays and Wednesdays too! *That* certainly never came from me, avoiding meat and multiplying fast days!"

He smiled, "And think on this. I was just about to sit down and eat meat, way over in the Holy Land, as I said, just when they burst in with the news from Assisi! I, Francis, about to eat meat on a day that the new ordinance said I couldn't! Well, I tell you, my friend in Christ, I commanded the little brothers to sit right down and eat with me!"

St. Francis then bent back down to his work, scouring the floor methodically. "So, what do I do then? I have to walk all the way back to Assisi and command them, by holy obedience, *not to fast all the time*, and to enjoy the meat that God provides for them, either by labor, or failing that, by begging. Fast only on the Church's fast days! Do not destroy the liberty given to us by the holy Gospel! Give thanks to God for sister cow!"

"Well, then," I said, "please sit down, St. Francis, and have at it. Sister cow is getting cold, and brother fries are turning into grease sticks."

"No, no, my friend. Not until I have earned it by labor. I insist that we friars are to labor for our bread, just as St. Paul did. But please, I beg you again, for the love of God and His Holy Mother, do not call me a saint," he said as he shot a slight reprimanding eye toward me. "I am the poorest of sinners. Now, if you would, please allow me to finish my work."

"But, I can't just *stand here* while you scrub the floor—a saint scrubbing my floor!"

"You are right, Master Wiker," he said, getting up from his knees. "Because I have not scrubbed where you are standing." He then kindly but firmly took my arm and walked me toward my beloved blue comfy chair. "You need to sit here instead."

But as he escorted me out of his way, he noticed a small crucifix on the wall, which made him let out a short gasp. "I did not see our Lord, the most Holy Crucified One! I am such a mule! I did not even see Him! See, what a blind fool and sinner I am!"

And he immediately fell to his knees and began praying most reverently and thoughtfully, as if he were really talking to God Himself. But of course, that *is* what he was doing, for that is what prayer should be. "Pater noster, qui es in caelis, sanctificetur nomen tuum. Adveniat regnum tuum. Fiat voluntas tua, sicut in caelo et in terra."

I felt very, very self-conscious, since I remained standing, not out of irreverence but more out of spiritual clumsiness. So I knelt down and mumbled along what I remembered of the Latin.

"Panem nostrum quotidianum da nobis hodie, et dimitte nobis debita nostra sicut et nos dimittimus debitoribus nostris. Et ne nos inducas in tentationem, sed libera nos a malo. Amen."

I had never knelt and prayed before my crucifix, least of all accompanied by a saint's radiant concentration on every word. It was more a kind of holy decoration for me—a sad comment on the state of my own soul, I must add. As I later found in doing more reading, this was St. Francis's practice. He would never pass by a crucifix without dropping to his knees in prayer.

He stood up as if this had been the most ordinary thing for anyone with any sense to do and continued escorting me to my chair. "I believe it will be best for you to sit here," and then he went back to scrubbing where he had let off, again singing in a kind of strange-sounding French.

There's no reasoning with him, St. Francis. Stubborn as a very holy mule! He's not from France, by the way, even though that's what his name means. "Francis" is a nickname of sorts; it translates roughly to something like "Frenchy," a name received because of his love of all things French, especially the songs of their troubadours—songs of romance, both the romance of love and the romance of knighthood and gallantry. He sang much. He was no dour saint. And he always sang in French, taking the tunes of the troubadours and substituting his own love songs to God. But he was not actually French, and his name was not actually Francis. His real name was Giovanni di Pietro di Bernardone, born about 1182 in Assisi, Italy, the son of a rich cloth merchant.

It didn't take him long to finish cleaning my office, most of which had been done while I was out picking up his makeshift meal. "And now, Master Wiker, I believe that I have finally earned the feast that you have so graciously provided for me—if you do not mind?" He gestured toward the desk, where the burgers and fries had, by now, released the majority of their grease into and through the bag.

"Please, be my guest," I replied.

After sitting down and saying grace, he lit into both burgers as if I had given him the finest cuisine, and in very little time they were gone. He picked up the fries. "You say these are French, no? I must confess that I have never heard of them." And they, too, disappeared. "I am most thankful for your gracious hospitality," he declared with a noble bow of his head.

"I must admit that I'm a little surprised that you eat meat, St. Francis, and further that you command your brothers to eat it, if it's what is set before them."

"Such zeal, but misplaced zeal! So, I must command them sometimes, as a matter of holy obedience, to feast. Feast, and be thankful to God, who gives all good things—including sister cow." He crossed his arms, putting them inside his tattered sleeves. "I tell you, it is not the only time I have had to correct them."

He wandered thoughtfully toward the window overlooking the garden. "We meet regularly at Pentecost, all of the little brothers from near and far, at the holy chapel—the Portiuncula. We gather just like the noble knights in King Arthur's time, around the round table! Do you know these fine tales?" he turned and looked at me.

"Yes, but probably not as many as you."

"Of that, I am sure! So, to return to my story, there we were at our regular meeting, on the day celebrating the descent of the Most Holy Spirit, and what do you think? There are all my little brothers, weighing themselves down with penances and wearing hair shirts and chains under their smocks. I told them, in the name of holy obedience: Take them off right now and put them in a pile!" He looked back out the window and sighed. "And what an enormous pile it was!"

He then turned around sharply, "Do you know that some of my poor little brothers died because of their foolish zeal for penances—just like the heretics, the Albigensians? You know who they are: They believe the body is evil, so they must kill it with penance! The body is not evil. It is given to us by the most glorious and high God. No, no, the flesh is not evil. The Word was made flesh, so how can it be evil? But our flesh," he patted his stomach affectionately, "it is like brother ass, the donkey, you know? He is stubborn, so sometimes you must give him a little discipline, or he won't move in the right direction. But if you beat him to death, what do you have, eh?"

"I'm guessing a dead donkey."

"And that would be a very good guess, my friend," he chuckled.

"But you yourself, St. Francis, you underwent rather significant penances."

"That is different. My body needs very little food and drink." But then he interrupted himself and became quite serious. "Master Wiker, I must insist that you cease calling me a saint. You do not know me the way that God knows me. So, I'm going to give you a little lesson, one that I had to give to one of my brothers once, Brother Leo."

He came over quite close and fixed his eyes on mine. "Now repeat *exactly* what I say, my good friend in Christ, for you will be speaking God's holy truth in what I am telling you to say to me. Are you ready?"

"Um, I think so," I replied, not actually knowing what I was agreeing to.

"Repeat after me: 'Brother Francis, you have done so much evil and sin in the world that you certainly deserve hell.' There now, say that back to me, word for word," he commanded.

I tried—really tried—but the words stuck in my throat, and then I blurted out, "But God performed so much good through you that we know, from Holy Mother Church, that you are a saint in Heaven."

St. Francis looked at me as if I had insulted him. "What? That's not right at all! I am asking you to repeat *exactly* what I say, and then you will know the truth about this sinner, Francis. You will not be talking about a 'saint.' Once again, let us try."

He firmly grasped me by the arms and looked into my face, speaking slowly so I wouldn't duff my part this time. "Please, word for word: 'Brother Francis, the iniquities of which you have been guilty against the Master of Heaven and Earth are so great that you deserve to be cursed for all eternity!' There!"

I couldn't do it. I gulped the words as if someone were pushing them down. And then out rushed, "But you made such progress in holy virtue that you merited to be blessed for all eternity, and have therefore inspired millions of people to imitate you, and thousands and thousands of churches bear your name."

The saint was very agitated now and started pacing around. "Why do you not say it the way that I said it?" He set his jaw and re-turned to grip me more tightly—a strong grip he had, I might add, and very bony fingers. "One more time, say as I say," he implored me in a tone by which I felt deeply the groaning of the saint's soul: 'Wicked Francis! Tremble lest you do not find grace before God, you who have so gravely offended the God of goodness and the Father of all consolation. You are certainly unworthy of pardon!'"

I gulped air again and must have looked like a fish pulled out of water. I couldn't force myself to say what wasn't true, however much I tried to honor his request. And so out came, "But God in His great mercy showed you His mercy toward all your sins, and not only pardoned them, but made you a great fountain for His mercy that to this day gushes forth over all the world."

"Why are you so stubborn as to insist on saying the very op-posite of what I say?" he asked, clearly exasperated.

"Because I must speak the truth. And the truth is this: that not only did God spare you His punishments, but He showered His graces upon you and has glorified you for all eternity. The Lord is Truth itself; that is what happened, and so Truth compels me to speak as I have." The words flowed out of me almost as if from another source.

He broke into a smile and bowed his head, as if relenting to a greater will. "You speak of me too well! Next you're going to tell me that a pope will someday take the name of Francis!" he slapped my shoulder affectionately and laughed at his own joke.

"Well, as it turns out ..."

Interrupting, he shook his finger at me in mock accusation. "But, as I tell others, don't canonize me too soon. A saint like me might still bring sons and daughters into the world, and I don't mean the spiritual kind! Never underestimate the devil and his temptations. That is a great lesson of humility. I would much prefer that you call me 'Brother Francis.'"

Thinking that my esteemed guest might like to sit down after his labor, I ushered him toward the chess table. "Perhaps we might have a seat, Brother Francis. You've earned a rest. After you?" I gestured for him to proceed me.

"After you, as you are the lord of this great house," he objected.

"And as lord of this house, I must insist," I countered.

"Then, I must then yield to your great courtesy." He chose the seat closest to the bay window. Settling in, he remarked, "Courtesy is one of the greatest virtues, the virtue of the chevaliers," he said, picking up a knight from the chessboard and inspecting it.

"Chevalier—French, for what we call knights."

"Yes, yes. Most courteous knights. Such courtesy is God's great virtue, the God Who deigned to become a mere man. As I tell my little brothers, courtesy is one of God's finest attributes, for God makes His sun shine and His rain fall on sinners and the just alike. And such courtesy is truly the sister of Charity. It extinguishes hatred and maintains love among men." He looked at me, and pointed heavenward. "The Most High God, He is very gentle and kind, to saint and sinner alike, and if we imitate His courtesy, we become His true and noble chevaliers, eh?"

I nodded.

"Yes, chevaliers," he said, a bit wistfully. "I spent my youth singing the songs of the great French troubadours, songs of noble battles and noble loves. I still sing, you know, always in French. I love French. I am God's troubadour! But even more, God's chevalier—what you call a knight."

"God's knight?"

"Yes! God, in His most merciful providence, gave me exactly what I wanted! From my youth on, I wanted to be one of the great chevaliers—knights, sorry!" He leaned forward. "I, the son of a wealthy cloth merchant, whose money I spent faster than he could make it, bought myself a horse and all the accouterments of a noble knight, and went off to serve my lord in battle. And then I was captured," he said with a smile, and then paused for effect. "First by the enemy, who threw me in prison, and then by the Almighty God, the true Lord, when I got out."

I must have looked a bit puzzled, because he then said quickly, "Ah, I see I am not a good storyteller, starting in the beginning and moving to both ends! Let me try again, from the beginning." He settled into his chair. "As I said, my father, Pietro di Bernardone, was a wealthy cloth merchant in Assisi, one of the wealthiest, and being a good boy—I was not a good boy, but we'll get to that!—but being a good son at least in some respects, I became an apprentice to my father when I was about fourteen years old—selling, buying, keeping an account of everything, even traveling with my father—especially to France! I love France—I mentioned that already, forgive me!"

"There's nothing to forgive," I assured him.

"So, anyway, I was a good apprentice, and I made a good deal of money for my father—but I spent even more than I made!" He got up and pretended to strut, "There I was, a big, young man in Assisi, tossing around money with others my age. We roamed the streets, threw huge feasts, drank like swine—you don't want to hear the rest!" Then he looked toward the crucifix pensively. "I've worn out God's ears on all that!"

"So, where was I?" he asked, slipping into his dramatic reenactment again, puffing out his chest. "Ah, a big sinner, with a purse that has a hole in it, letting all the coins slip through! Now, I don't know how much you know about Assisi, but like all cities it is divided by factions, the *boni homines*—you know, the old rich families—and the *populo*—the people, the newer families of the merchants. And they fight each other, just like they do in other cities, always fighting and choosing sides, some with the Italian popes and some with the German emperors who oppose them. If that weren't enough, the cities are always declaring war on each other too! Fighting, everyone is fighting!"

He smiled a bit grimly but maintained his prideful posture. "Fighting—that is good, is it not, for a young man who dreams of glory in battle? How could one become a great and noble chevalier without a battle? How else to get earthly glory?" St. Francis leaned on the back of his chair and looked at me. "I can tell you, I didn't dream of selling cloth, writing up ledgers, dickering with other merchants! I wanted to be like King Arthur's knights. I wanted to serve my lord nobly in battle and win great glory and renown for my chivalrous deeds, both on the battlefield and off—the lord of the city, not the Lord above.

"So, what happens next? My father belonged to the *populo*, and the *populo* had thrown out the old aristocratic families in Assisi, and these old families went to the city of Perugia. Are you following all this?"

I gave a "more or less" shrug and nod.

"So, what do you think? The city of Perugia declares war on the city of Assisi. And here comes Francis," he pretended to ride out, "rich enough to be able to buy a horse and my own armor. Here I come, on my grand horse, the 'great' twenty-two-year-old

Giovanni di Pietro di Bernardone, a young man who had never experienced real battle, but who hoped to be a great chevalier!"

He clasped his hands together, as if chained, and his countenance changed to grief. "Well, I was captured—*after* seeing a good many of my friends slaughtered like pigs, sheep, and cattle. The glory of battle!" He came to the back of his chair. "I rotted in prison in Perugia for over a year. When I came out, I was a sickly young man, not some noble chevalier." He receded into thought.

"And then?"

"God had knocked the wind out of me. I didn't want to carouse with my friends anymore. My soul felt as if it were filled with darkness and smoke. I was sick, spending weeks and weeks in bed. But after some months I began to recover—if not in my health, at least in my desire to fight for glory in battle under some great lord. Soon enough I had the opportunity to ride out and fight for the pope himself! I threw my money once again into all that a truly noble chevalier must have: hauberk, cuisse, greaves to protect my shins and feet, sword and lance, my buckler and my beautiful flowing robe. And don't forget the chain mail for my horse and the squire to serve me!"

"It sounds as if God didn't quite knock all of the wind out of you, at least not yet."

"No, the good God was showing His patience and His courtesy, using my desires to purify my desires. He sent me a dream, I am sure of it. I saw my father's house changed into a marvelous palace, filled to overflowing with all the equipment that a chevalier could possibly want. Every bolt of my father's cloth was transformed into lances, swords, shields, saddles, chain mail! And there appeared also a beautiful lady," his eyes were filled with love, "the lady to whom every troubadour sings, *his* lady, the lady for whom he fights. So I awoke and thought: God has granted me my greatest wish!"

"But you misunderstood the dream?" I hazarded.

"No, it is better than that! I awoke the next day and rode off, the noble chevalier. I got as far as Spoleto by nightfall. When I was finally able to fall asleep — you can imagine how excited I was — I had another dream. In this one, I heard a voice." Here, he began to act out both speaking parts of his dream:

"Francis, where are you going all dressed up like this?"

He turned as if answering. "I am going to fight in Apulia, I said."

Turning back to take up the first voice: "Tell me, from whom can you expect most, the master or the servant?"

"From the master, I replied, speaking the obvious truth."

Affecting the other voice, he asked, "Then why would you follow the servant, instead of the Lord, the true Master, on whom the servant himself depends?"

"By now I knew it was God who was speaking to me, so I asked, 'What would you have me do, Lord? What would you have me do?' And He said to me, 'Return home, and what you must do shall be revealed to you.'"

"And what was that?" he asked rhetorically. "It was the same dream again, the one about the glories of my father's house transformed into a palace filled with everything a knight needs to serve his Lord, and with the Lady whom he is to love — but this time it had been transformed by the Lord. I realized, I *knew*, that I would henceforth, forever, serve the Lord of lords, and love Lady Poverty — this was the great lady I had seen but not recognized in the first dream. I would sing her praises for all the world, and I knew that I would gather around me — that is, that the Good Lord would give to me — countless fellow knights from all the world. I would be the standard-bearer for Christ, the vassal to the holy Son of God, at the head of a great army of Christ, *Miles Christi*, who would all be my round-table companions — to fight and to die, not by and with the sword, but against sin and through martyrdom, in imitation of Jesus Christ Himself."

He stretched out his upturned hands and smiled. "And thus you see, God, in His mercy and wisdom, gave me exactly what I wanted—no! far more, infinitely more than I wanted—making me a humble servant of the most noble Lord of all, to whom I pledge my eternal fealty. I, a great sinner, and most unworthy knight, fighting not for earthly glory but for eternal glory."

And there he was before me, a knight in rags, a man who would conquer more by his embrace of holy poverty and his unearthly humility than any man with any sword ever has. And I offered, "I find that amazing, how God's providence works—just the opposite from how we usually think of it. Following God's will means giving up everything we've always wanted. But for you, He gave you more than what you desired—even though it doesn't look that way to the world."

He looked down at his patched robe and gave a mock look of surprise. "What? You are not blinded by the splendor of my armor?"

I laughed and then asked, "But this is what I find most interesting. We have all our worldly desires, and we think that God is saying no to them. But if you are not a 'special case,' and God treats us all as He treated you, it seems our strongest earthly desires are precisely what God uses, exactly what He transforms—if I'm not getting this all wrong."

I paused, musing over what he had said. "Do you think God put that great desire in you, from youth, the desire to become a knight, making you infatuated with all the courtly romances, all the Arthurian stories, the songs of the troubadours, knowing that He would take all those very earthly desires for very earthly glory and transform it all by grace, remaking it all into a knighthood aimed at eternal glory?"

As you might suspect, I was thinking simultaneously of my own "story," about my own deepest desires. Were they put there by God for a reason, or was I simply trying to justify whatever I happened to want? And what did I really *want* anyway? It depended on when you asked me, I suppose. I became lost in thought for a few moments.

St. Francis, noting this churning over of thoughts on my face, waited a bit—out of courtesy—and then said softly, "Well, in my own case, my friend, I would say, 'Can I read the Lord's mind?' Perhaps it might be safer to say the good Lord and Master *used* my vanity, like an old rag, to make a rich cloak—just like the one I'm wearing!"

I felt a bit deflated by his words, realizing I had been grasping at a kind of divine self-justification—not for the truth it contained, but for the excuse I might wring from it.

"Where were we?" the saint continued. "Oh yes. I went back to Assisi, following the Lord's command, waiting for all the glory I was going to earn by following Him into battle, and what do you think?"

By this time, I didn't know what to think, so I just raised my eyebrows questioningly.

"He tells me I must *embrace* what I most despise, for *that* is the way to both glory and wisdom."

Just as I suspected: There's no easy path to sainthood, even if God somehow does use our deepest desires. "And what was that?"

"I mean to tell you, the one thing I could not stand—I don't mind giving money to the poor, mind you, which I did quite freely even before the Lord called me—the one thing I could not stand was physical deformity. There was a poor old humpback woman in Assisi—I just couldn't stand the sight of her," he grimaced. "But even worse than that were the lepers."

I knew what was coming, as I had read of his life, and of course, being all too human, I wondered what this would mean for me if I were ever to have the courage of St. Francis.

"So, what does my Lord have in store? You may have heard this: He sends a leper to meet me on the road one day. I wanted to turn away, even run away, let me tell you, but God gave me the courage to embrace him, to embrace what I most feared and despised."

"That is a well-known scene from the story of your life. But most people just hear that story and think you had only one encounter with a leper — a spoon of bitter medicine you had to swallow only once."

"What? No, I immediately went to serve the lepers in the leper colony. I begged their forgiveness; I cleaned their wounds; I kissed them. And now, with my little brothers we serve them all the time. I demand of my brothers — and of myself — that they must serve the lepers every day, not just going in for a single little hug!"

"What happened next?"

"God was only beginning to mold and knead this pile of clay. Soon enough I heard God's voice again: 'Francis' — Frenchy, God calls me! — 'Francis, go repair my house, which is falling into ruins.' What does that mean, I ask myself. What does God want of me? I try to reason it out. I knew that many knights, to make up for their sins, would throw themselves into building churches or rebuilding ones that had begun to fall down. That, I thought, is what God must want of his new knight! It all fit together, and so off I went to rebuild the crumbling church of San Damiano, stone by stone, a bit outside of Assisi."

And he smiled, but his eyes revealed a deep pool of sorrow and weariness. "God shows us the big in the little, the great truth in the small, the universal in the particular. The Church, she is always in disrepair, always falling down, always in need of rebuilding. Nothing on this earth, even God's Holy Church, is unaffected by the forces of ruin — a menagerie of sins: avarice, gluttony, pride, sloth, lust, wrath, envy," he counted them off, one by one, like a bell tolling. "Pulling down the stones as soon as they are put in place. 'Repair my House, falling into ruins,' He commanded me. But it is always falling, always falling." He paused, and rubbed his arms as if they were sore from the labor. "There is nothing to do but keep picking up the stones."

I felt the weight of his words and felt myself standing over the history of the Church, indeed history itself, looking down upon it with the same resigned weariness. We all want things to be fixed for good, in our lives, in our countries, in the Church. We think there is some simple formula, some magic "architectural" discovery that would keep everything in place, solid and undisturbed by time. But it isn't time that wears things to ruin and pulls down what we try to build up. Time is an innocent creature. Other creatures are the source of ruin, some who also build and some bent only on destruction, some human and some more than human.

"But what am I saying—I'm leaving out a lot!" declared St. Francis. "I didn't just go marching over to San Damiano and start lifting stones with my bare hands. I thought I could just pay the money to have it rebuilt. I rushed home to Assisi, sold my horse and a lot of my father's cloth, and brought the money back to the priest, Don Peter. I don't need to tell you that my father was not pleased. To make a very long story short, my father renounced me," he said, looking at me directly, as if to ensure that I understood the seriousness of what he was about to say, "and I renounced him in front of the bishop, shedding the clothes he gave me right there. I then lived at San Damiano, building it up with my hands, begging for stones from others to repair the church as God had demanded of me."

"And how long ..." I began to question him, but a loud banging at the outside door, the one in my garden below the bay window, interrupted me. I got up to go to the window, saying to the saint, "Probably the pizza deliveryman."

"Ah, I see!" although it wasn't clear that he, in fact, did see. I knew they had pizza, or something like it, in Italy even during his time. It was a food for poor people.

"Just kidding!" I assured him, as I reached the window and opened the sash. "Yes, what is it? May I help you?" It was quite dark now, and the little garden lights didn't sufficiently illumine the dark form standing back from the door, looking up at me.

"I am Niccolò Machiavelli. Please open up your door. I am afraid I have become lost. I was on a diplomatic mission from my native Florence." He strained as he looked up at the window. I suppose my face was dark, given the strong light from the room flooding outward and around it. "You have heard my name, no doubt, as no one could be ignorant of my illustrious city, or my place in it. But I am afraid I will need to beg your hospitality, as I have had no food for the hours I've been wandering around like a dog without a nose. Fate has brought me to your door."

I had been expecting him, but as I've found out, expecting my guests and pinpointing the when and where of their arrivals are different things. "I've heard of you all right, Master Machiavelli—who hasn't? We were expecting you. I'll be right down to let you in," I informed him, pulling my head back in the window.

But he called out again, with some amount of impatience. "Are your servants in bed? Send one to let me in!"

Now, off and on I have wondered what it must be like to have servants living in my house—old-world envy, as you might say. But then I remember that in the old world, I most likely would have been the servant. "Umm, it's their night off," I informed him. "Be patient; I'll be right there. Please excuse me, St. Francis," I said as I strode across the room toward the door.

I hustled downstairs, through the hall, and opened the front door. And there he was, one of the most famous, or perhaps infamous, of men. He was not dressed in rags but had on a black velvet doublet that fell almost to his knees, which he wore over an even richer red satin shirt. I assume his stockings were of the finest silk.

"Please, come in. As I said, we have been expecting you but didn't quite know when."

He gave me a long stare, no doubt trying to figure out why the master of the house seemed to be dressed no better than one of his servants. He then walked in, breezing past me.

"Please, do come upstairs, down the hall here, and off to the right."

"I assume you might have some food for a man worn from travel," he more demanded than asked.

"Ah, yes, well I'm in a bit of a bind about the food," I responded, more than a little embarrassed at being caught up short twice in the same evening. We came up the stairs, to my office door, and went in. "If you'll just make yourself comfortable," I said, motioning to the blue comfy chair, "I'm going to call to have a pizza delivered. There's an all-night shop open across town."

"Pizza! — a poor man's food!" he said, looking disgruntled. "Your hospitality is … somewhat …"

"Quite grand and befitting!" chirped St. Francis, coming out from the shadows in the bookcase behind my desk. "Master Wiker is the very picture of courtesy, as I've found out." St. Francis then gave a bow and addressed our new guest with the greatest courtesy, "And who are you, my very good man? You appear to be of the noble ranks, by your clothes and bearing."

Machiavelli looked as if a passing carriage had splashed up mud and muck on him. "What is this beggar doing in your house?" he sneered, turning to me. "Should he not be sleeping in your barns at this hour, if you are the kind of man who would welcome such refuse out of charity?"

"He's my guest tonight, along with you," I said, somewhat offended, although not surprised by Machiavelli's reaction.

"I am beholden to your kindness in welcoming me, especially as I have no choice, but I am astounded at your judgment in welcoming *him.* He looks like one of those rotten Franciscan beggars — not the fat friars, mind you, but the *lunatics* who hail back to the original madman, the little poor man, Francis himself."

St. Francis only smiled.

Part 2

Machiavelli had, as yet, no idea that he was talking to the *poverello* himself—the little poor man, St. Francis. Of course, since Machiavelli was born almost three centuries after St. Francis, he was familiar with the Order of Friars Minor—that's the official name of the Franciscans—which had spread all over Italy and Europe. Indeed, he had plenty of negative experience with the mendicant followers of the saint.

Unfortunately, by Machiavelli's time—he was born in Florence, Italy, in 1469—some of the Franciscan brothers were not very holy anymore, and certainly not ardently seeking the hand of Lady Poverty. It was no wonder that Machiavelli was cynical about Franciscans, and about the Church as a whole. There's nothing like hypocrisy as an acid to destroy the achievements of holiness.

Now you've no doubt heard of Machiavelli because he is famous, or notorious, enough to have had his surname become an adjective: Machiavellian. A person who is Machiavellian is ruthless, a man without morals or scruples who does anything to get what he wants, a godless evil schemer and manipulator.

In Machiavelli's case, the adjective applies not so much to him as to his teaching. That is not to say he was a man overburdened with scruples. But his fame rests not on what he did but on what he taught, mainly in his little book of evil advice to rulers, *The Prince*.

I can think of no book of this small size that has had such damaging effects historically. On a pessimistic assessment, Machiavelli did as much harm as St. Francis did good, as if the devil, in jealousy, was anteing up. Taking the side of hope, we must believe that God's providence is continually victorious, even in apparent defeat. Isn't that the lesson of the Resurrection?

But that doesn't mean that we're not in a full-scale war, one that stretches from the temporal world to the eternal, from men to angels. Since there is a war, larger and far more comprehensive than any of our earthly wars (even while containing them), there is no neutrality. We must choose sides, good or evil. Not to choose is to choose. We're either with the saints or the scoundrels.

St. Francis and Machiavelli chose opposite sides, in the very deepest and most profound sense. I say this as a warning: Machiavelli was *profoundly* evil. That is, he used his most godlike gift, the one that sets us far above the animals, his reason, to serve evil knowingly. We forget, we moderns, the importance of the Christian doctrine that Satan is a fallen angel, a pure intelligence of such power that the greatest of human minds is dwarfed by comparison. But the evil that human minds can concoct is still great indeed, especially with the devil's aid.

Today, we often think of being evil as being stupid, as if one were merely making a slight but understandable error in calculation or a kind of slip-up of social etiquette. To be intelligent *means* to be good, so we think. And that is why we worship so-called geniuses, men and women of undoubted intellectual superiority. But worshipping human intelligence, as if it were an intrinsically beneficent trait, is as foolish as worshipping human political power as if it were unambiguously good.

As Plato and Aristotle knew, human intelligence is not unambiguously good; in fact, the greater one's natural intellectual powers, the more good *or* evil one can achieve—just as we've noted with St. Augustine and Rousseau and the gift of eloquence. We will be judged by how we *use* our gifts.

Machiavelli was gifted with a very powerful intelligence, and that is why he could choose to become such a profound teacher of evil. One thing he understood very clearly: Christianity was his enemy. A simple fact that points to the truth of Christianity is that all the great teachers of evil, all of our most wicked and destructive intellectual and political figures, regarded Christianity as *the* obstacle to their designs—Machiavelli, Hobbes, Marx, Freud, Nietzsche, Hitler, Stalin, Lenin, Mao. It's not for nothing that Nietzsche, the greatest of all teachers of evil, the atheist who summed up modernity's sustained attack on God, called himself the "Anti-Christ." Well, Nietzsche (whom we'll meet later) never taught anything openly that Machiavelli didn't teach at least implicitly.

So, here are Niccolò Machiavelli and St. Francis of Assisi. Two more opposite men could hardly be imagined, and I had a chance to learn from each, especially about the real nature of good and evil.

One of the greatest lessons of humility for Christians is found in how good and evil are "related." As we read history in an attempt to understand our Faith better, we find that the embrace of evil often comes about, in great part, because of the failure of Christians to live up to the demands of holiness—a very painful lesson, indeed. Yet the presence of evil in the Church often brings about the rise of great saints, such as Francis.

In the time of St. Francis, twelfth- and thirteenth-century Italy, the Church was in great need of renewal. Sin and corruption and extravagance had tainted priests and bishops. Since the great reforming popes of the century before St. Francis's birth, a number of bishops of Rome had been struggling for renewal. These same popes had been locked in a seemingly endless struggle with the Germanic emperors, who continually threatened the papal lands in Italy. The lands that the papacy owned were a constant enticement to kings and princes who wished to increase their land, wealth, and power, and (sadly) a constant temptation to the popes themselves to rule as earthly princes of Italy rather than humble and holy shepherds of the universal Christian flock.

As we've learned, God inspired St. Francis with the burning desire to embrace Lady Poverty. He did so not only because Jesus Christ Himself was born poor and among the poor but because he understood that a rich Church created churchmen moved more by greed than by the desire for holiness. St. Francis wanted to strip himself and the brothers of his order of every possession but the passion for holiness, the passion to imitate Jesus Christ Himself.

The pope at the time, Innocent III, sensed this holy zeal. We are told that, when St. Francis came to him to receive papal approval of his order, Innocent had a dream in which the Lateran Church, the cathedral church of the bishop of Rome, was falling over, but a little man from a religious order ran up and pushed it back up, straightening the church that was about to crumble. Pope Innocent recognized the little man: It was Francis, the man before him, asking him to approve his order's rule. This was the fulfillment of the call St. Francis received early in his life: "Francis, go repair my house, which is falling into ruins." It wasn't just the church in San Damiano that God wanted to be rebuilt. It was the Church Herself.

St. Francis acted like a kind of holy, cleansing fire, and the Franciscans became one of the great reforming religious orders, along with another mendicant order, the Dominicans, or the Order of Preachers, started by the Spaniard Dominic de Guzmán at nearly the same time as St. Francis's order.

But as St. Francis noted sadly, the stones used to build and rebuild the Church are always falling back down, repair followed by disrepair, reformation by deformation. This is not some kind of historical cycle of necessity; it is the result of sins of omission and commission. The good accomplished by St. Francis, it turned out, was followed two centuries later by the evil of papal corruption.

The popes at the time of Machiavelli were not reforming popes, to say the least. They were unholy men who had seized the papacy as a political prize. It shouldn't surprise us, with such corrupt popes as Alexander VI, born Rodrigo Borgia, that Machiavelli and many other people were very cynical about religion. When holiness is used as a mask for unholiness, piety hiding corruption, it's no wonder that Christianity was seen by many as the disease rather than the cure. And again, Machiavelli also saw very little holiness from the Franciscans of his time.

What if he had seen St. Francis himself? Would his life have been different? Would Machiavelli, with all his gifts, have become a great teacher of holiness? Or at least would he not have become one of the most influential teachers of evil?

Machiavelli translated his cynicism into atheism and was especially critical of Christianity, which he thought had ruined the world. He wanted to return to the greatness of the pagan world of Rome, the world *before* Christ. This world, he thought, had an earthly grandeur unspoiled by Christianity's call to live for the next life and to leave this world behind.

And yet we must still ask, *what if* Machiavelli could meet St. Francis? What difference might it have made? As you are now aware, depending on how skeptical you are of what my eyes and ears have experienced, this historical impossibility was made possible right in my office. I suppose we ought to get back to that.

As you recall, Machiavelli had shown up late, somewhat disoriented and quite hungry. By the time he arrived, the local burger joint Smokin' Joes had long closed and all that was left was a pizza parlor across town. I thought the most efficient plan was to call in an order for two pizzas and then drive across town while they were in the oven and pick them up myself. That turned out to be a rather stupid plan on my part, because it meant leaving the two alone. Would that I had just called it in and waited for delivery so I could have acted as a mediator between the two.

I realized this while I was waiting for the cashier to ring me up, and so I threw a twenty on the counter, snatched the pizzas, and bolted out the door. I went through quite a few "pink" lights on the way home.

As soon as I went in the house I heard Machiavelli thundering, "Enough!" and then a great thud. I ran up the stairs with the pizzas as he continued berating the saint, "I've had enough of your prattling on about my salvation. Keep your prayers and petitions to yourself!"

When I entered the room, St. Francis was next to my desk, picking himself up off the floor. "You have a good kick, my dear friend," he complimented Machiavelli, "and I thank the Lord from the bottom of my heart for the health and strength of your leg! You have given me perfect joy, the holy happiness of being beaten like my Lord and Master. It is not everyone who has the honor of sharing in the suffering of the King of kings, God incarnate."

Machiavelli rolled his eyes and looked away in disgust. I was shocked, and then quite angry, but St. Francis, seeing that, touched my arm and shook his head serenely. "Do not give in to anger, Master Wiker. This Machiavelli, he does not know what a great blessing he has given me with his foot. I beg of you, put your anger away, for Christ turns every curse into a blessing." He gestured toward Machiavelli, who was fingering some of the books in the case to the right of the chair.

I sighed, "I am no saint, I'm afraid," knowing full well my own shortcomings in regard to anger.

"You are probably not even very good at sinning! You should come to Florence—we are masters of the craft! We'll teach you, eh!" cracked Machiavelli from his chair.

St. Francis continued without acknowledging his remark. "The Lord says, 'Love your enemies; do good to those who persecute you.' Well, my friend, that person truly loves his enemy who is not hurt by an injury done to him, but, because of the love of Christ, is stung by the sin of his own soul. Let him show his enemy love by his deeds."

We think we're pretty good Christians most of the time, but that's because we've never been reminded by a living saint of how far we fall short of Christ's demands. I can tell you: It hurts to get a real baptism in humility. At this point, I confess, I was secretly wishing the saint was as harmless as the smiling concrete gnome outside. I'll probably have to carry a wheelbarrow full of garden gnomes around in purgatory for that one.

"I think this gentleman is in great need of some sustenance after his long journey. Hunger is enough to cause anyone to lack patience," the saint said, holding out his hands for the pizza boxes. "Might I serve him while you bring him something to drink?"

Obviously this was a polite command rather than a request. "As you wish," I relented, but not without misgiving as I disappeared out the office door to fetch something appropriate, trusting that somehow St. Francis wouldn't ignite Machiavelli's temper again. I hurried into the kitchen, snatched a glass, some cola, and ice, and ran back up the stairs.

St. Francis was standing by the chair, holding the pizza box for Machiavelli as if he were an obedient servant. "Might I get you a pillow, gracious lord? For you must be some kind of nobility, given the way that you dress. Forgive me, I did not quite hear your full name when you shouted it from outside. I have been trying to preach to you all this time, without knowing enough about who you are and where your home is!"

Machiavelli looked up at St. Francis as he chewed slowly on a bite of pizza. "I am Niccolò di Bernardo dei Machiavelli, of the great and illustrious city of Florence."

The saint looked pleased, as if he had met a potential friend. "And I am Giovanni di Pietro di Bernardone of Assisi," he said, bowing gracefully, even while holding the pizza box. "Your name, di Bernardo, and mine, di Bernardone—we have something in common, eh? I am also called Francesco."

The thought obviously struck Machiavelli as preposterous. "Francesco! Believe me, I have had my fill of the French! And I have nothing in common with a stinking beggar grubbing around for food!"

At this point I realized that Machiavelli not only didn't recognize St. Francis—how could he have?—but had discarded the notion that this "beggar" in front of him was some kind of a Franciscan, since he looked so different from the friars Machiavelli had seen.

"A beggar? No, I labor for my food. I am a poor man for Christ, a sinner begging for other poor sinners to repent."

"Oh, please! I have heard it all before." He looked over at me, "If this were my house, I would have given this 'thing' a beggar's boot when I opened the door at his knock."

As they spoke, I had been pouring a glass of cola over ice for Machiavelli, the usual kind of American go-with for pizza, without thinking that carbonated beverages were a rather new invention. Both Machiavelli and St. Francis stopped and stared at the glass as the mass of light brown bubbles surged to the rim.

"There we go," I said, handing the glass to Machiavelli. He looked at it closely and then took a sip. Almost immediately, he spat it out all over my bookcase. As I found out later, my cherished copy of Plato's *Republic* bears a stain to this day.

"What is this? Your wine is horrible!" he cried out. "Are you trying to poison me with your hospitality?"

"That's not wine," I responded, innocently. "My apologies. I do have some, however. If you'll excuse me."

St. Francis of Assisi and Niccolò Machiavelli: Part 2

As I went out the door, I heard Machiavelli say, "Well, beggar, I have had all of this I want. I suppose you may now jump right on top of the pizza with both feet!"

I quickly returned with the wine. "This should do it, a dark red should complement the pizza." I poured him a glass, which he took and sipped warily and then gave a slight affirmative nod. Seeing him at least moderately satisfied, I said, "Well then, Machiavelli, I've read your many works again and again over the years, and I have a lot I'd like to ask you."

Although I had not meant it this way, St. Francis thought this was a cue. "I see that you two have a great deal to talk about. If you will excuse me, I would very much like to have some fresh air and some time for prayer in your beautiful garden."

The saint left us, and I pulled my office chair over to where Machiavelli was sitting. "So, Machiavelli, I don't know whether I want to say that I'm honored to meet you, but perhaps ... curi-ous—that would be a better word."

"*You* are certainly curious—curious in letting that beggar into your house."

"That beggar is actually none other than St. Francis of Assisi."

Rather than express surprise, he merely grunted, "The beggar of beggars. What an honor!"

"But he is a great saint," I protested, "just as you are a great sinner."

Machiavelli seemed less upset by my dig than by my affirmation of the saint. He got up from the chair and started to wander past me to the bookcase behind my desk. "You think that he is a great saint?" he asked, as he ran his fingers over the volumes.

"The world thinks so. There is even a pope who now bears his name."

"A pope! A pope!" Machiavelli turned around with a scornful laugh. "The great and luxurious pope, bishop of Rome! Named after the little beggar Francis!" He narrowed his eyes as he looked me in the face. "Let me tell you about popes, what they are really like. They are hypocrites, wolves in shepherds' clothing, always scheming to fleece their stupid sheep."

I turned in my chair so as to be able to see him without straining my neck.

He continued, obviously enjoying his diatribe. "Franciscans and holy popes! I suppose you know about Francesco della Rovera—he was a Franciscan. He became pope when I was about two years old. He spent the thirteen years of his 'holy' pontificate stuffing the highest church offices with his relatives!" He lifted his eyebrows for effect. "Do you know about Alexander VI, eh? Rodrigo Borgia? There's a holy man sitting in St. Peter's chair! He became pope when I was—what was I then, about twenty-three years old? He did it through bribery! And he had I don't know how many illegitimate children by his mistresses—nine or ten! A holy pope. Make me laugh!" And apparently it did just that.

He wandered over to the window overlooking the garden and gestured toward the silhouette of the saint. "This Francis, he is a lunatic, just like his followers. Not the fat friars, the jolly ones with all the mistresses. They know how to live! But his 'true' followers, the beggars, dragging themselves across the earth moaning about Heaven. They know nothing about life, real life, life in this world." He turned and fixed his eyes on me. "The only world."

This was pure Machiavelli. I knew it by heart, but I let him preach to me nonetheless. His gospel was both simple and profound: There is only this world, and anyone who lives for anything else is a fool. Ergo, all Christians are fools.

So, quite predictably, he then declared, "This living for the next world—foolish dreaming of nothingness! There is no next world. The ancient pagans had it right, especially Epicurus and Lucretius—I do not mean Plato." He glanced up at the opposite

wall. "I see from the crucifix on your wall over there that you fall
in line with the folly of Christianity. That is why you praise the
'saint.' But I also see over the door two crossed swords, so perhaps
there is some hope for you yet!"

He pointed to the two double-edged swords, quite sharp, that
hung over the entrance to my office as a kind of ornament. I also
had several rapiers in the umbrella stand by the door. I must admit,
swords are fascinating — romantic even — in the original sense.
I've got quite a collection.

"Swords for this-worldly glory, for fighting! That is a man's pursuit! Christianity with all its 'cheek-turning' emasculates its ad-
herents by turning them into womanly cowards pining for a home
in the sky after death rather than earthly glory! But this, *this* is the
only world," he said, thrusting his finger at the ground. "*Here* is our
only glory, *here* our only pleasure, *here* our only pain."

He strode over to the crucifix, saying as he crossed behind me,
"Many have imagined some kingdom up in the sky, some kingdom
in an imaginary heaven. But let me tell you, if you are no fool and
you have ears to hear, that the only kingdoms are those built on
solid earth in this world."

Machiavelli then noticed a Bible I had sitting on a stand by
the door, on the side opposite where the umbrella stand stood
sentinel. It's a large, old Bible, rather fragile, and has been in my
family — actually, my wife's family — for generations.

The nobleman began leafing through it absently. "Kingdoms in
the sky, kingdoms in the thin air! This is all nonsense for women
and womanly men, eh? And let me repeat," he narrowed his eyes
as he imparted his worldly wisdom: "Christianity has made women
out of our men, turning them into meek little lambs like that
beggar down there in your garden. Always turning their cheeks,
always trying to beat swords into plows. Praying instead of fighting
like real men. That was not the way of the ancient Romans before

Christianity entered the world. *They* were real men, fighting men, fighting for the glory of the state, men who would rather beat their plows into swords!"

"So Christianity was a mistake," I said, baiting him, "and I assume the Holy Bible there is a rather long-winded children's tale?"

He smiled slyly, giving me an almost serpentine grin. "You have to know how to *read* it, how to find its *true* meaning. You may know, I wrote quite a bit about that — to those who could understand — about how to *truly* interpret Scripture."

Actually, I did know, as I had studied his *Prince* and *Discourses on Livy* and had written a chapter on them in one of my books.

"I had to be careful, of course," he confided in me smugly. "I had to write in a rather roundabout way, if you know what I mean, so that a few wise men could see the *real* truth about this 'holy' book. You can't let the religious fanatics know what you are up to! They'll persecute you. If they think that you don't believe in God, the next thing you know, you'll have your head removed."

Flicking one eyebrow up, to emphasize his own cleverness, he affected a conspiratorial air, "So, I had to tell the truth about the Bible to the very careful readers — so as not to get caught!"

"The truth! And what truth might that be?"

"The truth that was known to the ancient pagans, such as Polybius and Livy, and that truth is that all religion is a ruse, a trick."

"Including Christianity?"

"Truly wise men know that there are *no* gods, but they also know that in order to rule over others as kings, as princes, they need to *use* religion to control the masses, to control the foolish and superstitious people. So, the greatest and wisest men pretend that the gods have spoken to them. They pretend that their laws were, in fact, given to them by the gods, and that they are always speaking to the gods." He winked, "Say, on a high mountain, during a thunderstorm!"

He began pacing, or better, strutting back and forth, as he continued his discourse. "And why do the wise do this? Because this 'show' will make the people obey! Yes, the ancient pagan Greek and Roman philosophers and historians knew this was true of *all* religion. And all I have done, all I am doing, is reading this 'holy' book like a good pagan," he said, stroking a page of the Bible. "I am treating Christianity as just one more religion, one more foolish superstition. I am reading the Bible through pagan eyes, you might say. And what do I see? The real truth about Moses!"

Again, this was not a revelation to me, given my study of Machiavelli, but I egged him on, asking, "So you think that Moses was actually a charlatan, pretending that the God of Abraham was speaking to him on a high mountain, pretending that God had written the Ten Commandments on a stone tablet, when in reality, Moses was spending all that time on a mountain chiseling them in stone himself so he could lord it over the Israelites?"

I think he sensed I was less than convinced, but that took no wind from his sails as he blew forward. "He was a great and clever prince, this Moses! He knew not only how to trick the Israelites but also how to use the sword; that is, he knew how to make his followers into a mighty army who believed that it was God on high who would lead them into battle. He certainly made a good army for Joshua, eh?"

"And the miracles?" I asked, "I suppose they were just conjuring tricks—Moses the clever magician! The old turn-your-staff-into-a-snake trick?"

"Well, the Egyptian magicians certainly knew how to do such things," he said, stroking his chin. "Now I wonder if perhaps Moses might have learned a thing or two from the court magicians while he was living with the Pharaoh for so many years. Or perhaps from Pharaoh himself, who certainly knew how to rule a people by pretending to be a god!"

I pushed him to make his full admission of unbelief. "And Jesus Christ—no real miracles there, I suppose?"

He turned from the Bible and toward the crucifix on the wall, cocking his head. "Well, now we are treading in dangerous territory, are we not?" He looked back at me and gave a small shrug. "Let me just say that Jesus died a miserable death at a very young age, and He told His followers to put their swords away, while Moses died very old, and he told his followers to take up the sword." He looked up over his head at the crossed swords over the door. "So, if you are going to claim to speak for God, you had better have a sword to back it up, or you might die young, an unarmed prophet, so to speak."

At this point I thought I would stop pretending to be unfamiliar with his doctrines. I got up and began to walk around the room. "From what I've read of your works, your lesson about how to interpret Holy Scripture seems to be this: If you read it correctly, it really supports your own most famous—infamous—book of advice, *The Prince*. Am I right?"

He gave a little smile of affirmation.

"The lesson being that all religion is bunk, but useful bunk," I continued, "useful for a ruthless prince who knows how to manipulate others. In fact, since there is no God, there is also no good and evil, no Heaven and Hell. Therefore, so you argue, a prince is freed to do *whatever* he has to do—no matter how seemingly evil—if it will make him a more effective and powerful ruler."

I had ended up wandering over to the chess table with my back to my guest. "That's the lesson we really learn in reading about Moses—that he was a good Machiavellian prince who pretended God spoke to him so that he could lord it over the Israelites, and also that it was God who told him to slaughter his enemies ruthlessly."

"You are a fast learner," he replied.

St. Francis of Assisi and Niccolò Machiavelli: Part 2

I thought for a few long moments, wondering whether I should say what I was thinking, wondering whether it might have any effect on him or would just be waved away. I turned around slowly and asked, "What if *you* actually witnessed a miracle? Wouldn't that turn things upside down for you? Wouldn't one real, undeniable miracle make you have to rethink everything? Make you at least wonder if there isn't a God, and a Heaven—and Hell?"

"Hah! I have seen a thousand clever miracles and holy articles! Bones of saints, pieces of the true Cross, all of it, allegedly curing this and that! I have seen them attract money from pilgrims for fat and luxurious bishops! That's the miracle—that people are such perpetually gullible fools!"

Here, St. Francis came quietly into the room and stood in the darkness of the doorway, unseen by Machiavelli, who continued his oration. "And here's the miracle book that started it all! The Bible is truly a book for fools!"

"Do not speak of God's Holy Word with contempt, Master Machiavelli," the saint said firmly but quietly.

"What, the little brother himself is back," Machiavelli said as he turned toward him, "the captain of a whole ship of fools! Well, my little friend, you just missed a very good and enlightening lesson about the Bible."

"And what lesson would that be, my friend?"

"What lesson, what lesson, indeed! I am afraid you cannot learn this lesson. Your head is too high up in the clouds to understand what is happening on the very solid earth right under your unshod feet! And yet, and yet," here he seemed genuinely bemused, "why do so many other holy fools follow after you, a man without a sword, a wisp of a man. You probably couldn't even lift a sword," he added contemptuously.

"Oh, but I did lift a sword! As I was just telling Master Wiker, I fought for my city, Assisi, and I saw that those who live by the sword seem to die by it as well. But the glory of a knight, that's what you lift so very high, the glory to be gotten in battle?"

Somewhat taken aback, Machiavelli accused him, "You were listening at the door!"

"No, I was praying in the garden. For you."

He held the other's glare until Machiavelli looked down and away.

"This glory, I understand it," said the saint. "I did not lay down the sword or put on these clothes to avoid battle, as you must think —as a coward. I took up a greater sword, the sword of the Lord, and I put on this armor of poverty to fight in the greatest of all battles, fighting for more glory than all the kingdoms of the world added together!" He took a step toward Machiavelli. "That is what you want, is it not, glory? My friend, you do not aim high enough!"

"So," Machiavelli said, crossing his arms and walking around the *poverello*. "You want me to become a follower of you! Riding into glorious battle in, what, those rags? Why would anyone follow you? That is the mystery!"

"You wish to know why people follow me? You wish to know?" he said, with his head lowered. "It is because the eyes of the Most High have willed it. He continually watches the good and the wicked with those most holy eyes, and do you know what? They have not found among sinners any smaller or more insufficient person than I. And so I tell you this in all humility: He has therefore chosen me to accomplish the marvelous works He has undertaken. God chose me because He could find no one more worthless; in doing so, he wished to confound the nobility, the worldly strength and learning and grandeur, of all the world."

At that, Machiavelli shook his head and walked back toward the doorway. "Ah, little beggar Francis, it would take a miracle indeed for me to drop my sword of steel, for me to drop the real nobility and grandeur, the strength, the real learning, the real wisdom of the world. *That* is real wisdom, and I have learned it from the truly wise, the great pagan historians and philosophers," and he looked at St. Francis directly as he picked up the Bible, "not the supposed wisdom of this book."

"Again, I must warn you, for your own good, for your own soul's safety, do not speak with contempt of God's most Holy Word," and he put his hands together, pleading, "I beg of you."

"You do? Well," he said triumphantly as he strode quickly to the window, "let us see if one of your angels can catch this book of wisdom!" And he opened the sash and dropped the book into the darkness.

"There!" he said, turning around to rub the deed gleefully into the saint, but as soon as he had turned around—not two seconds after he had dropped the Bible out of my second-story window—in walked St. Francis holding the very same Bible, opened in his hands.

"What?! How did you ... what kind of trick ..." spluttered Machiavelli.

The little saint was absorbed in his reading, "'And what shall it profit a man if he gains the whole world and loses his own soul?' I have always been struck by that passage, deeply struck. And you?"

"You could not possibly have gotten ..."

"I believe you dropped this, did you not?" asked St. Francis, innocently, as he advanced slowly on Machiavelli, who was himself retreating toward the bookcase near the window.

"God give you peace!" he intoned as he laid the big Bible on my desk. "If you will pardon me for being so direct to a stranger, Master Machiavelli, I do not think that you are nearly as clever or wise as you believe that you are. You think that you see so very deeply, but you do not see deeply enough."

The saint stepped closer to the trembling figure. "Did you ever suspect that there was a deceiver far cleverer than you? Did it ever occur to you that your wisdom, your mind, was as small as a fly's in comparison with either God ... or the devil?"

Struggling to regain composure, Machiavelli asked, "What do you mean?"

St. Francis opened the Bible, which now lay on my desk. "Let us try a little 'trick,' as you might call it. I believe that you think Moses and Jesus are magicians? Perhaps Holy Scripture has a power deeper than magic, and a wisdom deeper than yours, a living wisdom sharper than any two-edged sword. If you would, please take that dagger hidden behind your cloak, on your belt there at the right side, the one with the eagle etched on the blade, and your family crest on the scabbard."

"What? How did you—"

"Now, Master Machiavelli, I will tell you what we shall do. I will fan the pages of this Holy Bible, and I want you to thrust your dagger in wherever you wish, and let us see if Holy Wisdom will speak to you in words that you can hear."

"The *Sortes Sanctorum,* the lot of the saints!" I announced, knowing that it played an essential part in St. Francis's own life.

"Some 'holy' superstition, no doubt," Machiavelli sneered, regaining some of his swagger.

"I can only say that when I opened the Holy Book at random some long time ago, and thrust my finger down without looking, I read, 'If you would be perfect, sell all you have and give to the poor.' I was trying to find out from God, from Holy Wisdom, what I should do. But I did not trust myself, or perhaps I did not want to hear God's first answer. So, I then I tried it a second time, and do you know what passage I had chosen randomly that time? 'Take nothing for your journey.' But, I admit, I tested the Lord. And so, to make sure, I chose again, and do you know what turned up? 'If anyone wishes to come after Me, let him deny himself, and take up his cross, and follow Me.' Three times the good God had spoken to me through His Word. And let me tell you, Master Machiavelli, that Word turned out to be very good; in fact, it pointed me to the very deepest wisdom. So, let us see what wisdom the Good Book might speak to you."

"Pious nonsense!" he cried.

"Come now, Machiavelli, you wouldn't want someone to report that you were *afraid* to give it a try. If there's nothing to it — a superstition, as you say — there's nothing for you to lose, is there?" I chided.

He paused and pursed his lips, and then relented, "Go on, let us get this over with."

"So, my friend, I will fan the pages of Holy Scripture, and you thrust your dagger in wherever you wish, and we shall see what the point tells us." St. Francis then fanned the Bible for Machiavelli, who, after some hesitation, stabbed the text — a bit more forcefully than I would have liked.

St. Francis put his hand over Machiavelli's to steady it while he read the passage at the end of the dagger. "Again, the devil took him to a very high mountain, and showed him all the kingdoms of the world and the glory of them; and he said to him, 'All these I will give you, if you will fall down and worship me.' Then Jesus said to him, 'Begone, Satan! For it is written, "You shall worship the Lord your God and him only shall you serve."'"

He let go of Machiavelli's hand and looked him hard in the eye. "All the kingdoms of the world and their glory! Do you find that tempting? What miracle would it take for you to see the wisdom in our Lord Jesus Christ *turning away* from the glory of all the kingdoms of this world?"

"I ... I ... that was mere luck, Lady Fortune, a mere accident. You ... you probably practice that trick all the time," he accused the saint.

But Francis was looking down curiously at Machiavelli's hand, the one that held the dagger. "You seem to have some blood on your hand, your lordship," and he took out a rag from within his own ragged sleeve. "Might I clean it off for you?"

As he did, Machiavelli pulled back violently, letting out a little shriek. And I must admit, I almost did the same myself, because there, all too clearly on St. Francis' right hand, was the stigma of Christ, the bleeding wound caused by the nails driven through His hands into the Cross.

"What is this — you — you cut yourself with some glass," Machiavelli rasped, "something in the garden? When you somehow caught the Bible, or went to get it, you cut yourself on something. Some thorns, that must be it! This is another trick, a magician's —"

"The name Machiavelli — that's an interesting one," the saint said, as he drew closer. "The Machiavelli crest, the one you have engraved on your doors, am I right? That family crest has four nails in it, four *clavelli* — or, more accurately, for your whole name, *mali clavelli*, the evil nails. *Mali clavelli*, Machiavelli. Those four nails on your noble family crest, these are the evil nails that were driven through the hands and feet of Christ, am I right?"

"Yes, that is my crest, my family name ..."

"You used to see these nails quite clearly, did you not, on your estate? When you washed your hands in the stone basin at the end of a long day, you would look at those nails carved into the door? I feel these nails," and he held out both hands, and both were marked by the open, bleeding wounds of Christ.

"This ... you ... this is a trick," Machiavelli whispered hoarsely, backing into the bookshelf. "This is no miracle.... You cut your hands, both hands, on roses in the garden, when you got the Bible," and he let fall the dagger that he had been holding ever more loosely. His eyes went involuntarily downward, and there, to his even greater horror, he saw the stigmata on the saint's feet as well. "This is impossible!"

"All things are possible with God," St. Francis smiled. "But you doubt, do you not, even when you see plainly. Perhaps you are like doubting Thomas. Would you doubt if you put your hands into my wound?" And with that, a dark red circle appeared on the right side of his patched cloak, expanding outward. Machiavelli was now speechless and wide-eyed.

"Do you remember when you were being tortured, Master Machiavelli?"

I knew of this incident in Machiavelli's life myself. When the Florentine was arrested as a traitor, he was strung up by his arms, which were bound behind his back, and very painfully hoisted upward by a rope from the ceiling and then abruptly dropped, again and again, a form of torture called *strappado*. How could St. Francis have known? This was the very question Machiavelli was asking himself, by the look on his face.

"You recall, do you not," continued St. Francis, "when you had your arms nearly pulled out of your shoulders, hanging there from the ceiling. Just for a moment, am I right, you felt like Christ hanging on the Cross."

Machiavelli blanched at having his private thoughts of so long ago revealed to him now.

The saint was not finished. "And then, sometime not too long after, walking in the streets, you saw the fat friars, as you call them, my fat friars walking together and laughing, and they made you angry because they had never hung like Christ on the Cross. But then you caught a glimpse of another of my little brothers, trailing behind. He caught your eye, did he not? He was no fat friar! You could see that he knew, like you, what it meant to suffer like Christ. You could see it in his eyes. And you, Niccolò di Bernardo dei Machiavelli of the great and illustrious city of Florence, you felt a sudden pang of love. But you immediately shook it off, did you not?"

A long pause ensued.

"Your soul hung in the balance there," the saint reported matter-of-factly.

Machiavelli was entirely shaken now. "How ... how can you know this about me? How do you know about all of this? No one could know—"

"But God, who knows all things, including the thoughts of man."

He stepped back from Machiavelli, who clearly needed some air.

"I told you: I am a poor sinner. God uses me as He wills. I am no magician."

He then put his hand on Machiavelli's shoulder and looked at him with love, seeming to breathe upon him a great, cool, life-giving wind as he said, "God give you peace, Machiavelli."

It seemed that Machiavelli felt that wind all the way down to his soul, which was, I believe, precariously balanced between the greatest of choices.

"I think you need to look very deeply at those nails on your crest, the *mali clavelli*," continued St. Francis. "On those nails your eternal peace now hangs, but you are dangling over Hell, my friend; you are dangling over Hell. And I would gladly pull you out," he said, extending his hands again, the stigmata glistening in the light from the lamp on my desk.

I did not have the privilege of seeing what may have happened next, for they both disappeared.

Reflections

Would it have taken a miracle to convert Machiavelli from his profound atheism? That is a very serious question that arose in my office, but as far as I know, it never did in Machiavelli's own life. Even here, though, Machiavelli and St. Francis both disappeared before I could see what long-term effect the witness of several kinds of miracles had on Machiavelli.

Of course, in one very obvious sense, it was too late. Machiavelli had already long ago made his choices, and the influence of his evil philosophy has malformed much of modernity. I have written about this elsewhere—that modern atheism owes an immense debt to Machiavelli. And by atheism I don't just mean theoretical, armchair atheism, but the "practical," political atheism that has given up on the distinction between good and evil, between acts that are permitted and acts that are too horrible even to contemplate.

Stalin was a dedicated Machiavellian, as was Hitler. But there are many followers of Machiavelli, less historically visible but no less deadly, teaching in universities, working in bureaucracies, trafficking stolen children in prostitution rings, shuffling papers and making appointments in abortion clinics.

So, profoundly evil ideas have profoundly evil practical consequences, and a very long book could be written about the immense historical influence of Machiavelli, beginning with the advisers to

Henry VIII, who consumed Machiavelli's work, and going right down to the present day.

A great lesson here is that his influence *could have been* for the better. I've said it already, but such an important point bears repeating: A man of his natural abilities could have been just as great a saint as he was a scoundrel. It's undeniable that the history of the world would have been *much* different if Machiavelli hadn't used his powerful intellectual abilities to craft books that asserted (and when they didn't assert, assumed) that God didn't exist, that Christianity was a sham, and that wise princes, knowing that there is no Hell, shouldn't be afraid to do *anything* that advances their political power and earthly glory.

Machiavelli is a perfect example of how intelligence can just as easily serve evil as good. That is the lesson of the fallen angels. But since modern atheists reject angels, they had to learn the lesson from watching some of their own cohort becoming devils who created hell on earth, such as the Nazis and communists of the twentieth century.

The Nazis and communists weren't stupid. Like Machiavelli, they were very intelligent, and hence, very evil.

Another serious, related error is to think that the more intelligent someone is, the more likely he will reject belief in God. This is a kind of perverse extension of the foolish belief that intelligence and goodness are identical, the twisted logic of which goes something like this: Intelligent people understand that belief in God is irrational; being irrational is bad; therefore, intelligence is unambiguously good.

But that is faulty reasoning, or, more accurately, an instance of reasoning from a faulty premise: namely, the assumption that being intelligent means rejecting God's existence. It is not *because* Machiavelli was so intelligent that he *therefore* saw through Christianity. Rather, he believed that Christianity was a sham, and then used his great intelligence as an instrument in the service of its destruction. This meant denying the difference between good and evil, and affirming the use of power to get whatever one wants by whatever means. To Machiavelli's credit, unlike many more-timid atheists, he understood and said out loud what subtracting God truly means for human society. It means that there are no moral limits on one's actions.

There is another obvious demonstration that the sheer intellectual power someone is born with doesn't automatically connect him to the truth. Very intelligent people disagree on the answers to the most profound questions—consider Plato, Aristotle, Epicurus, Lucretius, Cicero, St. Augustine, St. Thomas, Machiavelli, Rousseau, Kant, Hegel, Marx, and on down to our own heady disputes in the philosophy departments of modern universities. Profound intelligence is as likely to lead to deep disagreement as to consensus in regard to the most important questions human beings need to answer. That's why there are saints and scoundrels, even and especially among philosophers and philosophy professors.

Here, someone will argue that *science* is the cure for the frailties and confusions of philosophy, a common enough belief, especially among scientists and their eager followers who have not sufficiently studied philosophy or history, or who have not grasped the ambiguities in the development of modern science itself.

Modern science, in producing increasingly potent weaponry and in pursuing increasingly powerful means of manipulating human nature, has demonstrated conclusively that, when unchained from the concepts of good and evil, it is a tremendously destructive force. A casual glance at the twentieth and twenty-first centuries should make this evident. (Remember the famous speech in *The Devil's Advocate*, when Al Pacino, portraying the devil, exclaims, "Who in their right mind could possibly deny the twentieth century was entirely mine?") What counts is the philosophy, the understanding or misunderstanding of life, that guides their science. Here is where we find the great disagreements.

And so we are back with St. Francis and Machiavelli, and again we can ask: What if Machiavelli had witnessed a real miracle, as he did in my office? Would it have changed his very powerful mind, and hence, changed human history?

I strongly believe that the answer is yes, and I have good reasons for doing so. Machiavelli's atheism was rooted, in great part, in his acceptance of Epicureanism, a kind of philosophical materialism that denies the existence of immaterial beings—God, angels, demons, the human soul. In this materialism there is no room for God, and hence there is no possibility of divine miracles.

That means, however, that *if* a divinely wrought miracle occurs, the fundamental assumptions of materialism must be false. If Machiavelli witnessed a miracle, he would have to rethink *everything*, not only about God's existence but also about the nature of good and evil—and hence he'd be forced to rethink or, better, reconstruct his entire philosophy.

St. Francis was a living argument against Machiavelli precisely because of his gift for miracles, a gift that *followed upon* his goodness, his holiness, his complete witness to the truth of Christianity and its clear distinction between good and evil.

St. Francis was a man so entirely defined by Christ that he bore His bleeding wounds; a man so translucent to God's grace that he could read minds; a person so holy that those who were hopelessly sick, crippled, or epileptic were instantly cured by his prayers, or sometimes simply by touching him.

St. Francis didn't have to make an argument against Machiavelli's assumptions; he *was* an argument, a living demonstration of the falsity of Machiavelli's entire philosophy.

But does that mean that Machiavelli *would* have changed had he met St. Francis and witnessed a miracle?

Well, as I said, I think so, but it's certainly possible that he also could have witnessed a miracle and then denied what he had seen, dismissing the divine intervention in the same way the Pharisees responded to the undeniable miracles of Jesus by plotting to kill Him anyway. He therefore would have gone on denying that there are such things as saints and affirming that princes should all be clever scoundrels. God leaves us free to deny the obvious, to use our gift of reason to explain it all away so that we can hold to our precious and comfortable opinions no matter what.

We are free to be evil. That is a frightening truth. Free, even in the face of a miracle.

And if that weren't humbling enough, we must remember the truth that nothing produces someone like Machiavelli quite as quickly and surely as the fact that too many Christians do not live up to the demands of holiness that should mark them as followers of Christ. Machiavelli stressed the deep hypocrisy of the popes living in his time, specifically Pope Alexander VI, a man who did incalculable damage to the Church, both by inspiring Machiavelli's (and others') belief that Christianity was a sham and by convincing reformers such as Martin Luther that the Catholic Church was unsalvageable. But any number of shiftless friars, whose names history has long forgotten, brought this "lesson" to Machiavelli and Luther as well.

That leads us to a very serious final reflection: Each Christian is responsible for *being* an argument for the truth of Christianity, for if we are bad Christians, we then become an argument against the Faith. We all are given the choice between struggling to become a saint or falling all too easily into being a scoundrel. And if we do the latter, then we'll drag others down with us.

Flannery O'Connor and Ayn Rand

Part 1

Reading Flannery O'Connor has always been a great delight for both me and my wife. We enjoyed her works especially when we had just converted to Catholicism. Part of our attraction to Flannery is the fact that we lived in the South for some time, when I was in graduate school at Vanderbilt University, and we fell for the culture, the uninhibited friendliness, the graciousness, and the hospitality. But we also adored the quirkiness.

All of this is in Flannery, and it infused her Catholic faith and her rather startling stories. My children all grew up reading her, using her stories to illustrate points and quoting from her letters. I guess that has made us all a little bit strange. Her *Wise Blood* is one of my very favorite novels, and her short stories "A Good Man Is Hard to Find" and "Revelation" are, in my opinion, unsurpassed. You really need to read them if you haven't.

Ayn Rand? I struggled through her most famous novel, *Atlas Shrugged*, for a book I was writing in which I pegged her as a "false conservative." Since I had read about her life as well, I knew she was not only a false conservative but also an extremely unpleasant human being, and I was very glad I would never have to spend any time with her.

That was before people from the past started showing up in my office—in pairs. I wish that I had some control over who shows up. But certain people I read about, whether I like them or not, naturally fall into pairs, good and bad. As much as I wanted to meet Flannery O'Connor, just as much and more I didn't want to encounter Ayn Rand.

It happened anyway, and now that it's over, I'm glad it did, if only because the presence of Rand sparked O'Connor, and made her brilliance, the deep intelligence of her faith, and her lancet wit all the more evident. She had it out with Rand as an act of charity—tough charity, relentless mercy. That's certainly a lesson I learned from the encounter: You don't want to be on the wrong side of grace.

As I recall, I was cleaning my new pistol when I heard a knock on my office door. As already noted, if you look around my office, you'll see I'm a bit of a sword collector, not much of a gun man. One of my friends thought it might be a bit safer if I had my own handgun, seeing as an intruder in the night might not take me seriously if I was brandishing a rapier.

Since I am a fan of old rather than new things, he got me a Colt 45, a revolver with a beautiful wood stock—matching one of my favorite pipes, by the way. The revolver is from the late 1800s, so I keep it in a glass case on the mantel, with six bullets, each held in place by a blue satin ribbon. This is probably not the best place to keep it, given that it might be a bit difficult to get it out of the case and load it in real need.

But I had taken the case down and was polishing the gun when I heard a couple of sharp raps on the door, which I thought would be Rand but turned out to be O'Connor. Though either way, as it turns out, an O'Connor would have been at the door. Ayn Rand's real name is, or should have been, O'Connor—Mrs. Frank O'Connor, after her husband. Ayn Rand is a pen name. We'll get to that. Anyway, I set the revolver back in the display case and went to answer the door, ready to greet Mrs. O'Connor rather than Miss O'Connor.

"Oh," I said as I opened the door, "I thought it was … I mean, I wasn't expecting you quite this soon, Miss O'Connor." And then, fearing I had transgressed southern hospitality, "So this is even better. I will admit to you straight off, I am a great fan—as is my wife. Please, do come in."

There she was, looking frail as she leaned on her crutches, but with the same sharp, mischievous grin with which she writes her stories. "I'd be right happy to, if you could just take yourself a bit more out of the doorway."

"Yes, yes of course. My apologies," I said, feeling a bit stupid for standing there, gaped mouth and blocking the way. "Might I give you a hand?" I reached for her arm.

She was not to be treated as if she were an invalid, I quickly found out. Yet that is what she really was: Flannery was afflicted with lupus. Her father, Edward, died of it, and she was diagnosed when she was only twenty-five. Though her mother, Regina, kept the truth from her for a while, when Flannery finally learned that she had lupus, she knew, deep down, that it was a kind of death sentence, even though treatments had improved since her father's day.

She was born in 1925 in Savannah and would die in Milledgeville in 1964 at only thirty-nine years old, a Georgian lady from first to last. Almost all of her writing was done under the shadow of illness and impending death. Her spirit did not abide pity for her condition; rather, she mocked it with laughter.

So, when I reached for her arm, as if trying to help a little old lady, she waved me away. "Please don't, Mr. Wiker," which if spelled phonetically according to Georgia-ese would be "MISStuh WAAH-kuh." I will not attempt to reproduce her accent in reporting what she said, as that would be tiresome for me and the reader, and no attempt to capture it would be adequate. Happily, there are recordings of her reading her stories on the Internet, and these are well worth listening to.

"Them that tries to help me I usually shoo off," she explained politely but firmly. "Gets them out of my way, so they can't do harm by good deeds. Once they takes your arm or your crutch, they'll throw you every time!" She fixed her eyes on me, a smiling glint in each. "You are undoubtedly a gentleman, but in my experience there is nothing more dangerous to the safety of those on crutches than a gentleman's assistance." She laughed heartily at her own joke, as she always did.

"Where would you like to sit?" I asked.

"Preferably down, and sooner rather than later. I admit to being a little tired from the journey."

"I usually sit with my guests over here at the chess table, if that would be all right," I said, motioning behind me.

She stared across the room at the chess board and shook her head slowly. "I bought myself a chess set a few years back. I confess, I like the *feel* of the pieces. But I can't play." She took a few steps toward the table, leaning into each crutch as she made her way. "I reckon you have to be of a mathematical mind to get any enjoyment out of it, but I tell you straight up, Mr. Wiker, I can't even make change at the grocery store without agony!"

Pausing at the edge of the table, she picked up a chess piece and turned it around in her right hand as she leaned on her left crutch for support. "If I am going to play some kind of a game, I don't want to have to *think* about it. I suppose I might learn chess someday, if I could find someone to play along who didn't care about it any more than just pushing the pieces around on the board." She set the piece down again and turned back toward me.

"Somewhat my strategy as well," I laughed. "I take the blitzkrieg approach. Move as many pieces out as fast as I can and hope to confuse the enemy—all without the encumbrances of strategy."

She smiled. "If you don't mind, I'll just set myself down at your desk; then I can shed these 'flying buttresses.'"

"As you wish!" I circled around the front of my desk and brought one of the chairs by the chess table closer to her.

As she settled into the chair, propping up her crutches on the side of the desk, her eye caught the gun case amidst the general disarray of papers, books, coffee cups, and a pipe or two on the desk. "My, my, you are a gun enthusiast, I see."

"More of a sword enthusiast, actually." I gestured at the various examples festooning my office. "But a friend thought I needed something a bit more powerful in my armory."

"It's a mighty fine one!" She lifted the case lid and stroked the ornate wooden grip.

"Yes, a Colt 45, manufactured somewhere around 1890, I'm guessing."

"Well, it don't matter how old it is, as long as it shoots straight!"

"'Flannery O'Connor'—that's such an intriguing name," I noted, eager to get to know her in the little time we had, "especially for a Catholic writer from the deep south."

"Well, my full Christian name is Mary Flannery O'Connor. Flannery was the surname of one of my illustrious ancestors, a great soldier in the Civil War, and rich to boot! Captain John Flannery was a confederate officer in the Irish military corps of Savannah, Georgia. He made his money after the war as a banker and a broker in the cotton exchange. He left a million dollars that his daughter, Katie, used to fund the hospital where I was born—Old St. Joe's in Savannah. Captain Flannery's wife was named Mary. Now you've got my whole name!"

"I hadn't known all that. Interesting! Now, Miss O'Connor, I'd like a little time to talk with you about your stories before our other guest arrives, Ayn Rand—"

She cut me off as a look of disgust crossed her face. "Ayn Rand? Ayn Rand?! I hope none of your friends recommended her to you." And here she happened to notice a copy of *Atlas Shrugged* on my desk. "The fiction of Ayn Rand, if we can even call it that, is as low as you can get." She picked up the book and waved it in the air in front of me. "I once told someone if you found one of her books lying around, you'd best pick it up and find it a home in the nearest garbage pail."

And rather surprisingly, she did just that—dropped it straight into my wastebasket. Then she leaned toward me, as if issuing a final decree that should be carried out everywhere the offending volume was to be found: "She makes Mickey Spillane look like Dostoevsky! *She* is going to be here?"

This wasn't going to be very smooth sailing, I could see. Rand was as strong-willed as O'Connor.

"Um, well, yes, as it turns out. She'll be joining us later," I said with some hesitation.

As Flannery sat back in her chair and readjusted her gray sweater, I casually stretched my left hand down and fished the paperback out of the trash, setting it back on the desk.

"She's quite an influential writer, especially her *Atlas Shrugged*," I added. "I must admit, I'm not a fan—"

"Influential!" she thundered, slapping the desk. "Influential! You mean 'popular.' I'm afraid I have to be blunt, Mr. Wiker. The woman is an awful writer, and I say that quite apart from my deep disagreements about her subject matter."

She fixed her cat-eye glasses more firmly on her nose. "A writer writes about people, concrete people, real people, characters with a real personality and a real life. This Ayn Rand woman is all about abstract ideas, and the characters are just wooden posts to hang 'em on." She paused. "And they're bad ideas!"

This was a true judgment on Ayn Rand. I knew it as soon as she said it. I had a vague idea when I was slogging through *Atlas Shrugged* that I was reading an essay disguised as a drama, and even more, that Rand thought of actual people in the same way. By contrast, you read one paragraph into any of Flannery O'Connor's stories, and you feel all the sharpness and grit, the weight and presence, of very particular human beings.

"A story, Mr. Wiker, is about the mystery of personality," she elaborated, "presented through the drama. The primary goal of any story writer worthy of the name is how to make the action he describes reveal as much of the mystery of existence as possible, the mystery of real persons in all their vivid particularity." She shook her head. "And I can tell you, there is no mystery to Ayn Rand's characters, and no personality. They are lifeless advertisement boards for her philosophy, and a rotten philosophy at that! It's bad enough when you have a bad writer with a good philosophy, but a bad writer touting a bad philosophy is as low as it gets in literature."

She sat up a bit and said in a mock heroic voice, "'Serve yourself above all and only yourself. Damn the communists and the socialists! Go make money, and you'll be a Nietzschean superhero!' That's the whole theme of Rand's *Atlas Shrugged*."

I was trying to say something in Rand's defense, something polite that might bring Flannery's dander down a bit, as I didn't exactly want a scene when they would soon meet. The problem was that Flannery was dead right, so I got as far as a feeble attempts that amounted to, "Well ... uh."

Flannery brushed these aside like gnats. Her deep passion for the craft of writing didn't brook misplaced politeness.

"When you can state the theme of a story in a few shallow words or slogans, when you can separate these slogans from the story itself, the drama itself, and even from the characters, then you can be very sure the story is not a very good one. *Real* people are not, *cannot*, be reduced to slogans, however much this Rand woman thinks they can. That violates the God-given depth of personality, the profound mystery of each human being."

"So, every good story really is a mystery story?"

She smiled in agreement. "Yes, not in the usual sense, but in revealing the frightening depths of each human being, each and every one made in the image of God, not like some stamped-out cookie, but very real, very particular persons whose choices, desires, confusions, insights, loves, and hates all constitute the drama of their lives, all of which is set in the drama of God's salvation."

The more she talked, the more I realized what a great gap there was between her humorous, self-deprecating "hillbilly" congeniality, and her profound reflections on human life and art, as refined and deepened by her faith. O'Connor is a first-rate thinker, infusing a more profound philosophical understanding into her southern dramas than one would get from many thousands of credentialed professors — including myself.

"To state the obvious then, you think Rand's *Atlas Shrugged*, however many copies it happened to sell, is simply bad literature. It has no mystery, no personality, no real people. It's just a parade of ideas — or rather, one idea."

"That's why I said to throw the whole thing in the nearest garbage pail."

I moved Rand's novel a bit farther away from her, so I wouldn't have to fish it out of the trash again.

"There's a whole lot of people like this Rand woman," she added. "She just happened to make good."

Rather an understatement on O'Connor's part. Millions of copies of *Atlas Shrugged* have been sold, and she continues to sell well even today, decades after her death.

"Folks like Rand want to write about problems, not people, or about their favorite abstract issues, not the concrete situations of real life. They have an idea nagging them in their head, or more likely a kind of 'feeling' of some vaguely profound thought. You add to that, at least in some of them, an overflowing ego, and you got a recipe for bad literature. And that's Rand all over, if you ask me. Her ego mightily overfloweth! Well, people like that just want to be writers, to impart their 'wisdom' to the world in a simple enough formula for others to absorb it. Simple, just like real life ain't!"

"I must agree, I'm afraid. I had that very feeling in reading her book. But if you don't mind my asking, Miss O'Connor, why do *you* write?"

"Because I'm good at it!" she snapped back and then laughed. She smoothed out her brown skirt and added, "I know, that sounds a little bit prideful, doesn't it? But the truth is that no one should write fiction for the public *unless* he has been called to do so by the presence of a gift—any more than someone should sing or be a surgeon. A gift of any kind is a considerable responsibility. It is something one is given, not something he's earned. And that makes it a great weight, a kind of burden, a burden that is a mystery in itself, something gratuitously given by God, but wholly undeserved by the recipient. And because it comes from a source whose wisdom so far surpasses our own measly human understanding, the real purpose and impacts of that gift, from the divine perspective, will probably always be hidden from us."

She looked at her crutches for a long moment and then said, "Usually the artist has to suffer certain deprivations, afflictions, trials, so that he can use his gift with integrity."

I dared not interrupt the silence that followed, as O'Connor looked away at the window, lost in her own mystery—of writing, of suffering. She soon looked back at me and smiled, which I took as a cue to continue.

"If I might push a bit more in discussing your art, how does being *Catholic* affect your writing?"

"Let me make no bones about it: Whatever shock it may cause anyone—about which I care very little!—I write from the standpoint of Christian *orthodoxy*. I write with a very solid belief in every one of the Christian dogmas."

"Now I believe that's true, Miss O'Connor, but many of your readers might be more than a bit surprised at that. Your stories are often rather, rather," I searched for the right word, "grotesque, in the sense of the technical literary term, that is, fantastic, distorted, frightening, but also comic. And I use that term 'grotesque' accurately, don't I? That's the word you yourself have used to describe your writing." I got up to fetch a copy of her short stories from my bookshelf.

Flannery shifted in her seat to follow me. "I do reckon that a good many of my ardent admirers would be roundly shocked and disturbed to discover that the woman behind the stories is a thoroughly moral and thoroughly Catholic woman. My being Catholic is not mere religious decoration, Mr. Wiker. It defines the very soul of my writing."

"And one of my very favorite stories, and certainly one of the most famous and grotesque, is 'A Good Man Is Hard to Find,' where an escaped convict, the Misfit, kills an entire family on its vacation—a man and his wife, their two children, and, last of all, the grandmother. It is a story that is, as you insist, very Catholic, however shocking people might find it."

She slapped her knee and laughed, "And that is the one story I get the most requests to read out loud! Whenever I'm asked to read, I right away agree, Mr. Wiker—as long as it's not on the radio, that is, but I can do it in front of real live people. On the radio, I sound like an old woman with a cold who set her teeth in a dish in front of her! But when I can read it to a real live public, I must admit I'm pretty good, because I actually sound like a hillbilly!"

"Would you do me the honor?" I asked, holding up the book.

"Why sure," she replied, reaching for the book. "I've about memorized it, but a little cheating might help me through. Now I

warn you, Mr. Wiker, the funnier the story, the straighter your face
has to be in reading it. Serve it up dead-pan! The catch for me is
that I'm the kind of person who laughs heartily at my own jokes!
So, it'll be a struggle to keep from bursting out laughing, because
this is a first-order comedy."

If you've never read "A Good Man Is Hard to Find," or any of
Flannery's work, you'll wonder how she could consider to be hilarious a story in which a psychopathic killer, the Misfit, slaughters
an entire family. But all I can say is: If you read enough Flannery,
you'll understand. Like Dante, she sees everything in terms of,
or from the vantage point of, the divine comedy, but with a very
earthy amusement in the human peculiarities and foibles that make
up the drama.

I sat down in my chair for the performance, somewhat amazed
that I would hear, from the author herself, the story my wife and
I had read so many times. I had heard parts of a recording of her
reading this story in her thick Georgian accent and imagined her
sitting very still, but here she was up on her crutches in no time,
acting out the parts as best she could.

She just got to the part where the Misfit and his sidekicks, Hiram
and Bobby Lee, have already shot some of the family. The accom-
plices have taken the rest into the woods, leaving the grandmother
and the Misfit alone. The desperate grandmother is a manipulative,
self-centered woman; she's the one who got the family into this
mess by insisting that they turn off their main route to go see an old
mansion on a back road. She had smuggled her cat along, and it's
the cat, suddenly jumping out of a basket and startling the father,
that caused him to veer into the ditch.

The Misfit has a gun, and Flannery couldn't resist picking up
my Colt 45 to help add some realism to her dramatic presentation.
At this point in the story, the old woman begs the Misfit to spare
her life, insisting that he had "good blood" and "wouldn't shoot a

lady." "Pray! Jesus, you ought not to shoot a lady," Flannery cried out, acting the part of the grandmother.

But the Misfit, hearing the name of Jesus, turns the conversation from her life to the life of Christ. He tells her that Jesus should never have raised the dead, that by doing so He had "thrown everything off balance," because if He actually did perform all those miracles, then there's nothing one can do but follow Him. The problem is, the Misfit complains, that he wasn't there to witness the miracles, so he can't know the truth of what's reported in the Gospels.

If, on the other hand, Jesus didn't do any such things, then there's nothing left but to take pleasure in "meanness," including killing an entire family on vacation. "No pleasure but meanness," Flannery snarled, taking on the persona of the Misfit, and waving the gun dangerously close to me.

Sensing the Misfit's strange antagonism to Christianity, the grandmother tries to barter away her faith to save her life, suggesting to the Misfit that maybe Jesus didn't raise the dead. But this has the opposite effect from what she intended, bringing the Misfit to a kind of high-pitched declaration that if he *had* been able to witness the miracles, he wouldn't have turned out the way he did. As the Misfit bends down to make his point in the grandmother's face, she is overcome by an equally strange love, reaching out to him and saying, "Why, you're one of my babies."

The Misfit recoils in a kind of horror at her touch and shoots her three times in the chest, which Flannery acted out, pretending to shoot my gun. After the Misfit kills her, he pronounces to his fellow miscreants one of the most horrifying and just condemnations of human frailty, which Flannery spoke like a sentence from the midst of a smoldering divine vision: "She would of been a good woman, if it had been somebody there to shoot her every minute of her life."

I remained silent for some time. Finally, I was able to speak. "I've read that so many times, but every time I read it again — and now hear it from you — I feel like I've been hit by a sledgehammer."

She laughed and gently put the revolver back in its case. "Why thank you, sir! A sledgehammer makes a good tenderizer for grace sometimes!"

"Readers may very well wonder how such a ... terrible story — terror in the real sense of striking terror in us — could be deeply Catholic."

"Terror?" she mulled the word over. "I like that! I suppose that everything I've written is more terrible than it is funny — or maybe it's that my stories are funny *because* they strike terror." She thought again for a moment, "Or perhaps they are terrible because they're funny? Well, any way you slice it, even in Dante's *Divine Comedy* you got to travel through Hell before you get to Heaven."

She sat back down, a bit tired from the performance, and straightened out her sweater. "I guess the real question is something like this: Why strike terror in the reader? You might say that for the Christian writer today, the only tools in his toolbox that work are the blunt instruments. We are faced with a reading audience that is now largely defined by unbelief, a kind of comfortable and dull secularism. For Christians, the ultimate reality is the Incarnation, and nobody believes in it. But the audience doesn't even understand the nature of sin anymore, let alone the cure. They don't believe in sin; they don't believe in God. Yet, they are my readers, and so I've got to reach them where they are."

"They can't really hear Christian revelation and they can't see the Christian vision?"

"Near totally deaf and just about blind, like the prophet Isaiah said, deaf to grace, and almost blind to redemption. So a Christian writer must resort to ever more violent means, startling means, to wake up the near dead. When you can assume faith — that your audience knows what sin is and understands the need for redemption—then you can relax a bit. There's no relaxing anymore," she said, with a tired look. "Unbelievers need a shock to their system, a shock that can wake them. If you're a Christian writer, you've got to shout to the hard of hearing, and for those who can barely see anything, you'd better draw large, fantastic, and very startling figures—like the Misfit and the grandmother."

"The Misfit and the grandmother are startling figures, to say the least. Let's look at the grandmother. She seems to be some kind of a hypocritical … witch, a real hag of a woman who's ready to renounce her faith, to renounce everything, just to save her life. *She* is the evil one in the story."

I had thought about this story quite a bit, even taught it a few times in my classes, so I had formulated my own theories, which, I must admit, I was hoping to test out with the author herself.

"You sound like one of them university professors who always writes to me with all the wrong interpretations!" she chided me.

A bit red-faced, as well as a little crestfallen, I said, "Please, tell me about her then. I'm having the awful feeling that I've misunderstood your story all these years."

"The grandmother *is* a self-seeking hypocrite. She's annoying, petty, and her faith doesn't run real deep. If we were really honest, ain't none of us Christians are much different than she is. But the truth about grace—the Catholic Truth—is that it nearly always uses the imperfect medium, the purely human faults, including even hypocrisy, to get its work done. God didn't come to save the perfect, but those who are shot through with imperfection, and that's everybody! If you don't understand that, then you don't understand how God really acts, how He *must* act with *fallen* human beings. Like the old lady sewing a quilt for the bed, He uses whatever scraps He's got on hand—and that's us, sinful human beings."

"So, I had it exactly backward. The grandmother in the story is somehow a real medium for grace."

"That's right, Professor Wiker! Of course, as the Misfit rightly says, she was only purified as a medium for grace by having a gun put to her head."

She looked out the window for a moment and said somewhat distantly, "That's the sad but very real truth about us, ain't it? We're only receptive to the truth—about ourselves, about our need for redemption, about the terrible love of God—when we are standing face-to-face with death, looking at the barrel of a gun, like the grandmother. It's only when the terror of death is present that we begin to assess our lives, that we see the truth about ourselves, what we should have done, what we have failed to do. Death cuts through selfishness—the hypocrisy, the lies we surround ourselves with like pillows for our comfort—and forces us to ask about the real caliber of our lives. That's why the Misfit says, at the end, 'She would of been a good woman if it had been somebody there to shoot her every minute of her life.' I think that's about true of everyone, including me, and that says something about what sorry, sinful, thoughtless creatures we are."

"And the Misfit? Is he simply evil? An instrument of divine judgment? What?" I asked, afraid to hazard too many guesses, given my misunderstanding of the grandmother.

"Well, I reckon it's a bit more complicated than that, just like life itself. The Misfit has cut himself off from grace, that's for sure. But unlike many of our comfortable atheists of today, he *knows* what he's cutting off. He knows that if Jesus Christ did, in fact, do all those miracles and was raised from the dead, there would be no choice but to throw everything away, just like the disciples, and follow Him. Nothing else would matter. But if it's all a sham, then there's nothing to live for but the pleasure of destruction—of meanness, as the Misfit says. Modern men are not real unbelievers.

They *think* they're cutting themselves off from grace. But the Misfit really *is* cutting himself off, as a real choice of the will that affects everything, especially the very ground of the soul, and he *knows* what that choice means."

"Why does he react to the grandmother's reaching out to him in that way, pulling back violently as if she were some kind of poisonous snake?"

"The Misfit is touched by the grace that, for a very short moment, comes through the grandmother as she is confronted by death. Just as the Misfit, in self-consciously rejecting grace, is pushed to understand the full truth of a world without God—a world without redemption, without hope beyond the grave, without any moral structure—so also the grandmother is pushed to what it really means to follow Jesus, who, by love and through love, died on the Cross. For a brief moment, she truly understands what it means to love your enemy. Through her, grace reaches out to the rejection of grace.

"But the Misfit, having rejected grace, must destroy what he has rejected. He can't accept love. Love is, like you said, a kind of poisonous snake, or so it appears to him. But he doesn't escape God; he can't escape the wiles of divine providence. Even in rebellion, he is the unwitting instrument of grace for the grandmother, who dies with an angelic smile on her face, a kind of martyr who reached out in love to her murderer. That awful woman, as you called her, ends up dying among the redeemed. Against his own will and his intentions, the Misfit is an instrument of grace because he brings the woman face-to-face with her own sorry, sinful self, and, even more, with the love Christ had for those who were crucifying Him. But this is only for a moment—when the gun is pointed at her head."

"So, even in rejecting Jesus, the Misfit himself ends up being God's instrument of grace. Speak more about the Misfit's rejection of Jesus. Does he somehow work that way for the readers? That is, is he an instrument of grace for the readers too?" I asked.

"Well, as I said, we live in an age of unbelief, but generally those who reject Christianity don't really know what they are rejecting. They continue to live a comfortable existence because they don't understand the terrible choice — if I can borrow that word again! — the terrible choice that human beings must face once Jesus Christ, God Incarnate, has entered the world. If He was who He said He was, and if He did what the Church and the Bible tell us He did, then in the Misfit's words, 'He thrown everything off balance,' forcing us to make the deepest choice: yes or no. Most of us try to stay in the comfortable middle ground, neither accepting the fullness of what Christ demands nor truly living in a godless world. It's all or nothing, and the Misfit understands that, and he forces the grandmother to understand that as well. He understands that if there is no God and we do, in fact, live in a meaningless world, as the nihilist philosophers tell us, then there's nothing left to do but to take pleasure in destruction — burning down houses, killing, or doing some other kind of meanness, because that's the only pleasure left. You know, Mr. Wiker, unbelievers today think you can subtract God from the world, and we'll end up with a kind of permanent niceness left over. But while you might get niceness for a while, soon enough the real darkness of rejecting God, of rejecting a moral foundation for our lives, will burn through all the niceness, and leave us a world full of Misfits, whose only pleasure is destruction.

"That sounds, so … demonic."

"It is, Mr. Wiker, it is. That's what I'm shouting to the deaf. In Christian theology, demons are angels who, after explicitly and knowingly rejecting God — just like the Misfit — have one pleasure left. Since God is the source of all good, both naturally and supernaturally, the only pleasure left to them is the destruction of every good. As the Misfit says, 'There's no pleasure but in meanness.'"

"That would account for the deep cruelty, the grotesque inhumanity found in Communist regimes, or among the Nazis? A kind of positive pleasure in ruin, in torture, in violating human beings in every imaginable way."

She nodded, "We're made in the image of God. If we reject God, sooner or later we've got to attack that image with everything we've got; that is, we've got to attack our own selves. The world can't have a Church of Christ without Christ, all the benefits of Christianity without God, niceness without real goodness. That's what the liberal Christians and humanists want—a worldly kind of religion with a church that preaches niceness but without a crucified God. They don't understand the actual depth of sin, of evil—either in themselves or in others—and *that* is why I bring them face-to-face with the Misfit. *And* his gun," she added, patting the revolver.

"That rings a bell, 'The Holy Church of Christ without Christ'! Of course you are referring to your novel, *Wise Blood*. One of my very favorite novels—a masterpiece!"

Here, I do believe she blushed a bit at my enthusiasm. I got up and went to the bookcase as I prattled on. "But in that novel, the 'Misfit,' the main character, Hazel Motes, tries to reject Jesus *and* His Church—yet *he* ends up redeemed." I found the slim volume. "I don't suppose you'd do another reading?" I asked.

"I am truly flattered, Mr. Wiker, really I am. But I'm afraid I don't have the strength, with my illness. Seems like I have never been anywhere but sick. In a sense sickness is a kind of place, one where one must go alone." She added, more thoughtfully, "Sickness before death is a real mercy, though most folks don't understand that—like the Misfit's gun, I suppose! Wonderfully concentrates the mind and the soul, so to speak."

She leaned forward and gathered her crutches. "I'm very tired now, Mr. Wiker. I wonder if I might ask a little northern hospitality from you. You must have a spare bedroom in this big ol' house where I can rest a spell."

"We certainly do. It's just down the hall, the second door on the right."

She struggled up and waved away my efforts to help her. "I can take myself down there, sir, and save you the trouble." She paused on her way out the door. "Now, if that Ayn Rand gets here, you be sure to wake me. I would hate to miss the opportunity to meet her. I think I got a message she might find right refreshing."

"Will do, Miss O'Connor, will do."

I watched her as she disappeared out the door, and I could hear her making her way down the hall. I had no idea how this would all turn out, but I was more than a bit worried that Flannery might have a bit of divine mischief in mind.

Part 2

While Flannery was resting, I thought I'd read one of my favorite stories of hers, "Revelation." She wrote it the year before her death. As with all her fiction, it is frightening, fantastic, shocking, hilarious, and deeply orthodox.

Before I say more about that story, I should mention the obvious: Flannery O'Connor is not a canonized saint. But she certainly is an example for us of heroic holiness. She understood her talent as a real gift, a gift guided and deepened by the Church, a mysterious gift that made her a kind of prophet, shouting the deepest Christian revelations to an age deafened by unbelief, an age comfortably numb to the fire of the Holy Spirit. O'Connor's story "Revelation" is an excellent example of her prophetic literary voice, a sign of her deep holiness.

I will not relate the whole of "Revelation" here; there is no substitute for reading it. But one part of it is important for the "message" Flannery decided to deliver to Ayn Rand later that night. In the story, which takes place in a doctor's waiting room, the main character, the exceedingly self-obsessed Mrs. Ruby Turpin, is given a soul-searing revelation through an unlikely prophet: a bookish, acne-ridden eighteen-year-old girl named Mary Grace. I believe Mary Grace is Flannery's self-deprecating image of herself: Recall that Flannery's full name is *Mary* Flannery O'Connor.

We hear Mrs. Turpin chattering away smugly the entire time she's in the waiting room, condemning others and praising herself, all the while posing as a sincere Christian. Finally, overflowing with self-affirmation, she exclaims, "When I think who all I could have been besides myself and what all I got, a little of everything, and a good disposition besides, I just feel like shouting, 'Thank you, Jesus, for making everything the way it is!'"

At this, Mary Grace throws the book she was reading across the room, hitting Mrs. Turpin above the eye. She then leaps upon Turpin, trying to strangle her. The doctor and nurse wrestle the girl off the plump Mrs. Turpin's neck and give her a sedative.

But Mary Grace, as the story's prophet, isn't finished. She must reveal the truth about Mrs. Turpin *to* Mrs. Turpin. The "revelation" she utters is horrifyingly blunt, put in the form of a command, almost an exorcism: "Go back to hell where you came from, you old wart hog."

The revelation entirely crushes Mrs. Turpin's pride in being a "good" Christian. At bottom, her sin — pride — is revealed as the very sin she shares with Satan. A chastened Mrs. Turpin then has a vision of all the other fools and lowlifes she so cheerfully dismissed as beneath her, dancing and singing their way into the glory of God's Kingdom, while she drags in at the very end, the first becoming last and the last becoming first.

It was not long after Flannery finished writing "Revelation" that her health took its final downturn. I imagine that after death, she danced and sang her way into the glory of God — crutches left behind, along with her lupus-broken body.

Do I *know* that she is among those honored on All Saints' Day? God alone knows. I like to think so, given how patiently (and humorously) she bore her illness, and how she forced herself to write about the deepest of Christian mysteries under the shadow of death.

So, as I said, I was reading this favorite story again when I heard a scuffling and banging, and then suddenly Ayn Rand came through my office door. She was wearing her typical 1950s-style black dress, made even more dowdy by her short, chewed-off dark hair framing a most unappealing, almost vampire-like face.

"So here you are, Mr. Velker," she snapped. "I am wandering around looking in different doors but could not find you—until now." She squinted. "You are Mr. Velker, are you not?"

"Wiker, actually. Like 'biker' or 'hiker,' but with a W. And please forgive me for not meeting you properly. I didn't hear you come in." I held up the book. "I was engrossed in reading a story by Flannery O'Connor—'Revelation.' Perhaps you've read it?"

"Flannery O'Connor? Who is he?"

"*She.* She's a woman, a Southern short-story writer, one of the very best." Not seeing any glint of recognition, or even polite interest, I continued, "Never mind.... Well, please come in. I've been waiting for you."

"O'Connor? Interesting. That's the last name of my husband, Frank. So this Flannery O'Connor, she wrote a story called 'Revelation'? Is she one of these *Christian* writers? I will not read about revelation. It is a waste of my precious time. There is no God, and nothing but reason and reason alone is the proper guide for man. If man wants to live on earth, and to live as a human being, he has to hold reason as an absolute, as his *only* guide to action. He must, to be a man, live by the independent judgment of his *own* mind, not of some supposed god."

"Well, I see we're not going to be wasting much time on pleasantries," I said, forcing a smile. "So please, have a seat, and we can talk about your ... philosophy of life. I usually sit with my guests at the chess table."

I ushered Rand in that direction, and we exchanged some rather forced chitchat while settling into our seats. At least that's how it seemed to me, as I was very conscious of my intense dislike of her.

"Some of my guests like to play, others don't—chess, I mean. Are you a chess player?"

"I wrote an essay on chess, you know, as an open letter to Boris Spassky, the great Soviet chess master, pointing out the contradiction between the game of chess and the communism of his own country. I wanted him to see the truth, the truth of *my* philosophy, through the game of chess, which he loves so very much."

The torrent of words continued to pour out, and I dared not interrupt. That's how Rand is, a kind of rapid-fire deliverer of her judgments on nearly anything you might care to mention. She had a strange way of talking, I might add. It may have been because English was not her first language. Rand was from Russia; her real name was Alisa Rosenbaum. But she spoke in a very clipped, deliberate, almost robotic fashion, as if her words had been memorized and were now being mechanically reproduced. And she had a pronounced Russian accent against which she seemed to struggle. If that weren't disconcerting enough, she had a strange habit of shifting her eyes, continually flicking them off to the right or the left.

"Chess depends on one man applying his own individual intelligence," she continued, glancing at the board, "for *his own victory*, and hence *his own happiness*. That is how we each should live; that is what it means to be moral. To win by our own efforts and only our own efforts, and for the sake of our own happiness and only our own happiness."

"Well, I—"

She plowed forward, gaining even more steam. "No! Not communism, not socialism, not egalitarianism, not democracy! In chess and in life, each man must play his own game. Each man must seek his own victory. Each man must strive for his own happiness, and do so by the use of his own reason, for his own self-interest. Not for someone else do we play the game of chess. Not for someone else do we play the game of life. And the victory goes to the most intelligent, the best player."

She looked at me for a few seconds, and then her eyes flicked away. "That is the essence of my philosophy."

I tried to restrain myself out of Christian charity, which I find in short supply in my own veins, but also for the sake of giving her more rope, so to speak, in which she might entangle herself.

"I find it a little strange that you keep referring to it as *your* philosophy. If it is true, wouldn't it just be ... philosophy. Not yours or mine, but just the truth?"

"It *is* mine!" she snapped. "I created it, so I am being entirely accurate to say that I have discovered it; indeed, I have *revealed* the truth."

She shifted in her seat, not out of nervousness, I suspect, but from some other cause of unrest. "I am primarily the creator of a new code of morality that has so far been believed to be impossible—namely, a morality not based on faith, as it is for this O'Connor woman," and then, looking around and seeing a few religious paintings, she added, "or perhaps for you. My philosophy is not based on an arbitrary will or on some kind of emotion, such as kindness or compassion. And it is not based on someone's arbitrary edict, such as that of a communist dictator or the majority in a democracy. My morality is not based on any mystical notion or idea of social goodness or altruism. No! None of this. It is based solidly *on reason itself*, and so my morality is based on logic itself. And so—unlike all these others—*my* morality can be demonstrated to be true and necessary!" She sat back triumphantly.

I thought she was indicating the possibility that I might talk, so I began, "I see. Well now let's look at—"

"What this means, Mr. Velker—I will tell you what this means precisely. It means that the highest purpose of man is the achievement of his own happiness, by his own efforts, by his own reason. He must not force other people to work for his happiness, nor allow them to force him to work for their happiness—as happens in communism, and as happens more and more in the United States, as the socialists gain power. No! Each man must be free to follow his own rational self-interest in pursuit of his own happiness, and expect nothing of other men, nor let other men expect anything from him. That philosophy is what I reveal in my novels."

She smiled grimly and leaned toward me. "You no doubt have read my *Atlas Shrugged?*

"Yes, as a matter of fact, I have, and I was just going to—"

"The heroes in it make a mutual binding pledge: 'I swear—by my life and my love of it—that I will never live for the sake of another man, nor ask another man to live for mine.'"

"Yes, I have read it and remember quite well the oath. In fact—"

This time it was Flannery O'Connor who interrupted me, and I was very glad of it.

"So have I," she said, entering the room. "Why you must be Aay-yan Ray-yund," she said, drawing out all the syllables in her thickest Georgian accent.

Rand just stared, utterly flummoxed, not only at Flannery's brassiness, but even more because she was unable to translate Deep Georgian into a form of English she could understand. Rather than helping, Flannery simply looked at her and smiled innocently.

Suddenly, a bit of light dawned on Rand's face. "Oh, you are saying my name. It's pronounced 'Ine,' as if with a long *I*. Ayn. Ayn."

"Rhymes with 'mine, mine,'" I blurted out, unable to restrain myself from a bit of a jab after her rather tiresome monologue.

"And who are you?" she asked Flannery disdainfully.

"Why, I'm *Mary Grace* Flannery O'Connor," she said, giving me a bit of a mischievous wink. She had something in mind, but at this point, I didn't know what. Why add "Grace"? Why use her real first name rather than her more famous "Flannery"? And then I remembered the character Mary Grace in her story "Revelation." An "uh-oh" feeling ran through me.

"Well, Miss Eye-an Ray-und, I do a little writin' too. I told Mr. Wiker how much your writing reminds me of Mickey Spillane, and that I advise all my friends that if they see your novel lyin' around somewhere," she said as she walked toward my desk, "they ought to pick it right up and put it in a *very special place*." She knocked her right crutch casually against my wastebasket.

Again, Rand stared at her, working through a translation. She then said rather coldly, "I take that as a compliment, although I am having a bit of trouble with your strange accent. Where are you from?"

"My accent?" Flannery chortled. "Why, I hail from Georgia."

"Not the one near Russia in the Caucasus, obviously. I was born in Russia, you know." She stared at Flannery and then looked back at me. "But you are interrupting," she said dismissively. "I was just outlining my philosophy."

"My apologies, Miss Ray-und. I'll just set myself down here at Mr. Wiker's desk and listen to your ponderous explications."

As she worked her way into my seat, leaning the crutches on the side of the desk, Rand continued as if Flannery were of as little consequence as the chair she sat in. "As I said, I was born in Russia."

"Not Ayn Rand, but Alisa Rosenbaum, so I've discovered," I interjected. "You are, or you were originally, a Russian Jew?"

"Yes, but my parents were not devout." She thought for a second, "My mother, Anna, she was a bit religious, perhaps just by custom. But my father, Zinovy, not at all! He struggled in this life, and was quite successful. This was Russia *before* the revolution of the communists. My father earned a degree in chemistry. He built up his own business—an apothecary. What is it called here in America again?"

"A drugstore, a pharmacy," I offered.

"Yes, that is it. He built it up, this business, this drugstore, by his *own* efforts, with his *own* hands, by his *own* mind, with his *own* sweat. And then, do you know what happened? The communist revolution! The communists took over his business, snatched it from him in the name of 'the people.' The people! Through their idiotic incompetence, their laziness and stupidity, they turned a thriving business into a failure." She rocked back and forth in an agitated way. "And *that* is why I am a champion of capitalism against all attempts of the state—of stupid committees of bureaucrats, of the so-called people and their common good, of the parasitic socialists—to take what one man has built up by his own mind and hands and ruin it. What they did to my father, they did to the whole of Russia!"

She looked off in the distance for a moment and then added, "I admired my father very much, though he was not very interested in me."

So much becomes clear about Rand's philosophy when one hears about her life, especially the effect that the real stupidity and brutishness of the communists had on her father. Had I witnessed such things, perhaps I, too, might have adopted a philosophy like Rand's and become a radical capitalist touting radical individualism. There but for the grace of God go I?

"And your mother, could you tell us about her?" I asked.

She hesitated, as if weighing the consequences of bringing her into memory. "Well, I was their first child. My mother ... she did not want children. She made that very plain to us. She told us right to our faces, me and my sisters, that she never *wanted* any children at all, but did so only out of duty. She always seemed . . . angry."

I could see the pain each word caused her.

"She broke the legs of my favorite doll once. In every way, my mother disapproved of me: I was not athletic; I did not care about other girls. She was proud of only one thing: my intelligence. She was proud to show me off—or at least that part of me—to the rest of the family. I suppose you could say that my reason was the only thing she loved."

My passionate dislike of Rand was, I must admit, softened quite a bit as she talked. A loveless family, a father who ignored her, a mother who bluntly told her she was unwanted: It was no wonder she craved attention. And the only attention she ever got was for her intelligence, *her* reason. That's why she was so insistent about *her* philosophy: She still wanted to be loved for her mind, which was the only way she had been loved, if we can call it that. In any case, I did not answer her or offer vapid condolences for a sorry childhood. Frankly, I was unable to think of anything to say.

"I did not like being a child at all," Rand continued. "I did not like being attached to a family at all, and that is why I decided never to have any children of my own. And *that* is why I support abortion as a fundamental right!"

She looked at me as if issuing a challenge to a duel. I declined, thinking that I was getting much further by letting out more rope.

"*Individualism*—that is my theme song, my obsession, my mania, you might say. The individual—not the state, *not the family*—is supreme!" She paused, lost in her thoughts for a moment.

"But enough of that," she suddenly continued, shaking off whatever memories were bothering her. "I knew I had to get out of the Soviet Union as soon as possible to escape the madness of communism. And America was the land I already loved!"

She smiled warmly (at least for her), but then a wave of cold appeared on her face. "So, I left the Soviet Union and came to the United States. And what do I find here? In the universities? In the media? The intelligentsia? The Stupid Left? The Liberals in America?" she said, increasing the decibels with each rhetorical question. "They are praising communism, of which they are entirely ignorant! They speak against the so-called evils of capitalism, while they are living off all the benefits of capitalism! Ignorant parasites!"

She was nearly shouting now as she slapped the chess table hard enough to cause a kind of revolution amongst the pieces, with kings and queens, knights and pawns crashing to the board. I picked them up and reset them as she continued.

"If they could have tasted communism, if they could have experienced what real communism was like, they would not have chattered and twittered about the glories of the communist state. The fools!"

She stood up and started walking around, pacing in anger. "I will tell you this, Mr. Velker, my family was well-off before the 'glorious' communist revolution. We even had servants. Jews with servants! Think about that! But within a very short time, after the communists took over, everything of value was ruined. All the beautiful colors turned to gray, all the fruit of my father's labor spoiled and trampled upon by swine. My father's business, snatched and ruined."

Tears began to form in her eyes, tears of rage rather than a more tender emotion. "We were starving, literally starving. I remember begging my mother once for *just one more dried pea*. I dressed in rags. I ... I had to rub kerosene in my hair to protect me from the lice that brought typhus! That is communism! That is socialism!"

She then allowed a small smile and lifted up her hands, gesturing around her in approval. "But here, here in America, I am already rich! Here, I have been rewarded for the work of my own mind. *That* is why I shall put a big dollar sign above my coffin when I die—not a cross!" She looked at me in what appeared to be a clumsy attempt at being coquettish. "I am a radical for capitalism, you see!"

Well, it was certainly all coming together now. No wonder she had such an abiding hatred for socialists and especially communists, and such a virulent disgust with American leftist intellectuals of the 1950s, spouting off about the wonders of communist Russia. Put this together with her rotten family, and her philosophy becomes more understandable—even though, ultimately, repugnant and wrong. Errors are errors, however we may come to accept them.

But again, I must admit that I was feeling rather subdued after all this—less inclined to be on the attack, more inclined to sympathy, even with a dash of compassion. As I sat there meditatively, thinking what I might say, I heard a great cackle from across the room.

"A dollar sign on her coffin!" guffawed Flannery, laughing so hard she was nearly doubled over. "Lordy, I think I feel a story comin' on!"

Uncontrollable laughter was exactly the reaction Rand wasn't expecting, and it left her, for an all-too-brief moment, speechless. I searched for something to say.

"You said your family was not devout, was not religious. I assume your father was a purely secular-minded Jew. Did he have a great influence on you? When did you become an atheist?"

Here, she picked up her chin and said proudly, as if it were a precocious achievement, "At thirteen years old, I remember writing in my diary, 'Today, I decided to be an atheist.' Yes, Mr. Velker, I was completely convinced, even at that very young age, that the very concept of God, the idea of God, was completely degrading to man. To affirm that God is perfect means that mankind can never be God's equal. But that is simply wrong! To think that man is low, that man is imperfect, and that there is something above him, always above him! No! There is nothing above man. I will not allow it!"

I was going to suggest that thirteen years old is a bit young to come to such a conclusion, but Flannery chimed in before me, spoiling for a tussle.

"So, you make the sin of pride into the greatest virtue? Sounds like you agree with the devil himself!" she said, crossing her arms in disgust.

"I agree with the philosopher Nietzsche," she barked back. "There is no God. There is only man, and what he makes of himself. If there is going to be any perfection in this world, it must come from our efforts *as men*, from our *human* reason. And I came to America to do just that—to succeed by my own efforts. And I did."

She walked a few steps toward Flannery, arms smugly folded across her chest. "I started writing movie scripts almost as soon as I got off the boat. How I loved the American movies!"

"That explains the caliber of your later writing," Flannery said to herself, as if it were a private conclusion, but loud enough for us both to hear.

If Rand heard her, she chose to ignore her. "Soon enough I went all the way out to Hollywood, the place I dreamed of going when I was a young girl trapped in the darkness of the Soviets. And believe it or not, I, an atheist, got a job right away! I was an extra in Cecil B. DeMille's epic *The King of Kings*! Think of that, if you would. An atheist in a film about the last weeks of Jesus Christ before He was crucified!"

"I couldn't have written a more ironic plot," added Flannery, "though I might give it a try."

"And that is where I met Frank O'Connor. It was love at first sight!" she said rapturously—or anyway, as romantically as she could. She then turned back to Flannery. "That is your name, is that not what you said? You are Miss O'Connor?"

"Yes'm. *Mary Grace* Flannery O'Connor, at yer service."

Rand continued her story. "Frank and I married about two and a half years after we met."

"And has it been a happy marriage, Mrs. O'Connor?" Miss O'Connor asked with a kind of exaggerated innocence.

"It is a marriage of destiny! Frank was so dashing, just like my childhood hero, Cyrus Paltons, in that wonderful book I read again and again when I was a young girl," and here she let out a sigh, "*The Mysterious Valley*."

As I found out later, *The Mysterious Valley* was written by Frenchman Maurice Champagne in the early twentieth century as an adventure story for young boys. It was by no means a literary classic but was originally serialized in a boys' magazine. It was roughly the equivalent of, say, the Indiana Jones movies. For some reason, it fascinated Rand when she was young and deeply formed her later literary efforts.

Flannery barely stifled a laugh. "Do you mean that you picked your husband from a pulp-fiction action-adventure book?"

Rand fumed. "Do not laugh! From the hero Cyrus, I understood at a very young age what my philosophy should be. Cyrus was a man of action. He was totally self-confident—and no one, *no one*, could stand in his way. No matter how bad things got, no matter how difficult and dangerous the circumstances, Cyrus would always find the solution."

She glared at Flannery, as if her very soul had been directly assaulted by her, but her passionate defense seemed to me almost that of a child defending a favorite superhero. "And Cyrus helped *me* to develop in my fiction what I have called 'my kind of man,' the ideal man, the man of intelligence, of independence, of courage. The heroic man!"

Flannery was entirely unruffled by having raised Rand's ire. In fact, she seemed to be enjoying herself a bit too much.

"And this ... hero from your childhood book, he's the idol at the center of your adult philosophy?" She shook her head back and forth slowly, as if to say, "What a shame," and then looked Rand directly in the eye and said with lovely bluntness, "You ain't grown up much, Mrs. O'Connor, philosophy-wise."

Unsurprisingly, this did little to soothe Rand. "I have held the same philosophy I now hold for as far back as I can remember! My philosophy, in essence, is defined by the concept of man as a heroic being. He is heroic if and when he seeks his own happiness, making the achievement of *his own* happiness—and no one else's—the moral purpose of his life. What he makes, he makes for himself. What he produces, what he achieves, he does it for his own happiness. That is man's noblest activity, and it is only when man holds his own reason as his only absolute that he can be heroic. That is why the fruit of what he produces should be his, and his alone. That is why capitalism is the only moral system. The producers are our true heroes, the capitalists, those who lift our society out of the animalistic stage by the invention and production of technology—the work of the hands and minds of heroic men!"

I thought I might step into the argument, not only because I had something to say but also to bring down the temperature of the exchange between the two O'Connors. But Flannery was quicker on the draw.

"So, your husband, Frank O'Connor—he was, or is, for you, that ultimate heroic man? Let me hazard a wild guess here, Mrs. O'Connor. I just bet Frank is *the* famous John Galt, the 'Who is John Galt?' in your *Atlas Shrugged*? Am I right?"

Here Rand seemed to hesitate, as if untwisting confused strands about her life's relationship to her most famous book.

"Well … John Galt is the *ideal* heroic man, a literary creation of mine. Frank is … very dashing, very handsome."

She paused, uncomfortably. Her discomfort, it turns out from a little reading on my part, had its source in a distinction between Frank and her ideal man. Frank may have been dashing, but he was more of a pussycat than a lion, so to speak, and certainly no philosopher. No, that's unfair on my part. Frank was just an ordinary guy, a man who preferred to garden rather than to chase pirates or sinister figures from the orient like the fictional Cyrus. He even wanted children, which Rand refused him. Poor Frank was a captive of the expectations of his wife's rather childlike romantic fantasies, a handsome man on whom Rand could pile her unreal expectations. And since they were unreal, Frank could never meet them.

Rand continued, "But John Galt, he represents, in concrete literary form, the abstract idea of the heroic man, the real Atlas on whose shoulders society actually rests, the shoulders of the brilliant producers, the makers." She scowled. "Not the takers and the moochers, not the parasites who live off the great men, the socialists and Left-wing intellectuals who so cozily criticize the capitalists even while they enjoy the fruit of the labors of these heroic men."

She walked over to the window and looked out as if she were surveying the battle portrayed in her fiction on the landscape. "That's what I show, as you know, in *Atlas Shrugged*," she said as she spun around abruptly. "I show what happens when the real heroic men, the men of industry, the men of capital, the Atlases holding up society, shrug off the burden of being the only producers upon whose back society rests. I show what would happen if the real heroes *just leave* and let the nonproducing, parasitic socialists and intellectuals, the coddled Marxist university professors and hack journalists, try to run society on their own!"

She smiled triumphantly. "What happens? When the real heroes of society withdraw, they go on to start their own society, a society that consists *only* of producers, of makers, of real men. And in their absence the old society decays under the rule of the moochers, the takers, the parasites, those who have no real knowledge or skill. As I show, what happens is that the society the heroes leave behind ends up looking like communist Russia! Not the communist Russia that the Leftist intellectuals fantasize about, but the one I experienced, the one where fools and incompetents destroy everything they touch—and they touch everything!"

She paused for effect. "And that is my warning to America. The creeping socialism of the welfare state will eventually drive away all the real producers, the heroic men who are the real creators and sustainers of civilization, of industry, of plenty, and leave only the parasites, those who live off others' capital, off others' labors, off others' minds. The state will collapse into chaos!"

"Mrs. O'Connor," began Flannery, as she sat forward in her seat, "if I may call you by your *married* name again, I want to speak to you writer to writer. I do agree with some of what you've said. I do a fair share of shoutin' down the communists and socialists myself. But as a *writer*, Mrs. O'Connor, you've just stated your theme in a very short space. There's not much mystery beyond that."

Ayn Rand just looked at her in utter incomprehension at the route she was taking the conversation. Having expected philosophic acclamation, she was unprepared for literary critique. But as I suspected, Miss O'Connor's literary critique of Mrs. O'Connor's *Atlas Shrugged* was soon going to turn into a criticism of her ideas.

"Now, as a fellow writer, one who's struggled through reading *Atlas Shrugged*, a long-drawn-out drama of well over a thousand pages, it certainly seems to me that the whole thing is merely an illustration of a single abstract idea, a very long song with only one theme, one that you've just put into a nutshell in John Galt's thirty-some-page speech at the end—which I could barely get through, I might add. Now, what I want to ask you, Mrs. O'Connor, is this: Why did we need the novel? Just give us the thirty pages, and be done with it! Up with the makers, down with the takers! I got it all real quick."

Flannery looked so fragile, so demure, but she was actually quite sharp in her criticisms of writers and would-be writers, as anyone who has read her letters can attest. This so caught Rand off guard that she was able only to listen, rather than to speak—a rare situation for her, I surmised.

"But here's the problem," Flannery explained. "In real life, real human beings are much more complicated, much more mysterious, much deeper, both in their goodness and in their evil, than you make them out to be. I don't find any real characters in your book, any real personalities. I find a mess of *ideas* walkin' around on two legs, but they are thin ideas on wobbly legs. So forgive me for bein' a little bold," she said, drawing out her accent, "but your characters ain't much more than billboards advertising your philosophy. And I got a feeling that's how you see actual people too. They're either carrying your philosophy, or they're not. But in either case, they're just something to hang your pet ideas on, not real flesh and blood men and women. I consider that real dangerous, Mrs. Frank O'Connor. Seems to me that's just what the communists do."

"Ouch," I whispered.

Rand finally shook loose of her tongue-tied surprise and hissed, "If you insult my novel, you insult me. My personal life is really a postscript to my novels, a very short one. I have always lived by the philosophy I present in my books, always lived by rational and radical individualism, where my only goal is my own happiness. This philosophy has worked for me, just as it works for my characters. The details of my life and of my fiction differ, of course. But the abstractions—the ideas—are exactly the same!"

"So, you live by the philosophy you outlined in your *Atlas Shrugged*?" asked Flannery, already knowing the answer. "That the sole concern for your own happiness, the pursuit of your own self-interest is the *highest* virtue? And so you believe that if everyone quite literally minded his own business and expected only the fruit of his own labors, then everything would be just peachy?"

"Or, just to clarify a bit," I jumped in, "if we each followed only our own self-interest and pursued own happiness, then we could create a kind of utopia, a truly good society, just like the one created by John Galt and all the other 'Atlases' at the end of *Atlas Shrugged*? And that would be a harmonious society of self-interested individuals, each pursuing his own individual happiness?"

"A truly good society with no need of God?" Flannery chimed in.

"Yes, yes to everything you have both said. It is both that simple and that profound," she replied, turning away from Flannery and toward me, her arms folded across her chest, her chin high and haughty.

Flannery looked down and spoke to herself, "Hmmm—ummm. I do think I feel a prophecy comin' on."

She then looked up at me and gave an "insider" smile, as if to warn me what that might mean. And then—and you will understand how difficult it was to keep my composure—she casually reached for my revolver and began pushing the bullets out of the ribbons that held them in the case.

Flannery gave me a "go ahead" nod, so I pushed Rand a bit more on just those things I very much wanted to ask her.

"You must forgive me if I get personal now, Mrs. O'Connor, because you did say that you live by the philosophy in your books. I call you 'Mrs. O'Connor' because I would like to bring up something about your husband."

"Yes? What do you want to know?"

I looked her directly in the eye, which was difficult because of her habit of averting her eyes from anyone's direct gaze. "It is true, isn't it, that you had a long-standing affair with a married man, Nathaniel Branden, one of your disciples, and that instead of trying to hide the fact from your husband, you told him and Nathaniel's wife, Barbara, quite bluntly—and I quote—'You know what I am, you know what Nathan is. By the total logic of who we are, by the total logic of what love and sex mean, we had to love each other. It's not a threat to you, Frank, or to you, Barbara. It's something separate, apart from both of you and from our normal lives.' You sat them down and told them just that, didn't you?"

I looked up from the sheet of paper that I had written her words on, words I had gotten from one of her honest biographers. "Mrs. O'Connor?"

Rand had become significantly unraveled as I had read, and would have become more so if she had turned around and seen Flannery loading the bullets into the revolver.

"Where ... where did you get this?" she gasped. "How could you have—" "From Barbara Branden herself. She wrote a book about you," I interrupted.

"And this little 'arrangement' sure sounds familiar to me. Doesn't it to you, Mr. Wiker?" added Flannery. "I think I recall reading something just like that in Mrs. O'Connor's *Atlas Shrugged*."

She pushed herself up and got on her crutches and then picked up the loaded revolver she had laid on the desk.

"Doesn't the main heroine of the novel, Dagny Taggert, move up the romantic pecking order, jumpin' from the bed of one heroic producer to the next, until she finally beds the greatest hero, John Galt? And all the lesser heroes just cheer her on?" She was waving the gun to emphasize her words.

Once more unable to resist a pun, I muttered, "Whoa, a good man is hard to find!"

"So, you think *you* are Dagny Taggert?" asked Flannery, pointing with the gun instead of her finger. "And you wanted Frank O'Connor and Barbara Branden, your disciple and the wife of your 'lover boy,' to cheer you on? In real life with real people? You actually thought that was going to happen, like in your book?"

Rand had lost all her high-handed confidence and could only rasp out, "I am ... you are violating my privacy. I have a right—"

But Flannery pressed her, "But you said that you *lived* your philosophy, and so we should judge your philosophy by your life, and your life by your philosophy? Am I right, Mrs. O'Connor?"

I closed in on Rand as well. "And in your book, you have each of the lesser heroes rationally affirming the heroine's bed-hopping climb up the ladder of heroes because your philosophy claims, morally, that the most rational man should be united sexually to the most rational woman? I believe I've got that right, don't I, Mrs. O'Connor?"

"Now ain't that convenient!" Flannery smirked. "And so when a more 'rational' hero comes along, the rational heroine is free to hop to the next bed up? That's how you wrote it in *Atlas Shrugged*. And you thought real life should work just like your little old story?"

Rand managed to sputter out, "I ... I am outraged at your—" but I drilled home the point even more deeply.

"Nathaniel Branden, your lover, was intellectually superior to your husband, Frank. Poor Frank—he just wasn't John Galt, your *abstract*, fictional hero. Didn't have the brains! So you bed Nathaniel, more of a philosophical guy, who was, I believe, a *quarter of a century* younger than you? And you just sent your husband away during your trysts to walk the streets and drown his misery in drink? I have this from both Barbara and Nathaniel Branden."

Rand shrieked, "I have … I have cut them off! I have thrown them out! They are no longer in any way associated with me!"

"Ah, yes, I checked up on that as well," I added. "You threw Nathaniel and Barbara out because you were furious when Nathaniel had an affair of his own, with a much younger woman! A bit of your own medicine, but too bitter for you to swallow?"

"Whew-woo! I get the story!" Flannery hooted. "You could do it to your husband for *your* self-interest, for *your* happiness because you considered yourself to be the very pinnacle of rationality, and so it was necessarily *rational* and *logical* for you to commit adultery, even though it made Frank and Barbara miserable. But when your lover did a double on you for *his happiness*, well, that was somehow morally wrong, somehow irrational!"

"You do not understand my philosophy, who I am!" she exploded. "How could Nathaniel ever have dared to aspire to *me*!" she thumped her chest with the flat of her hand, as if indicating she were a goddess. "If he had been the man that he pretended to be, a man entirely devoted to *my* philosophy, then he would have valued me *romantically* above any and every other woman, even if I were eighty years old!"

"Whooeee," hooted Flannery again. "You are a world-class narcissist, if ever there was one. I give you this compliment, Mrs. O'Connor. I write about the grotesque and fantastic, but you are a character more grotesque and fantastic than I could imagine! I couldn't have written this plot in a thousand years, Miss Eye-un Ray-und."

"And I also know, from very reliable sources," I added, "that however happy you've made yourself—and I suspect that's not actually very happy—you've made almost everyone around you miserable, including your most devoted disciples."

Flannery looked at Rand and tilted her head on one side thoughtfully. "You know, I think you could be in one of my stories after all, Mrs. O'Connor, maybe one or two I've already written." And here she gave me another wink. "And it just might cure you of the 'philosophy' that ails you!"

She walked a couple of steps closer to Rand and leaned forward on her crutches, "I, Mary Grace Flannery O'Connor, mean to deliver you a revelation, Miss Rand, one that might save your sorry soul. *You* are a wart hog straight from hell!"

Rand reeled back and fell into the chair by the chess table. "What?!" she gasped out, as if she had been impaled by the sharpness of the words.

Flannery stood back up, and a strange look came across her face, the same one that she affected when reading the Misfit's lines. "Miss Rand, I thank you for bringing me your truth, your philosophy. You see, I started out today believing in Jesus Christ, the Incarnation, love as sacrifice—all of that 'irrational' stuff. I was a kind of Bible salesman, so to speak."

She flipped out the cylinder of the revolver and spun it, checking to see if all the bullets were there. "But now, after your inspiring words, I see it plain and clear, plain and clear as if I had never believed in anything since I was born. You're right, Miss Rand. There is no God, just like you and Nietzsche said. There's nothing above us, nothing above whatever kind of happiness I can get out of life by my own efforts. And that's because Jesus didn't do what He said He did. He didn't do any miracles. He wasn't raised from the dead."

She stroked the barrel of the gun, musing over her own words. "Well, as far as I'm concerned, then, it's nothing for you to do but enjoy whatever time you got to live in this world in the best way you can, and for me that means by killing somebody, or burning down his house, or doing some other meanness to him. Without God, Miss Rand, there's really no pleasure but in meanness."

Flannery leveled the gun at Rand's chest, and Rand responded with a kind of squeak, "What are ... what are you doing? That gun ... it is not real." She looked to me desperately for assurance. "It is not loaded?"

Flannery answered the question by turning the barrel slightly to the side and shooting a vase full of flowers on a stand to the left of Rand, which shattered and crumbled to the floor, flowers, water, shards, and all. If I had not realized that Flannery was reenacting her "A Good Man Is Hard to Find" for the benefit of Rand's soul, I might have been a bit more worried.

"Seems to be loaded and ready to go! Now I want to ask you, Miss Rand. I got the 'no God' part of your philosophy down pat. And seeing as there is not a God, and I get to pursue my own happiness, my own self-interest, I'm going to pursue a little meanness that I think would make me right happy. Miss Rand, I am going to shoot you."

"No! What are you—"

"So I'm going to count down, as a little favor to you, from ten, so's you can enjoy your last moments. Ten, nine, eight, seven ..." She cocked the gun.

"No! Please ..."

"Six, five, four ..."

"You wouldn't kill me! You are a Christian ... you ... are a Christian.... You wouldn't—"

"*Was* a Christian, but you done convinced me otherwise, Miss Rand. I am now one of *your* disciples, not His. So, here we go! Three, two ..."

"Why, you … you … you're my mother," Rand spilled out, as she broke down crying. She began to plead to Flannery, "Mama, why would you kill me? Why don't you love me … why …"

"One!"

A shot rang out, and Ayn Rand slumped over in her chair, passed out from the sheer terror. Another hole had appeared in my wall, just to the right of the one made by the previous bullet.

Flannery stared at Rand for a moment, sternly but a bit wild-eyed, and said slowly, "She might of been a good woman if it had been somebody there to shoot her every minute of her life."

She worked her way back over to my desk and put the gun back in the case; she then looked over her shoulder at me and smiled. "Worth a shot, so to speak. You won't know till she recovers from her little fainting spell."

She surveyed the two holes in the wall, the glass shards, flowers, and water on the floor. "Sorry about the collateral damage, Mr. Wiker. I didn't see any other way to bring her around but a little visit from the Misfit."

Flannery started walking toward the door, but then stopped, thought for a moment, and turned around. "When she comes to, can you give her a message for me? She's got *some* good things to say, though she's a terrible writer. But tell her she don't know the real depth of evil in the world, or the true glory of goodness. That's why she wants a dollar sign on her coffin instead of a cross."

She looked at Rand, who was still crumpled in the chair. "And tell her I shot at her because I love her—at Christ's command, not because I find her very lovable. Did it to wake her up. I didn't think anything else but a little visit from death could do it. Tell her Jesus loves her even if her mother don't—loves her enough to let her shoot Him."

She turned again and walked toward the door.

I thought I should go to minister to Rand somehow and looked back that way, but I discovered that she was gone—and then, so was Flannery.

I slowly found my way back to my desk. The gun was in its case, as were all the bullets.

Reflections

I know that there are many folks, perhaps even some reading this book, who consider Ayn Rand to be a kind of secular saint, a twentieth-century champion of the individual in the face of the stifling, dehumanizing threats of socialism and communism. The problem with Rand was that her reaction in favor of radical individualism — a philosophy based on an entirely self-centered ethical system — was equally erroneous.

This was demonstrated most clearly in the thoroughness with which Ayn Rand lived out her philosophy: The single-minded pursuit of her own happiness brought about the misery of everyone around her. If that's the effect of living out the philosophy of Ayn Rand in the life of Ayn Rand, then how much good can it do for anyone else?

That philosophy formed the heart of her literary endeavors from the beginning, as one of Rand's biographers, Anne Heller, makes clear. In an early novella Rand developed in the late 1920s, she says, approvingly, of her murderer protagonist: "He doesn't understand, because thankfully *he has no organ for understanding*, the necessity, meaning, or importance of other people. Other people do not exist for him and he does not understand why they should." Commenting on this, Heller says, "This, by the way, is practically a diagnostic description of narcissism, and also a description of Rand herself."[2]

Narcissism reduces everyone to an object to be maneuvered for the narcissist's pleasure. Just as Rand described the murderer in glowing terms, other people aren't real for the narcissist; they simply don't matter. And that's how she lived her life, and she fabricated her philosophy accordingly. She therefore had no guilt in cheating on her husband; she even commanded him to acquiesce to her affair with a much younger man. He descended into alcoholism, and the marriage of Nathaniel Branden, her "lover," collapsed. Rand never admitted any moral fault in all this; rather, she mercilessly chastised those whom she immiserated for complaining.

From all her disciples, she demanded complete intellectual surrender. As Barbara Branden, wife of Nathaniel and a Rand disciple herself, reported: She wanted to be worshiped as a goddess, the greatest philosopher and novelist who ever lived. This is one more symptom of narcissism: an exaggerated sense of self-importance. In truth, she had very modest literary and intellectual talents.

Flannery hammered Rand for her writerly shortcomings, but this was a *moral* as well as a literary criticism. I think—no, I'm sure—that Flannery O'Connor had a very refined theological sense, one that permeated her understanding of all aspects of her life, including her writing. She picked up immediately that Ayn Rand's writing was defined by her narcissism, by her refusal to see other people as real, in all their particularity. For Rand, other people were just two-dimensional figures that illustrated her philosophy of radical individualism. But there were, as it turns out, no other real individuals besides Ayn Rand herself, no

[2] Anne Heller, *Ayn Rand and the World She Made* (New York: Doubleday, 2009), 70.

other real people. Everyone else was a prop or a puppet for her to manipulate.

That's why there are no real characters in Rand's *Atlas Shrugged* with the kind of depth that we find in any of Flannery O'Connor's (much, much shorter) stories. Rand, unlike Flannery, didn't believe that real, particular flesh-and-blood people were worth studying in depth. *She* was all that mattered.

But Flannery O'Connor believed that each human being is made in the image of God, that is, with a depth that goes beyond what we can ever hope to plumb. And so she studied people in their true individuality, in their quirks, their warts, their insipid vices, and their hidden virtues, as creatures capable of the greatest magnificence and the most astounding malignance, not as cut-out figures for some philosophy, but as real-life players in a divine drama. She understood evil in a way that Rand couldn't, but she also understood a far more splendid goodness. Her stories reflect that depth of understanding.

Another way to sort out the difference between the two might be this: Rand was a prophet of her own philosophy, of which she was the self-proclaimed goddess; Flannery was a prophet of the Most High God and was therefore completely repulsed by the self-worship of Rand, a pristine example of the very worst kind of idolatry.

In her stories, and in her meeting with Ayn Rand, Flannery delivered a kind of grace, hence her choice to refer to herself as Mary *Grace* Flannery O'Connor. This was not cheap grace, but sharp and therefore piercing grace. She had no room for weak charity, for the kind of politeness that doesn't address the depth of the disease for which grace, won through the Crucifixion, is the cure.

Sometimes the disease is so bad that only an encounter with death can cure it. Flannery decided that the only way she could penetrate Ayn Rand's armor was with a bullet, as with the grandmother in "A Good Man Is Hard to Find." She taught her a theological and a literary lesson all at once by incorporating Rand the narcissist into this very story, with Flannery playing the Misfit.

The more I thought about this, especially as I fixed the two holes in my wall, the more I realized the brilliance of Flannery's brashness. She recognized that the atheist Rand, with all her bluster about accepting a godless world and all her praise of the archatheist Nietzsche, didn't really understand what a world without God would look like. She had to be confronted with someone who did—the Misfit.

But the real masterly stroke was that in bringing Ayn Rand face-to-face with the muzzle of a gun, with the real possibility of death, she broke through the ice that had, for so long, made Rand the cold and calculating individualist-narcissist. And in so doing, she revealed a fragile, helpless little girl, rejected and unloved by her mother.

It seems that Ayn Rand built a loveless philosophical system around her loveless life as a way to make a home in her misery. Love is the very opposite of radical individualism, the very antithesis of narcissism. God is love. Rand was never loved; therefore, Rand couldn't understand God.

Does that let Rand off the hook? Are everyone's moral failures to be blamed on his or her parents, a process that would go back endlessly so that no one has ever been accountable for anything except the first set of parents? Are we all just helpless products of the first sin of Adam and Eve?

No. Part of Flannery's affirmation of each person's dignity and individuality was her insistence on the importance of the particular choices each one of us makes that move us toward either redemption or damnation. She did not have a Calvinistic view of predestination any more than she embraced a kind of psychological or social predestination. The drama of people's lives are written by what they do or fail to do as much as they are by what others have done or failed to do to, or for, them. That is what makes the plot of life, and of Flannery's stories, so intricate and interesting.

St. Thomas More and Henry VIII

Part 1

Having one of history's great tyrants in one's office is a bit daunting, but things started off rather mildly. Henry VIII and St. Thomas More appeared more or less simultaneously—not through the door, but at my window, right next to the telescope.

As I said, I generally hide most of the technology when I'm expecting guests from the past. I don't want it to distract them from the conversation. Imagine showing them a movie, or surfing the Internet, or playing a CD of a symphony! But I forgot to remove the telescope, and a sudden inspiration led me to introduce them to it. They were both absolutely fascinated.

Obviously, they had no idea what a telescope was when they arrived in my office—such a thing would not appear for a century after their deaths—but they were both avid gazers upon the heavens. They used to spend hours together, when Henry was a younger and less bitter king, staring up into the night sky, looking at the stars and the planets, so their mutual fascination with the telescope helped renew the roots of their old friendship.

"Absolutely amazing, astounding!" declared Henry, as he bent over the device. The king stood up and rubbed his lower back. He was a big man, much taller than St. Thomas More, and, as is well known, very much wider. He must have weighed about four hundred pounds; he was much larger even than he appears in the famous portrait by Hans Holbein, where the artist did some felicitous trimming of Henry's bulk.

"No one will believe us if we are not able somehow to take this miraculous device back with us," he declared, nearly as giddy as a schoolboy. Then he turned to me. "What do you call it, squire?"

"It's called a telescope, Your Highness," I responded.

"Telescope," he said pensively. "Ah yes, from the Greek adverb *tēle*, meaning 'far off' or 'far away,' and the verb *skopein*, 'to look or gaze at.'" Henry was quite well educated, including in Latin and Greek, I should note.

"And I cannot help gazing," he added, as he bent down once again and peered through the lens. A moment later he stood up abruptly. "But, my good Thomas, you must have another look!" he said, slapping the saint on the shoulder.

St. Thomas More gladly obliged his king. It was far easier for him to bend over the telescope since he was not just shorter but much, much thinner. More was as much an ascetic as Henry was a gourmand. The only thickness he had was from a hair shirt he wore hidden under his robe and doublet as a kind of perpetual penance.

More was silent for some time, entirely engrossed and enchanted, just as Henry had been. Henry watched him intently and then squinted up at the sky, exclaiming, "I cannot believe that Saturn is robed round with such a ... a ... what? What could we even call such a wonder, Sir Thomas?"

"A skirt, perhaps," answered More, "or should we say a tunic, since he is a Roman god. I must confess that I am at a loss, my Grace, to see Jupiter so dazzlingly arrayed. Can God be thanked enough? A beautiful mystery hidden for man to discover, as a kind of half-buried jewel in the heavens. Our Creator is exceedingly kind and fatherly to have hidden such gems for His sky-seeking children."

"And spy again upon Mars, the great war god!" Henry added excitedly. "A redder planet than my mere eye would ever have seen. We are twice blessed, with this device and a conjunction of these two planets this very night. A great enchantment, indeed!"

Sir Thomas More stood up straight and stroked the bristles on his chin thoughtfully. "Mars, the great god of war, and Saturn, the god of the golden and peaceful age, feasting, plenty, gift-giving — and the god of speech freely given and received as well, I make bold to add. It is a wonder that they can dance so closely together in the sky, is it not, Your Grace?"

More was exceedingly witty, almost a jester in his delicate innuendos that were meant to instruct the king gently without riling his famous temper — no small feat. But that left Henry perpetually trying to unfold hidden meanings in whatever More said.

"You always speak in riddles, Thomas, hiding your real meaning amidst a bramble of well-chosen words. Speak freely, for once!" the king said in good-natured frustration. At least it was good-natured for now.

"I will, under the inspiration of Saturn, for Mars always leads to tight lips. I merely mean that while the movement of the heavens brings Mars and Saturn together as God sees fit, the war god and the god of peace cannot come together on Earth without Mars swallowing Saturn, harsh and pitiless war devouring golden peace. I suppose that is, in part, what is meant in our great prayer."

"Go on, you riddle again. Speak your mind, Sir Thomas, so that I do not have to pry it open!"

"You know the answer well. *Fiat voluntas tua, sicut in caelo et in terra,* 'May Your will be done, as it is in the heavens so also may it be on earth.' Such is the Lord's prayer, is it not?"

"And who could deny it, Thomas More?"

"But More adds more," he said, punning on his name, which he did frequently. "More is expected from us here on Earth than from the planets in the heavens. While Saturn and Mars will spin round above us and each leave the other graciously be, on our

Earth, Saturn, peace, is prophesied in Holy Writ to swallow Mars, war, the swords of Mars being beaten into plowshares suitable for Saturn, who is also the great agricultural god. So the great prophet Isaiah tells us!"

Here, Sir Thomas had cut a bit close, for Henry immediately became angry.

"Do you mean to assault me once again on my policies toward France?"

Henry was a restless king, right from the very start of his reign. He loved merriment—dancing, singing, playing games, and, above all, feasting. But he also itched to prove himself in battle, and there was no more obvious foe than the king across the channel. For Henry, it probably seemed more like play than real war, but Thomas knew of the great dangers and misery caused by inciting a war merely to gratify a king's lust for glory. And so, as a member of the Privy Council and then as Lord Chancellor, the saint always pushed hard against Henry's desire to tangle with the French. Such are the problems with monarchs, who underneath all the royal trappings are mere men, men whose whims and peccadillos, crimes and vices, can bring an entire people to ruin.

Rather than cowering at Henry's anger, he replied gently and patiently, "I thought, given Saturn's blessing on speech freely given, that we could learn lessons from the heavens that would serve us well on Earth. Surely there is some message for us in these wondrous new glories just revealed with this ingenious telescope?"

"Mars is the guardian-god of kings," Henry said, rather threateningly. "War brings glory to a king and riches to his realm. So it was for King David, and so it shall be for me! God has made me a king so that I may *be* a king!"

But the saint would not give up, which is, of course, why Henry had him thrown into the Tower of London. He would not consent to the divorce of Henry from Catherine of Aragon, or to Henry's bold assertion that he was the head—the pope—of the English church.

That, by the way, is where he arrived from that night, the Tower. I failed to mention that previously, but, as should be both very obvious and very strange, my guests always arrive from a particular place and time in their lives. They don't just show up generically from some misty, vague past.

In this instance, St. Thomas More had come from his imprisonment in the Tower, and his face and body showed it; he was worn, tired, dirty, and bearded, but was still the man who refused to yield, whatever the earthly cost. He refused to bend the truth to save his life.

"Yes, Your Grace, God has made you a king," agreed the saint, "but let us bring to mind the King of kings! I seem to remember that so many centuries ago the heavens brought a message not of war but peace when this King became a suckling babe who was laid in a most humble feeding trough in Bethlehem. If I recall the message of the angels, *Gloria in altissimis Deo et in terra pax in hominibus bonae voluntatis*, 'Glory to God in the highest, and on earth *peace* among men of goodwill.'"

Henry cut him short with a shout. "Confound you, More! I do not need a Latin lesson from you, and much less do I need a lesson on how to be a king," he snarled, moving uncomfortably close to the saint. "I think sometimes—as good a servant as you once *were* to me—that you have always stood in need of a lesson on how to be a good subject. A good subject is always a willing servant of the king, rather than a master!"

The king began to finger the knife on his belt, and I knew I had better do something to distract him and to restore the feelings of friendship between them—for they once were very good friends. Henry was, I understood from my studies, sometimes easy to distract, being rather mercurial in temperament.

"Your Highness," I trumpeted, "I think Venus should be rising any time now, shouldn't it, Sir Thomas? Dawn isn't all that far off. I wonder if you might take the most royal highness out on the hill just beyond those hedges—with the telescope, of course. I believe he'll get a wonderful vision of Venus, even more so than of Jupiter and Mars." I looked at Henry in a sly, knowing way, as if we were in on a private joke. "The goddess of love is certainly something he pays the greatest attentions to here on Earth."

He was at first pleased with my remark. "You speak the truth, squire. My reputation is certainly such!" But then a look of suspicion clouded his face. "But I suspect you have some double-meaning or mockery hidden in your words, just like Thomas."

"May it please you, Your Grace," the saint interrupted, peering out the window. "I see the hill he speaks of, and if this magic looking glass performs its wonder once again, I say you will never get a better prospect of the morning star. I suggest we make haste. I will set this telescope upon the hill for your majesty, and leave you with the heavens, while I attend to some matters with Master Wiker here."

More picked up the telescope and graciously ushered the king toward the door.

Henry was perplexed. "Are there no servants to carry this burden?"

"Fresh out, your royal highness," I replied, a bit too glibly. "I mean, they are themselves out in the fresh air, preparing for ... a great feast. So forgive me."

"Worry not. I have carried greater burdens, and carry them still."

Sir Thomas More folded up the legs of the telescope and set it on his shoulder. The king was already on his way out. As the saint caught up to him, he said, "This searching the heavens brings back to memory times of the greatest friendship, Your Grace, when you and I would stand atop the towers at night and gaze for hours at the night sky." Henry stopped and smiled, very warmly, and St. Thomas added, "I could have had as much hope for you as an astronomer as a king, so learned were you in the march of the stars and the wanderings of the planets."

The king cheerfully clapped More on the back. "You are right, Thomas, far better than the king of France, I might add!" and he roared at his own joke. Thomas gave a polite smile.

They are certainly a pair, St. Thomas More and the ruthless king who eventually took off his head. Never was there a man more fit for Heaven than St. Thomas More. And Henry VIII? Never was there a man more fit for Hell. When I think of Henry VIII, C. S. Lewis's brilliant "Screwtape Proposes a Toast," from the end of his classic *Screwtape Letters*, always comes to mind. The devil Screwtape, in lamenting the tepidly evil damned souls of contemporary democratic times, waxes nostalgically, "Oh, to get one's teeth again into a Farinata, a Henry VIII, or even a Hitler! There was real crackling there; something to crunch; a rage, an egotism, a cruelty only just less robust than our own. It put up a delicious resistance to being devoured. It warmed your innards when you'd got it down."

So, like Lewis, it seems obvious to me that someone as evidently evil as Henry VIII is among the damned. But in truth we are not able to judge the eternal destiny of even someone so clearly wicked as Henry. God's mercy is beyond our understanding. St. Thomas More understood this better than anyone. It was his prayer, until his dying day, that he would someday be "making merry" in Heaven with his earthly king, the very man who unjustly condemned him to the chopping block.

And he meant it, too. Rather than cursing Henry in the last days before his death on July 6, 1535, St. Thomas More composed, in his cell in the Tower of London, a "Devout Prayer before Dying," which ended: "Almighty God, have mercy on my enemies" — in this case, Henry VIII, as well as his wicked counselors, such as Thomas Cromwell—"and on all that bear me evil will and would harm me. And by such easy, tender, and merciful means as Your infinite wisdom can best devise, grant that their faults and mine may both be amended and redressed; and make us saved souls in heaven together, where we may ever live and love together with You and Your blessed saints. O glorious Trinity, grant this for the sake of the bitter Passion of our sweet Savior Christ. Amen."[3]

I don't think that I could have composed, let alone uttered, such a prayer had I been in St. Thomas More's place. But the saint had a special, lifelong devotion to the Passion of Christ, and we all know how Jesus treated His enemies from the Cross, and so we know how God wants us to treat our enemies. Thomas More prayed for Henry because Jesus Christ prayed for those who crucified Him.

The year 2035 will mark the five hundredth anniversary of St. Thomas More's martyrdom. He was born in 1478, so he was a few years shy of sixty when he was executed. He was named after St. Thomas Becket, another English martyr under another English king—in fact, another Henry, Henry II. Coincidentally—or providentially—Thomas More was born in London only twenty or so yards from where Beckett had been born about 360 years earlier. Henry II did public penance for his crime. Henry VIII did not. One wonders how much, or how little, Henry VIII mourned the death of his old friend. God knows.

But it isn't just for his martyrdom for defending the faith that Thomas More was canonized. Even if Henry's attempts to wring a divorce out of the Church had never happened—and England had kept its faith and Thomas More his head—he would most likely have been canonized.

---

[3] See Gerard Wegemer, *Thomas More: A Portrait of Courage* (Princeton, NJ: Scepter, 1995), 219.

St. Thomas More and Henry VIII: Part 1

From a very early age Thomas More desired holiness above all things. He was raised in a very prosperous household, but he deeply desired to become a Carthusian monk. And, in fact, he did stay with the Carthusians for about four years when he was younger, but in the end he chose to marry and follow in his father's footsteps as a public man: a lawyer and a government official.

He was the kindest of husbands and fathers—deeply religious, but by no means dour. He was always cheerful and ready to liven every conversation with his considerable wit. He ensured that his children received an excellent education, but also that they had fun (and so he provided his home with both a jester and a pet monkey).

More was known as a scrupulously honest lawyer and public official, praised for his impeccable character and just decisions. It is no wonder that he is the patron saint of lawyers, civil servants, and politicians.

But he always seemed to be a monk at heart, even in fulfilling his wedding vows. (I should mention that he was married twice: His first wife, Jane, died six years after they were married, and he was married again, this time to Alice.) From his eighteenth year onward, he wore a hair shirt under his clothes and woke every morning at two o'clock for study and prayer, just like the Carthusian monks he so admired. He fasted often and regularly invited the poor to dine with him. One year, during a famine, he fed a hundred people a day at his home.

And, as I mentioned, he had a deep devotion to the Passion of Jesus Christ. So, as he sat in the Tower of London, imprisoned month after month and awaiting his execution, he ever more thoroughly identified his own sufferings with those of his true Lord, Master, and King, Jesus Christ. And that is why he prayed so earnestly for the forgiveness of those who persecuted him—especially his king.

St. Thomas More's alleged crime? Treason. We all know the story. Henry VIII was married to his late brother's wife—Catherine of Aragon—but he fell for Anne Boleyn, so he wanted to get a divorce. He felt justified, in part, because Catherine had given him no male heir, but he also tried to make the case that his marriage was contrary to Leviticus 20:21: "If a man takes his brother's wife, it is impurity; he has uncovered his brother's nakedness, they shall be childless."

But More was not fooled by the king's attempts to justify his divorce, so he bravely sided with Queen Catherine against Henry and the scheming Anne Boleyn. He refused to allow that Henry's marriage to Catherine was somehow null and void, and when neither Thomas More nor the Pope would budge, Henry VIII took the history-altering leap of declaring, in effect, "If the Pope and the Catholic Church shall not grant me an annulment, then I shall declare myself the only Supreme Head of the Church of England."

So Henry declared himself pope over his own church, thereby creating the Anglican church. Well, needless to say, when you're both king and pope, you get your annulment, and quick. You get anything you want.

And so, Henry set Catherine aside and married Anne Boleyn. And since he was simultaneously king and pope of his own church, it stood to reason that to deny that his marriage was licit was an act of treason. Hence the charge against St. Thomas More (and many others).

As it turns out, Anne didn't produce a male heir either. Soon enough Anne found herself accused of treason, and she was executed in 1536, a little over a year after More. Henry waited nearly an *entire day* after Anne's death to announce his engagement to Jane Seymour. She would die after childbirth, leaving Henry to marry Anne of Cleves, a union that would very quickly (even by Henry's standards) be dissolved, as he found her entirely unsuitable and undesirable (as she found him as well). That convenient divorce allowed him to marry Catherine Howard—his fifth wife, if you're counting—a girl in her teens, over thirty years his younger. In less than two years, he had her executed for committing adultery, which Henry considered both a violation of their marriage vows and an act of treason. She was not yet twenty years old when Henry sent her to the chopping block. Finally, there was number six, Catherine Parr. She managed to outlive Henry, who died in January of 1547.

To return to our evening in my office, Thomas wasn't gone all that long. He had settled the king on a hill just beyond my house, where he could get a good view of Venus. As I had hoped, the walk and the inviting prospect of viewing a planet with the wondrous telescope deflected his anger.

"Is His Majesty all settled in on the hill?" I asked as Sir Thomas came back through my office door.

"As settled as an unsettling king can be," More replied, ever ready for a little word play.

I led him over to the chess table, as he appeared very tired, worn down by the many months he had already spent in the Tower of London.

"I must say, Sir Thomas, for a man kept in a dark cell in the Tower, you are quite deferential and amazingly courteous to King Henry. I think I would be more than a little angry with the man."

"Ah, here you are wrong, Master Wiker. My king has done me the greatest of favors, despite his intent, just as Joseph's brothers did to him by throwing him in the pit." He looked at me as he smiled. "They meant to kill him and instead made him Pharaoh's favorite and the savior of the Israelites when the famine hit! So you see, God uses evil for good. That is the way of Holy Providence."

"And what favor is that? What favor is King Henry doing for you?" I asked rather petulantly.

"Well, good sir, he has put me in a cell by myself and thus graciously given me both day and night to devote to prayer, reading of the Gospel, and even writing." And then his features became a bit dark. "Though I soon think he will deprive me of all but prayer. And so he has unwittingly made me a monk, for no Carthusian has had so fine a private cell, nor more chance for penance than good King Harry has given me!"

I was amazed at his good humor; that alone, I should think, would be enough of a miracle for his canonization. "You refer, of course, to the desire of your younger days, when you seriously thought of joining the Carthusians for a life of poverty, penance, and prayer." He gave a slight affirmative nod. "I have heard that your father was against it — joining a religious order, that is. I take it that's why you chose marriage and public service as your vocation?"

"In great part, though even so, a life of public service was not my favored choice. I would have much preferred to live the life of a scholar, studying the glories of Greece and Rome, spending my time among the wise dead rather than the foolish living." He laughed gently. "But here again, my father most strenuously objected," More said, throwing his hands up. "He nearly disowned me, I should have you know. Sir John More was a great public man, a good servant of the realm, and he would have me do the same. I am thankful to God he saw me become Lord Chancellor, the greatest man under the king, but even more thankful that his days did not stretch to see me give the Great Seal of England back to the King when I renounced the chancellorship."

"How long ago was that?" I asked.

He looked off into the distance. "Has it been three years yet? I must confess, since I have been in the Tower, the days and months both drag and run together."

"You couldn't serve Henry in good conscience, and that's why you handed the Great Seal back to him?"

"Yes, I knew that I could no longer serve a king who demanded of his subjects a loyalty no king can ask: that I take an oath confirming the legitimacy of his marriage to Anne Boleyn, and, even more impossible, that I swear unto God that Henry VIII, rightful king of England, was also rightful Supreme Head of the Church of England." He smacked the table with his open palm. "I *could* swear he was rightful king. That I would do even now. But never could I consent to a marriage that was no marriage, take an oath that what was not, was. Nor that a king could also be a pope! And so he accused me of treason, for he made it treason to trespass against his will."

"Many others took the oath, I assume, out of fear. If I'm right, the punishment for treason is very harsh: drawing and quartering, that is, disemboweling a man while he's alive and then cutting him up into four pieces when he's dead." I immediately regretted bringing this up in so clinical and callous a fashion.

"I thank you for reminding me," he said with a wry smile.

"Sorry about that, my apologies. I'm sure you've meditated on that all too often in your cell."

"Usually it is the devil who delivers that message, trying to tempt me to yield to Henry's unlawful and unholy demand." He brushed some dirt from his sleeve and then looked me in the eye with a graver expression on his face. "But here is the more important point—and this I told Archbishop Cranmer and Thomas Cromwell when they dragged me from my cell and attempted to win me over. While a great majority of men and women in England may have taken the oaths prescribed by His Majesty," he said as he leaned in and spoke more softly, "and I will not say that those who did acted from fear or from the desire for gain; let God be the judge. I know, however, that I have a majority of Christians from other lands and times on *my* side," he said, his voice rising again, "the side of the one, holy, catholic, and apostolic Church. I stand with all of Christendom against England, the realm of my birth. And I will not disown that great majority — no, I shall not — I will not disown Christendom, merely to save my head, that it might sit atop my neck a few more pitiable years, years spent in a small corner of this dark and fallen world. I will do no such thing, for in so doing, I should lose my soul for eternity. A poor trade, do you not think?"

He had gotten up during this stirring speech and now walked pensively toward my desk, hands clasped behind his back. After a quiet moment, he turned to face me again.

"They offered me every worldly honor, you know — Cranmer and Cromwell. Before threatening me, they offered me land and riches, honors and titles, beyond anything I had owned and lost." And here he smiled and shook his head. "That is where they made their mistake. They sounded to my ears all too much like Satan when he tempted our Lord Jesus Christ with all the kingdoms of the world! Man does not live by bread alone, and, since he has an immortal soul, even by his *head* alone." He wandered back to stand behind his seat. "And so I will not escape death, but I do hope for the lesser punishment — I must admit my weakness. I would rather die by the quick blow of an axe, losing my head quickly rather than the extended agony of drawing and quartering. May God and King Henry grant me that mercy."

He leaned on the back of the chair, seeming to gather some great inner strength, and then said a bit mischievously, "But here is a case that a man may lose his head and come to no harm, is it not?"

"No harm! How could that be?"

"The greatest harm, as even Plato well understood and our Savior Christ Jesus declared, is to keep one's life while losing one's soul, to win this world, which passes away, while losing eternal bliss with our only true King. The king is doing me a favor, a great grace from my grace, by constructing for me a cross upon which I may follow my Savior to eternal salvation. Henry may have my head, if he wishes it. And if he does take it, I shall leave it full of good cheer!"

I couldn't help laughing, a little anyway, at his grim humor, but then I remarked, "But it is sad for you, isn't it? You and Henry were friends. You were his closest acquaintance, at least for a time. And I believe you had a lot of hope for him as king, at least at the beginning."

"Yes, Henry and I spent much time talking and jesting, discussing the great works of Rome and Greece, as well as Holy Scripture. And as I may have mentioned, he was well educated in math and science. We would spend long hours into the night peering at the heavens together—without benefit of your telescope, but using only the eyes God gave us!"

"Then it must be difficult to understand how he could so quickly have changed," I remarked.

"Not so very difficult, no, not so very difficult at all." He rubbed his forehead, as if trying to smooth out the weariness. "Even when we were at our closest—when I was Lord Chancellor, that is—I always knew that if my head could win King Henry a castle in France, off it would go!"

He walked over to my copy of Michelangelo's *Last Judgment* hanging on the wall and peered closely at the souls in bliss and those in distress. "One of the great lessons we learn from history is that the power of kingship rarely falls upon a man without making him worse rather than better. Human nature is too fragile to bear the weight of earthly power without bending down and becoming entirely earthbound, forgetting about the immortal soul. Likely, more are damned than saved by having a crown placed upon their head—unless it is a crown of thorns, in imitation of our Lord."

"The chain of office you wore around your neck as Lord Chancellor—not exactly a crown, but I imagine it was heavier than it looks with the weight of the office."

"The livery collar? Yes, the gold is heavy, but the weight of the office heavier by far," More replied, "as heavy as any cross could be. A most uncomfortable yoke, with the weight of the world, or at least of England, hanging on it. I was mightily glad to return it to him."

He walked back to the table and sat down again. "Master Wiker, I tell you that many a man lusted for that gold collar as if it were a crown, so much did they wish to advance in worldly power. But I did not want to become Lord Chancellor, you know. I had to be dragged into it, and I consented only because I thought it was God's will that, through my poor efforts, I could make the realm better and bend the king more upward than downward."

"And were you ever able to make any progress with him?"

"A little, but nothing lasting," the saint said as he picked up the black king from the chessboard and looked more closely at its chiseled features. "He is a lustful man, King Henry is—for war, for women, for earthly glory." He sighed and put the king back in place. "Yet he was so handsome, so talented, so well taught, so full of promise." He sat forward, with a bit of a smile, "He composed some very beautiful songs. I might sing one for you, on his behalf?"

This was a bit of a disquieting suggestion. Thomas More may have been a saint, but he would not have gotten into Heaven for his singing. As I had read, he wasn't quite able to hit the right notes straight on, but just gave them glancing blows as he passed through to another key. As I searched for a polite response, More read my apprehension.

"Ah, I see! My fame as a singer has preceded me, so you know that I am famously bad!" He laughed at his own joke. "But I did always love to sing, especially in Mass. The Good Lord—as well as some of His flock—must often have graciously turned a tin ear in my direction to protect themselves from my tuneless dinning! When I am alone in my cell, I bother no one with my hymns but the rats and mice!"

"I wonder how you can keep your humor so well in such awful circumstances, but you are also famous for that."

"As the pagans Lucian and Juvenal both understood well, much more can be done with a laugh and much more can be said with a smile and a jest than can ever be done or said with an angry tongue. Humor soothes the soul. When the soul laughs at itself and at our poor lot as human sinners, it is healed of pride and thereby made the better. Such laughter is the froth and fruit of the great virtue of humility. And, if one is serving a king as irascible as Henry, there is no better and more soothing tonic for his troubling and troubled soul. I found that I could serve up many lessons to the king as a jester that he would not have found so digestible if I had not seasoned them with a laugh." He shook his head, and perhaps even shuddered a little. "Believe me on this, it is no easy thing to speak to a king—especially to speak the truth."

"It seems as if your time with Henry was a continual exercise in roundabout speaking, circumlocution, cat and mouse—anything but dishing him up the truth straightforward and unalloyed."

I leaned forward and asked him a question that he must have answered so many times, but silently: "And what would you say to him, if you could speak with him freely, if you could tell him the straight truth, as simply and plainly as it can be told, a simple and plain as it is to you, in your own mind and heart?"

This seemed a painful thought, something he had kept buried within, but which was burning his very soul. He spoke with evident emotion; in fact, tears were forming with his words. "I would tell him, as I think he knows I would if free from his abominable threats and even more abominable thoughts, to stop this madness, to put Anne Boleyn away, and to take back his right and lawful queen, Queen Catherine. And even more dire, I would tell him he must renounce headship of the Church of England, for there is no such thing!"

He stood up, his voice rising in anger with him. "It is not a true body—this Church *of* England—it is not a true body for which there can be a true head."

More then began pacing, as he must have paced his own cell, more upset about what Henry was doing to the Church than about his own fate. "There is only the universal Catholic Church, *in* every nation but *of* no nation. To create a church in one nation—a king's church, the church *of* a king—is to allow that each nation, each king, shall have his own personal church."

He turned around sharply from where he had wandered, at the corner of my desk. "That is what it will come to, given King Henry's lead. I can easily make that prophecy if this breach of faith is not mended. There will very soon be as many different religions with their own peculiar churches as there are kings with crowns upon their heads! What will that give us? I will tell you! Christianity will be hopelessly splintered, a body torn asunder, and the pieces torn asunder in turn."

The saint came closer to me but spoke no less forcefully. "I would tell him, my king, if I thought he had ears to hear rather than a hardened heart, that he is lustily seduced by a power he can claim only at his own peril."

He straightened up and looked toward the window, where somewhere off in the distance Henry was still staring contentedly at the heavens. "And how powerful that seduction is! Stronger than any woman—even for Henry! What earthborn and earth-bent king would not like to control both the bodies and souls of his subjects by taking hold of both the crown and the miter, the state and church? Yes, that is complete power, so complete that it corrupts all but God Himself, who came to earth as King of kings and highest priest, and yet shed earthly glory for heavenly.

He was silent, clearly upset, and wiped his eyes with a hand-kerchief he produced from his sleeve, which I could see was quite ornate. He ran his fingers around the edges and seemed to be gathering strength to continue.

"I would tell King Henry to remember every day, in prayer and penance, on his knees before the true Heaven, that there is one King we must all obey, one King over all kings, one King only who has our ultimate allegiance and to whom we swear our most binding and most holy oaths, and that is Christ the King."

He was almost breaking down now. I felt awful, as if I had dragged him into the darkness myself.

Clearing his throat, he struggled with every word. "I would tell Henry, then, to let the Pope be the Pope and care for the universal Church, so that he, Henry, may be a better and holier king and care for this realm of England—rather than destroy it with his lust, ambition, and pride. And I would tell him ... ask him ..." And here he broke into tears, his shoulders shaking.

"Ask him what?"

"I would ask him, having given up his madness, to release me so that I may go back to my wife and children and live out my days in domestic love and private peace, unburdened by any service other than that of a good husband and father."

He walked back toward his chair and paused, gathering himself together again. "But that is too much to ask," he fairly whispered, "though I have been asking it of God. The madness is too deeply worked into the king, into his marrow, both of his bones and his soul. Too many scoundrels have risen to aid in England's self-destruction, ruining and deforming what they think they are saving and transforming—men whose lust for worldly power is nearly the equal of their maddened sovereign's."

"There is no hope, then?"

I asked this question knowing how history had already turned out. But again, the very strange thing is that my visitors, my saints and scoundrels, really do seem as if they are somehow given a new chance, a new hope that they could choose another destiny from what appears before them. What effect would that have on history?

"Is there hope, Master Wiker? There is always hope, and faith and love, these great theological virtues, as long as we hope in God and His Church for our ultimate deliverance from this fallen world. We are fools to hope for anything less than Heaven, yet there are so many fools who hope for nothing more than this 'less.' They should, rather, settle for nothing less than this more, the 'more' that God promises those who obey Him."

"Amen. I wish I had your courage, Sir Thomas."

This caused a great laugh, which I think was more than anything else due to a desire to climb back out of these somber depths.

"Be careful, Master Wiker, be careful! God may bring about a circumstance in which you'll need such courage!" He stood up and readjusted his doublet. "But I think it may be time to fetch His Highness. He may wonder, in this strange land with such strange and magical devices, whether he is in a dream! And if he starts wandering because he is wondering, he may brashly trouble the peasants who do not know him as their king."

"I think you're right. I would like to hear the king speak on his own behalf, to see what defense he might make."

Thomas More exited, and I sat down at my desk, thinking hard about the whole strange thing. I wondered if Henry VIII's mind could have been changed if the saint had been allowed out of the Tower, so that the two could speak privately—without any meddling ministers such as Cromwell around. More was a great speaker, immensely persuasive, a witty, learned man, who knew English law more thoroughly than anyone else of the time. And he certainly knew the Scriptures and canon law inside and out as well. That's why his enemies—who became the king's "good" servants by telling him whatever he wanted most to hear—kept

More from speaking publicly or from speaking to the king directly. They feared the power of his words, and the power of his integrity.

We wonder about these things, don't we? How much history could have changed if only one man had changed his mind? What if Henry VIII could have been persuaded to change course? What if St. Thomas More could do that now, in my office?

Part 2

King Henry VIII returned from his stargazing in much better spirits, helped along by St. Thomas More's diplomatic use of humor to settle his master's flammable temper. I wondered, watching them interact, just how much exhausting effort More had to devote to the task—until Henry turned entirely against him. But here they were, laughing and acting like old friends.

As you might suspect, a man of such large appetites as Henry wanted to refuel after his junket to the hillside and back. More ate little, as I expected, but Henry kept shoveling faster than I could cart the food upstairs. I will say nothing of his etiquette. He was especially keen on a bag of Doritos; you'd think he had never tasted anything more divinely delicious in his life. He'd probably weigh eight hundred pounds if he were a modern-day tyrant.

After Henry was finally filled, he gleefully challenged the saint to a game of chess. I'm sure my humble chess set was nothing compared with what a king would have, but he seemed not to notice. I wondered, of course, whether anyone ever beat Henry at chess fair and square.

The king was big on athletic games—before he became so fat. I suppose I should also explain here that in his youth he was knocked from his horse in a jousting match, hurting his leg. The injury kept him from his usual boisterous activities—but he kept eating as if he were an active young man. So he's got at least a bit of an excuse for his unseemly girth.

But the point I was making is that he was a man for games, but one — as a king — who didn't like to lose. I recall hearing that he was especially good at tennis and that few ever beat him — or ever dared. The saint was obviously more intellectually gifted and probably could beat the king in chess. My suspicion was that More would be as deft in this regard as he was in his speech.

There they were, playing away, as I sat at my desk and watched. Henry remained in good humor, fairly licking his lips in anticipation of the More's next move, which he made after much head rubbing and hesitation.

"Ha! I thought you might fall for my trap!" Henry cried, bouncing up and down on his seat, giggling like a young child. I suspect, in having the crown thrust upon his head so early, he might have missed aspects of a real childhood — or, having received power before becoming a man, in some ways never grew into adulthood.

The king moved his bishop across the board and declared, "And that, Sir Thomas More, is checkmate!" He then slammed his fist on the table, causing some of the pieces to topple, and let out a roaring laugh.

More sat back in his seat and smiled, spreading his hands, palms up, in acknowledgment, "I gracefully admit defeat, Your Grace."

A steely glint entered Henry's eyes as he fixed them on More. "And do you, Sir Thomas? You seem stubborn beyond all reason in our larger and much more serious game."

Oh well, I thought, the peace couldn't last.

More didn't flinch from the king's innuendo. "Here, in this game, the stakes are small. I did not have my soul and its eternal fate wagered for this match, but only a few shillings — and these I borrowed from you, my Grace, for I am reduced to poverty."

The king's eyes narrowed. "Then let us raise the stakes." He paused, and I thought things might explode again, but he suddenly smiled and sat back in his chair. "I mean, for another match be-tween us here. Let us recall our friendship, Sir Thomas. Remember how we used to play chess long into the night, you and I, and how we talked and laughed and made merry?"

The saint nodded but remained silent.

Henry continued, and did so with obvious, real affection — at least for the More in his memory. "I have often thought that if we might rekindle the fires of our friendship, you would happily and faithfully walk from the Tower of London to my Court and be my good servant once again."

Again, More gave no answer but merely raised his eyebrows slightly.

"So, shall we play another game," asked the king as he sat up to the chess table again, "and thereby more deeply renew our former friendship?" Henry gave a mischievous grin. "How about a half crown on a match — unless you are afraid of such great stakes on a game?" And Henry began setting up the pieces for rematch.

More did likewise. "Not in the least, Your Grace. Shall we make it a whole crown? Sixty pennies is not much for a crown from a king!" The saint loved wordplay — in English money a crown is worth sixty pennies, and four crowns made a British pound.

"You are right, Thomas. Then let us make it four crowns from the king. That brings us up to a pound!"

"I do not know whether I can match Your Grace, pound for pound."

"Ah, you make merry at my girth! Then, in payment for that jest, you shall put up two pounds to play with the crown!"

"I will yield the honor of the first move, as the king's good ser-vant." Here, much to my chagrin, it seemed as if More was actually baiting the king. This, I think, was a sign of the saint's integrity.

He could have been entirely obsequious and deferential to Henry, but instead he pushed into dangerous territory—not for himself, I suspect, but in charity to the king, to try to save his soul as well as the realm.

The king took the bait. "If you were my good servant, Sir Thomas, you would be as easily moved as this knight," Henry said as he moved out his queen's knight. "It was, after all, I who bequeathed you the honor of being knighted."

"It is because I am the king's good servant that I so carefully and prayerfully make my every move."

Henry picked up a pawn, the one in front of his bishop. "The pawns at least do good service, and move where I will them."

"They are indeed loyal footmen who take their feet wherever you move them, even to make queens." He looked over the board as he considered his next move and then picked up a pawn. "I have always thought it is strange that a pawn can make us another queen merely by crossing the board to the other side," he said absently, as if referring to the chess rule that allows one another queen if he can move a pawn to the opposite end of the board. He then set it down, two spaces forward. "And then such newly made queens could move wherever they will—such a curious innovation." Then he added casually, "These pawns are carved much like the bishops."

Henry lurched forward. "Your double meanings are not very well hid, Thomas. I put you in the Tower for defending Catherine, who was never queen, as my theologians so well and so thoroughly proved! That marriage was never valid, for I unwittingly married my brother's wife, having gotten a false dispensation to do so from Rome."

As I said earlier, this was all a king's ruse. The dispensation wasn't false. His brother had died, and so his brother's wife was free to marry. No one was fooled by Henry's attempts to prove that his first marriage was invalid, except those who wished to be the king's fool, either for advancement or out of fear. He had the gall to send his court theologians all over Europe to try to find more evidence for his case among scriptural scholars. At home, in jolly England, no one at court thought there was any other reason for the whole debacle than Henry's own lustful infatuation with Anne Boleyn.

The king stood up, quite angry, and shook his finger at More. "And then when you would not, as I had bidden you, attend the coronation of Anne — the true queen — that was, *and is*, too much for a king to bear!"

More was all innocence. "Your Grace mistakes my meaning. It was only a lesson in history I wished to mark. Your Grace is younger than I and therefore does not remember when queens in chess had not the power to move wherever they will, as they may according to our present-day rules. At first, queens could move only two spaces, straight or diagonal."

I had to look this up later, and everything More said was indeed true. Yet as Henry intuited, the saint's history lesson was not idle trivia.

"It was about the time of King Richard III, the great tyrant," More looked off into the distance, "that things began to change — in chess, I remind you. Where one day, queens could barely move, tethered two squares hence. Soon, about the time of that dread tyrant, there came a great innovation in this courtly game, and queens could suddenly move as far as they wished in any direction, and became so powerful that, when this novelty was introduced, the game came to be called Mad Queen Chess."

Henry understood all the pinches and prods that were meant for him under the veil of innocent speech. He moved out his own queen. "And is your queen mad, mad with power?"

The saint picked up his queen and examined it thoughtfully. "Mine is not." He then put it back down next to his king and moved his arm dismissively. "But a lesson in a mere game is a poor treasure to dig from history." He sat forward so as to look Henry more closely in the eye. "I wonder whether you did read my *History of King Richard the Third*, speaking of that tyrant. I penned it just after Your Grace became king." He moved his knight onto Henry's side of the board. "I have referred you to it many times in our walking and talking, thinking it would be good reading for a king. History is a good lesson book, if it is read with care."

I thought Henry would explode at this, but oddly he laughed, as if being teased, and hunched himself over in mockery of Richard's deformity. "You are calling me another Richard, then?" As with all tyrants, he didn't see himself as a tyrant.

"You certainly look nothing like him, and you were, when I penned that history of Richard, inside and out quite his opposite. Your Grace, if I might say so, was as handsome and well formed a prince as ever became a king."

All of this brought a smile to Henry's face as he moved a pawn out in front of his rook. More's mode of flattery here was, apparently, too subtle for the king to detect — or perhaps his character too vain to suspect any deeper intention.

"The malignant Richard was, as you know — if I recall how I put it," he said stroking his beard, "'little of stature, ill featured of limbs, crooked-backed, his left shoulder much higher than his right, hard-favored in appearance.' His soul matched his body in deformity. 'He was close and secret, a deep dissembler, lowly of countenance, arrogant of heart, outwardly friendly where he inwardly hated, not omitting to kiss whom he thought to kill; pitiless and cruel, not for evil will always, but for ambition, and either for the surety or increase of his estate. Friend and foe was much the same; where his advantage grew, he spared no man death whose life withstood his purpose.'"

The saint's eyes fell on the board as he searched out his next move. After some pause, he brought out the bishop on his queen's side. Looking back at Henry, he continued from his history of Richard III—words he must have thought over long and carefully, both before and after they were written. "'And a sign of his bad end was his bad beginning. No crowd in the realm could be made to cry up "King Richard! King Richard!" and throw up their hats in joy when the Duke of Buckingham, in conspiracy with Richard, tried to whip up their support for the usurping king with his great and windy speech, but the citizens of the realm sat in stony silence.'" He paused for effect, and then became more animated, acting out his words. "And that soured crowd was entirely unlike the crowd at Your Majesty's coronation where the realm bubbled over in the truest and deepest joy and hope and love that ever met a king ascending his throne. All cried from their inmost hearts and with utmost sincerity, 'King Henry! King Henry!'"

Henry obviously traveled back in his memory to that exhilarating moment as he smiled and said fondly, "Indeed! I remember well.... I well remember." He stretched out his massive leg next to the table and rubbed his great thigh as if trying to soothe a knot of pain.

"You would do well to remember such good promise as a good beginning, for a good beginning can bring a good end if we do not turn from the course first set out." He nodded at Henry. "It is *your* move, Your Grace."

Henry awoke from his pleasant daydream. "Mine? My move? Yes, yes. Let's see now." After refocusing his attention on the board for some time, he moved one of his knights to St. Thomas More's side.

More continued carefully wheedling the king: "Much, much unlike like Your Majesty, Richard, the foul usurping king, began mischief immediately upon stealing the throne. He got the crown by evil and, as I have noted, a 'thing evilly got is never well kept; through all the time of his reign there never ceased cruel death and slaughter, till his own destruction ended it.'" The saint paused and looked at Henry more closely, as if trying to peer at his soul through the window of his eyes. "And there was no peace in the realm—neither *for* Richard, nor *in* Richard."

Henry moved his other bishop, sat back, and looked at his opponent. "*In*? What do you mean *in*? Speak plainly and freely, Sir Thomas."

"As freely as I am able, being a mere knight on the realm's board," he said again, moving his knight closer to Henry's king. "By saying there was no peace *in* Richard, I mean that his nights were more disturbed than his days, for that is the lot of all tyrants."

And here the saint again threw himself into a kind of dramatization of what he was saying about Richard, as if he might thereby bring Henry to a kind of catharsis. "So it was, Your Grace, that 'King Richard took ill rest at nights, lay long waking and musing, sore wearied with care and watch, rather slumbered than slept, troubled with fearful dreams—suddenly at times he would start up, leap out of his bed, and run about the chamber; so was his restless heart continually tossed and tumbled with the troubling impression and stormy remembrance of his abominable deeds.'" And then he sat back, as if stepping off the stage, and said with apparent casualness, "But again, that is not like Your Majesty, for I know you must sleep well and deeply."

Henry snorted indignantly and moved his rook out. "I sleep well enough!"

"Your bed is somewhat softer than mine, perhaps."

At this Henry lurched forward and growled. "You would have the softest bed in the realm if you were not so hard of heart! Confound you, man! I would send you home, and you would sleep on three feather beds made from the finest geese in England—*in* your own home *with* your family—if you would only come to your senses!"

More seemed entirely unfazed by the crouching king and merely remarked, "No one ever got to Heaven on a featherbed, Your Grace, as I have told my dear daughters."

"You invoke Heaven," rasped Henry, "but you act against the king and against his law—and you have sworn to Heaven, have you not, to remain loyal to both?"

The saint's calm came to an end, and he spoke words that seemed to boil over out of him: "And I remain the king's loyal servant, all the more so since I serve most faithfully your eternal good, which will outlast any gain for your realm in this fallen world. I am indeed faithful to you, Your Grace, more faithful than those who have escaped the Tower." Henry was a bit stunned, as I'm sure no one had ever used this tone with him. But More only continued with ever greater indignation. "You remember—I know you do, Your Highness—when you first asked me to enter into your service, when no one else was there to witness our private conversation but ourselves and our God. You assured me then, at my request, that I should look first of all to God, and then to you, and that was the promise upon which I made my oath of loyalty to be your chancellor. And that is why I cannot swear an oath that goes against my first. I cannot swear allegiance to an Act of Parliament that declares you to be the Supreme Head of the Church, for such is directly repugnant to the laws of God and His Holy Church, the supreme government that no temporal prince may presume by any law to usurp. Ecclesial authority rightfully belongs to the See of Rome, a spiritual preeminence given by the mouth of our Savior Himself, personally present upon the earth, to St. Peter and his successors."

As More said "Savior," Henry stood up in a blind fury and threw the entire chess table halfway across the room; the saint's concluding words were spoken as the pieces rattled across the floor. I must confess, at this point I was barely able to keep from standing up and clubbing the king a good one, but with greater self-control than I thought I had, I waited on St. Thomas's response. I knew, somehow, that my actions could not be as effective as More's in bringing Henry around, if it could be done.

Henry thundered, "And is that how you speak to your king!"

The saint's head hung low, as he realized the king's character was not to be changed. "I speak freely because I now realize that I have only one end to accomplish, and that is to obey God first, the King of kings, and to do so to my last. I repeat that I am the king's good servant, but God's first, and in being God's first, I am most deeply yours, most of all when I strive to turn you from evils that appear to you as good."

Henry was red-faced and began stalking around as More continued: "You throw this board and these pieces so easily into the air. Ignited by your anger, queens, knights, bishops, pawns wiped away with a blow of your hand. And so you may do in your own realm on your own board—no, so you have done *to* your own realm, where those who merely displease the king, let alone those who dare to stand against him for the good of his soul and the good of his realm, are swept away, as were just now these chessmen, like so many bothersome flies."

"I will have your head, More!" he snarled. "You know that I shall have your head—and that is an act of mercy, for it is in my power to do far worse! To stand against a king is treason. You are no loyal subject, and you are, by resisting me, teaching others to resist and giving them courage to band together as vile villainous traitors. Do you design to throw England back into another great war? Is that your wish?"

Henry angrily looked around and snatched up one of my many swords, this one standing upright by the bookcase near the window—a rapier, to be exact. Now I don't want to be made out to be more heroic than I am, but I own swords and I have learned how to use them, and so, as soon as I saw the king reach for the rapier, I grasped a broadsword—a nice one, with an intricate basket hilt, a replica of one from the late sixteenth century—from the other side of the bookcase. As Henry brought his rapier up to threaten the saint, I brought my much sturdier and sharper broadsword down on his blade.

"I would reconsider, Your Highness. The funny thing is, I've just had this sword sharpened, but I entirely forgot to sharpen that one."

Henry looked at me as if he had just seen me for the first time. Being a royal all his life, he was quite used to having people in the room for whom he had no more regard than the furniture, so that wasn't surprising.

Throwing the rapier to the floor in disgust, he said condescendingly, "And just who are you anyway, who would so boldly, so foolishly address your king—and threaten his person? Perhaps your head may not rest so tightly on its shoulders as you may think. A word from me, and *you* shall be in the Tower with Sir Thomas, for to threaten a king is treason!"

"Actually, Your Highness," I replied walking back toward the desk, "you aren't My Highness. I'm not under your jurisdiction, so to speak."

"A foreigner! I suspected such a thing all along—especially with your barbarous speech. You can barely pronounce the mother tongue."

"Not exactly a foreigner. More like a breakaway colonist," I said, making my way casually to the world map hanging by my comfy chair. "You see, I know this may be hard to believe, but you've heard of the new voyages westward across the ocean?" I turned to look at him as I indicated the direction of sailing from England to America's shores on the map. "Well, in the time of your father, Henry VII, a certain Christopher Columbus sent his brother, Bartholomew to the English court to see if it would support his expedition." Here, I leaned casually on the ledge of the bookshelf under the map and said a bit too smugly, "Turned him down, your father did, a huge mistake on his part …"

My little display of insouciant swagger was too much for Henry, for he suddenly pulled back his coat to retrieve his dagger hanging tight next to his doublet, and threw it before I realized what he was doing. It stuck into the wall right next to my head, and I must admit I was stunned and quite shaken.

"You speak very freely and evilly to a great monarch, directly under God in his rule of the land. Is that how you speak to your own king?"

"No, indeed! I speak to my king, Christ the King, on my knees in prayer, and try to obey Him—the same King that Sir Thomas More so dutifully, so courageously obeys—though he is a far better servant than I'll ever be."

"Do not banter with me! Who is your earthly king?"

"Don't have one," I replied, and I walked slowly in his direction. "Sometimes I wish I did. There is no splendor like that of a king and queen and their court—the glories of knighthood, the romance of the sword, the great castles. And I think, a greater dignity, refinement, and elegance. We 'colonists' decided not to have kings, in imitation of the ancient Romans. We are self-governed, what we call democracy—though it should properly be called a republic."

"Ha! As Aristotle said, the rule of the rabble, governance by the lowborn, the vulgar, the groundlings. No wonder you are so impertinent!"

"You're right, unfortunately, to a great degree," I conceded. "Graft, corruption, scandal, fraud, demagoguery, every kind of foolishness and inefficiency—and all without the romance of royalty. No children want to play at being a politician or a bureaucrat or even a president or first lady, shuffling papers in offices and giving tedious speeches. Every little girl wants to imagine herself a princess or a queen, and every boy a noble knight or a king. Our government is entirely without such romance, entirely devoid of such splendor."

"Then you have some sense in you yet!" he snorted as he shook his finger in my face. "Why do you not choose to serve a king then, rather than mix with a government by the rabble?"

"There are no kings to speak of anymore."

"No kings!" he said, in genuine astonishment, if not a bit of horror.

"But that's not the main problem. Like Sir Thomas More, I know my history well enough, all too well. If I ever get tempted by the romance of earthly kings," I leaned very close to him, and whispered, "I simply remember *you*." Then I straightened up, and with a flourish of my right hand added, "Cures me immediately!"

As he scowled, I walked away, offering him the interesting news from the future, "You are—history has judged you—one of the great tyrants."

"History? A tyrant?"

More stood up and interrupted, "It need not be so, Your Grace. You may yet write your own history. Rewrite it well now; scratch out what should not be and reedit for what should. Take courage and take the pen of repentance in hand," he pleaded, holding up an imaginary quill. "Do not be like the infamous tyrant Richard, who grasped at glory by foulest means and now is known only by those inglorious deeds he so evilly wrote with other's blood." More's eyes were tearing up, and he was having trouble speaking. "We do not in this life have to continue to walk in a path that leads to destruction. God grants us that grace, my Grace, freely to walk back and to find our right way again. Be the good king God called you to be! I beg of you, as your servant most loyal to your truest good, I beg of you!"

"But I am a good king," he countered, "and a good king must sometimes choose being feared rather than loved."

"That sounds all too much like the advice of the infamous Machiavelli," said More, shaking his head sadly. "I feared that Your Highness was reading the murderous Machiavelli."

"I have not," replied Henry, coldly, "but Cromwell and my other advisers have. And I think there is much sound advice in his book, *The Prince* — what I have heard of it, anyway."

"I would have you take your counsel from another prince, the Prince of Peace, the prince who warned you that you may gain the world — as the prince of this world so readily promises — but lose your soul to eternal Hell, where the promising prince resides." More hung his head as if searching for words. He then looked back at Henry, imploring him, "I tell you now that the warm love your subjects once had for you is fading into cold fear as they taste more violence than wisdom from their king."

"A king must be violent, sometimes, to keep the peace in his realm. He must punish with violence those evildoers who would do violence to the realm, and who is eviler than he who commits treason?"

"And what if treason means only this," I piped up, "to go against the will and whims of the king, no matter how foolish, prideful, and destructive?"

The king had no patience for any interruptions on my part. "What do you, a commoner, know of what a king must bear?" he thundered at me as he walked back toward his seat, kicking the chess pieces that he had scattered on the floor. He turned to More and shook his finger severely: "And I fear Hell well enough, mind you, Thomas, well enough indeed. As Supreme Head of the Church in my realm, I have been given by God Himself the ultimate care of my subjects' heavenly fates as well. And so I quote Scripture to you: 'Fear God, and honor the King,' as St. Peter himself tells us. What says your piety to this?"

"But we are not to fear the king as if he were a god," replied More quietly, "and that is what happens when the king rules by fear over the church as well. The church becomes a mere department of the king's estate, a political church instead of a holy one. And then, quite suddenly, to disobey the king is not only treason, but a kind of blasphemy, as if the king were God Himself."

"But it is treason!" shouted Henry. "And so I have charged you with treason for not swearing your fidelity to the Act of Supremacy by which I have been rightfully declared king of the church in my realm. The king receives his power from God Himself," he pointed upward, "and is answerable to Him alone. Can a king rule in his realm, I ask you, if his subjects ultimately are ruled by a foreign sovereign, a *Roman* bishop, a pope who acts more like a prince than St. Peter? Will a house so divided not fall into ruin, Sir Thomas? Will it not do so?"

"I agree with Your Highness in saying that Jesus Christ, in proclaiming that His kingdom was not of this world, thereby divided every man's loyalty," the saint replied softly. "For that greatest of kings rules over all kings, and we must choose the greater king when the lesser kings rebel against His rightful and holy rule."

"But Christ and the pope are not the same!" he spluttered. "I would like to remind you, *Sir* Thomas More, that you were not always so keen on the Roman Pontiff and warned me early on not to give in too much to him, or he would encroach on our realm! I recall your warning well."

"And so I did, but then Your Grace himself gave me a good lesson, making me wiser by your foolishness." He said this not looking at the ground but straight on, glaring right into Henry's astonished eyes. "Yes, I came to understand the importance of the primacy of the office of St. Peter—as given directly by Christ—and even more, the necessity of the Church being separate and distinct and free of the king's governance." He walked away from the chess table and picked up a crucifix standing on my desk. "Caesar and St. Peter may not share the same throne; I saw that with ever more fearful clarity as Your Highness tried to use the power of the Church to serve your ill-begotten ambitions. *You* taught me the lesson, more than anyone, that Caesar and Christ must be kept separate, and that Caesar can never be allowed to rule over Christ."

Henry shouted over the saint's last words, "And have we not been taught by that same Christ that we render unto Caesar what is Caesar's?"

Unflustered by Henry's anger, More replied succinctly — and with a pun, "And not a bit more, Your Grace, and not a bit more, says More."

"You render nothing but treason to *your* king!"

"Again, I serve you best by serving God first. And indeed, even now I serve you with most loving loyalty. I pray for your soul in the very cell where you have unjustly sent me. I have made it the work of my own penance and prayer, pleading to God that you would 'make merry in Heaven' with me one day. I thus serve *you*, on my knees and with my tears."

"I do not need your prayers, but your obedience!" he roared, so red in the face, so fuming with anger, that I took a step forward in case I needed to provide some protection for the frail saint. Ignoring me, he stepped under Michelangelo's *Last Judgment* so that he quite literally appeared to be coming under the discerning eye of the King of kings, his own head among the writhing and wretched damned. "You pray only that I will give up my queen, Anne, and take back Catherine, and that I will give over my rightful title of Supreme Head of the Church in my realm. I will be *damned* before I do such things!" He defiantly put his fists on his hips and gave a royal scowl.

I could not resist remarking, "Truer words were never spoken. A king as well as a prophet. Let us hope that St. Thomas More's prayers save you, did save you, from your prophecy."

Henry turned on me, almost hissing like a snake, spewing out a string of rather old-fashioned expletives. "And blast you, man, you abortive rooting hog, you muddy-mettled rascal, craven crapper-clawed lout.... Where is my knife?... I'll give you a taste of kingly wrath!" He was searching for the blade he had so recently sent my way. As a man who quite enjoys knife-throwing—I have a target out back; it's all very relaxing—and also a man who believes in returning property to its rightful owner, I sent it back to him. It stuck right next to his head, in the wall to the right of the painting.

"I believe you dropped it earlier," I added nonchalantly.

Henry was livid. He snatched the knife out of the wall, meaning to throw it back again, I assume, but as soon as he yanked it out, he simply disappeared. I had not previously witnessed another of my guests so suddenly removed in front of my very eyes.

More looked down at the floor and rocked back and forth on his heels a few long moments, weighing it all. "He will not change, that is clear enough," he said at last, "My prayers may reach my God, but my pleadings have not reached my king. I have nothing left but my cell and my prayers then."

"No, St. Thomas, that's not true. There is more on the other side of that cell."

"Do you then see More there?" he said, as usual unable to resist a pun, even when his heart was filled with dust. "Do you spy More making merry with his king?"

Compelled to tell the truth, I replied, "He is making merry with his true King, but even we, who know how it all turned out for you, do not know how it turned out for Henry."

The saint rubbed his red, swollen eyes. It was clear he was worn out, in body and in soul. "I had always feared for Henry's eternal destiny, even with his good beginning, and that is why I feared for my own head when I entered his service. When a man ascends to royal power, he is not made stronger, as those who judge with a worldly eye suppose. Put a crown on his head, and he is made weaker by his own ambition and festering pride, however much power his scepter seems to wield. He rises only to fall. He sees all below him on bended knee in his court and soon cannot see God above him even while he bends the knee in prayer. It is very strange that the very man who received the title *fidei defensor*, 'defender of the Faith,' should become such a monster by rejecting it."

"Defender of the Faith! What an unpleasant and inappropriate irony!"

"Yes, it was a title he received from the pope himself for his writing a fine treatise, a *Defense of the Seven Sacraments*. I helped him, of course, as did the good and holy John Fisher." He paused and looked off sadly. "He too stands with me against Henry, this holy Fisher of men. He too will not bless this union with Anne, nor will he consent to Henry's taking the crowns of England and the church." He looked at me imploringly, his eyes tearing again. "I suppose he will lose his head."

"I'm afraid so."

"And I mine."

I tried to answer him, but I must confess I was completely choked with emotion, unable even to croak out a reply. I just looked down at the floor.

Oddly, More smiled, a smile of relief, one that welled from a deep and holy resignation to God's will. "Well, then, there is no more to be said about More, is there?" He patted me gently on my shoulder. "I go to my cell to await the opening of the door that leads home, home to the great hall of the King—a door Henry shall open for me with an axe! And for this great favor, I shall pray for him until the end."

He vanished, and it felt like a great weight had withdrawn from the room, a profound presence of a holy man who filled more than the space of his body.

I sat down at my desk and tried to think it all through. Henry would not change; history had not changed. Off the saint went to his punishment, and then to his reward. It is reported that he joked to the very end. When an officer gave the weakened More his hand to help him up the steps of the scaffold, he said, "When I come down again, let me shift for myself as well as I can."

The executioner was in tears, and More kissed him kindly and joked about the shortness of his neck and the resulting difficulty in chopping off his head. The joking saint, the merry saint, the martyr, the king's best servant.

More kept his promise to Henry VIII, the promise he made right from the beginning to serve God first, and the king second, and he always believed, rightly, that in serving God first, he served the king best.

The real traitors were the ones who let Henry have his way. While they helped lead Henry into ever greater tyranny, More prayed for Henry's soul to the very end—and whose prayers could be more effective?

More was just like St. Stephen, who prayed for those who stoned him, just as Christ had prayed, "Forgive them, Father, they know not what they are doing." And so at his final trial for treason, he didn't curse the unjust judges. Instead, he recalled that St. Paul, who had held St. Stephen's clothes while he was stoned to death, is now with him in Heaven. "So I verily trust," said More to his accusers, "and shall therefore right heartily pray, that though your lordships have now here in earth been judges to my condemnation, we may yet hereafter in Heaven merrily all meet together, to our everlasting salvation."

So, perhaps St. Thomas More and Henry VIII are making merry in Heaven, or will someday, as More so ardently wished.

Reflections

Very famous people are actually real people. It's easy to forget that and to treat someone like Henry VIII as a kind of historical abstraction, a painted portrait, or a legendary idea rather than a flesh-and-blood individual with his own particular features and foibles making daily choices for good or ill. We feel as if famous people are larger than life because they had so much historical effect, and we fail to remember that they had so great an effect precisely because they were actual men living real lives.

I stress this because we are inclined to talk of history as if it were some kind of magic force that has a life of its own and that men of such stature as Henry VIII were merely abstractions who act out a predetermined part. But when you come face-to-face with the actual man, you realize that history doesn't have a life of its own apart from the lives of men and women. History is what happens when particular human beings freely choose to do one thing or another, the right or wrong thing, the brave or cowardly thing.

That's all to say that Henry VIII didn't have to be Henry VIII, or more accurately, he didn't have to be the notorious Henry VIII that history hands down to us. He could have made quite other choices than he did; in fact, he could have become St. Henry VIII, God willing.

But for the same reason, St. Thomas More could have been merely Thomas More if he had, like so many others, chosen the wide and easy path of accepting Henry VIII's divorce and remarriage and his claim to be both the king of England and the pope of his own national church. He would have had his life spared; he would have been restored to his family; he would have been showered with gold and lands in reward for his obedience.

Instead, he took the narrow and difficult road. He chose to serve God first, out of both love and fear, holy love and righteous fear. He feared—to recall the Gospels—the one who had power over his eternal soul rather than the one who had power over his temporal body. But this fear was really an aspect of his holy love of God, of Jesus Christ who Himself faced a horrible death. Thomas More preferred to follow his Savior to the Cross, and hence to lose his head, rather than to add a few more years to his life.

It all sounds so good and so easy. Who would we not want to be known as the man who stood up to such a tyrant? But while I like to think of myself standing up to Henry VIII as More did, when I honestly take stock of my soul, of my fears, of my weak virtues and weakening vices, I shudder as I realize that my courage would likely have failed me. I'm afraid, if I'm to be honest, that, were I living way back then, I'd be among the nameless wretches who sought to spare their lives. At least I can count this honesty among my acts of virtue!

I say this because we often have only a vague notion of the heroism required in extraordinary historical circumstances. We blithely believe we would have acted just as boldly as the great saints such as Thomas More, as boys imagine themselves with their toy guns bravely running into battle amidst flying bullets. It's easy to be courageous in our imagination, but very hard to be so even in the littlest trials of our actual life. I imagine myself standing boldly beside St. Thomas More, waiting my turn for the wooden block, but in Lent I tremble not to have sugar in my tea.

Meeting these two men gave me a much more vivid understanding of what it means for an actual man to face death rather than give up his faith. One thing that was very clear was how much *training* it took for Thomas More to meet the pivotal moment with courage. Just as boys misunderstand how much physical training is required for soldiers before they can fight bravely in real battle — being inexperienced children, they think just having a *feeling* of courage is *having* courage — so also we Christians think our present *feelings* of piety and resolve would steel us for a great trial.

But Thomas More was *St.* Thomas More because for years he was a saint-in-training. He prayed and fasted; he studied Scripture and deeply contemplated its revelations; he treated foolish and irascible people with undeserved charity; he dutifully cared for his family in all the daily details that define real love; he wore the finest robes and gold chain of the chancellor but a hair shirt underneath. It was all this, years and years of it, that made him, by the grace of God, able to cling to his faith against the vile tyrant Henry.

This also brought me to reflect on the nature of political power and political tyranny. We today think that we are so very superior to those who were ruled by kings, especially kings such as Henry VIII. But as Aristotle knew well, democracy can be just as tyrannical as monarchy, and that means we Christians can be just as cowardly in the face of a raging crowd as a raging king.

I don't mean to disparage politics in saying this. St. Thomas More is one of our finest examples of a holy political servant. He understood that no political order — whether ruled by a king or by a congress — is automatically good. Like a garden, the political order we happen to have is the one that we cultivate and care for.

If we neglect the proper care of our common political life, then we can expect weeds to grow: the petty and profound corruption, the seizing of power by the lovers of power, the manipulation and deceit, the endless expansion of taxation and public debt, and the lies that patch it all together.

St. Thomas More understood that it was his Christian *duty* to bring integrity and holiness to his political office, and when he was asked to leave both aside, he gave up the gold chain of England's highest office under the king. But that did not end More's troubles. Henry could not allow so great a man to stand as an example against him, even out of office, and so as a perfect tyrant he had to hunt More down in his private life and demand undue obedience.

I fear that our own democracy is becoming a different kind of tyranny, one that bids us to remain comfortable amidst growing chaos and moral disorder. In return for our acquiescence we are implicitly promised, as Henry promised Thomas, featherbeds rather than crosses.

You might say that, in our time, we are ruled by invisible kings, men who have been able to amass a thousand, thousand times more riches than Henry VIII or any other king in history, and it is they who rule over the politicians and bureaucrats who, in turn, rule over us. These invisible kings do not ask for our heads in the barbaric way of King Henry; rather, they ask for our souls, or more exactly, for us to give up all our silly notions of becoming saints like Thomas More and to settle for far less. We are offered a long life of convenience, titillation, gustatory and sensual satisfaction, and the medicinal repair of the ill effects of our hedonism, and the peace to enjoy it all in. But compared with Heaven this is less than a pittance.

Saints are dangerous, as tyrants of any kind realize, because they would rather lose their heads than lose their souls. They choose

Heaven over lives defined by worldly satisfaction, whether it is the life of royal prestige or the life lived in the fulfillment of the most trivial pleasures, amusements, and comfort.

And so we must ask ourselves: What form would a saint like Thomas More take in our day?

Edith Stein (St. Teresa Benedicta of the Cross) and Friedrich Nietzsche

Part 1

Sometimes, when I know that particular historical figures will be visiting me, I have something brought in that I hope will make things go more smoothly. I was a little worried when I understood that Edith Stein and Friedrich Nietzsche would be my next guests. Casting around for some way to get a Jewish woman philosopher-saint to interact peacefully with a man who joyfully declared that reason is destroyed by the will, that God is dead, and that Christianity itself is a horrifying plague, I came upon the fact that Nietzsche was a great lover of music and quite an accomplished piano player. So, I rented a piano for their arrival.

I'm a bit of a duffer on the piano, to say the least—out of practice now, and bad even when I put time into it as a much younger man. But I still retain some sense of how to play. When I understood that Nietzsche was coming, I quickly did some research into his compositions and purchased the sheet music for a few, thinking I could peck away at them, and that they might give me an interesting insight into his volatile character.

Nietzsche is certainly one of the most famous of modern philosophers, both for his strident atheism and for providing a great part of the intellectual foundation for Nazism (which is ironic, because Nietzsche, who was German, wrote that he hated Germans *and* anti-Semites). Yet, despite the attempts of many to distance Nietzsche's philosophy from the horrors of the Nazi regime, there is no getting around the great influence of his work on that movement.

I should mention that Nietzsche died in August of 1900, long before the Nazis came to power, so there's no *personal* connection between the philosopher and the movement. Nietzsche went insane about a decade before he died, so he is even more distanced in time from the rise of the great evil of Hitler.

But his philosophy lived on after his death. Even though he may have been repulsed by the crude German anti-Semitism of his time, he was also an outspoken enemy of Judaism, which he despised because—so he argued—it raised the lowest and weakest human beings to power over the strongest and best, all in the name of a pathetic concern for the lowly and poor. To Nietzsche, the strongest and best *should* rule, using the weak as their instruments. Nietzsche, we could say, was on the side of Pharaoh, rather than of the Jews, in that great biblical contest.

As much as he despised Judaism, he hated Christianity even more because its expansive concern for the poor and the weak, the outcast and the downtrodden is accentuated by the fact that *God Himself* became one of the weak. Nietzsche did not believe in God, but he especially loathed *that* God, the God-become-man who offered Himself as a sacrifice. He was much more comfortable with pagan gods who called for the sacrifice of human beings.

Now you can see why I was concerned about Nietzsche meeting my other guest, St. Teresa Benedicta of the Cross, that is, Edith Stein. She died in 1942 in the infamous gas chambers of Auschwitz concentration camp. Her crime? She was a Jew, and even worse, a Jewish convert to Catholicism, specifically a Discalced Carmelite nun, but a Jew by birth nonetheless.

We can truthfully say that Nietzsche's philosophy and Edith Stein's life converged at Auschwitz. For Nietzsche, someone like

Edith Stein had a double strike against her: She was both a Jew and a convert to Christianity. The Nazis despised her for the same reasons.

Despite all this, Nietzsche and Stein did have some important things in common, which made their meeting with me even more interesting. Both were German. Both were philosophers. Edith Stein received her doctorate in philosophy in 1917, the year World War I ended, and studied with the most influential philosopher in Germany at the time, Edmund Husserl. In fact, she was so intelligent and well read that she was Husserl's assistant for some time. One of the philosophers she read closely was—you guessed it—Friedrich Nietzsche.

Miss Stein was the first to arrive, a tad earlier than I thought she would. It was late at night, the usual time of my guests' arrival, and I had been reading her autobiography, *Life in a Jewish Family*. I had nodded off in my chair, not because of her book, which is fascinating, but because I had been up quite early that morning. She must have quietly knocked and gotten no response, because I was awakened by her after she had entered of her own accord.

"Excuse me, you are Herr Doctor Wiker, I assume?" she said softly, as she peered around the corner of my chair.

I shot up, embarrassed a bit and feeling rather disheveled and nap-headed, and replied with only modest coherence, "Yes, Miss Stein, or Frau Stein, or no. I'm sorry, I should have gotten this all straight, knowing you were coming. Things just seem to slip away before I can get to them."

I tried to straighten my hair and recoup my appearance. "It's Fräulein Stein, isn't it, because you are not married?" And then I hesitated. "But wait, that's not quite right, since you've got a doctorate ..."

She graciously rescued me from bumbling any further and smiled gently as she held out her hand in greeting. "It would be

Fräulein Doctor Stein. But I think we would both be more comfortable if we would use the English form of address. I am quite fine with Doctor Stein."

She wore a very plain brown dress, with a thin black sweater that was worn but not tattered. Her hair was drawn up into a bun.

I crossed over to my desk, saying rather humbly, "Yes, I'm afraid I was never very good at German. Took me three times to pass my Ph.D. language requirement in it. I know you are very good with languages," I said as I ruffled through the papers scattered across the oak top. "Did a bit of research. Ah, here we go! Let me see, you obviously know your native tongue of German, and English, but also Latin, and ... and ..."

"Greek, French, and Dutch as well. But I always loved Latin the best, especially the crisp Latin of St. Thomas Aquinas, and even more the beautiful Latin of the Holy Mass. I learned Latin in school when I was quite young. I felt as though I were learning my mother tongue—and I was, of Mother Church!" She smiled affectionately. "Yes, that was the language of the Church, but how could I know that later I would pray in this language! Such a thing never even occurred to me at the time."

"A beautiful act of Providence, as I see it!" I added.

Suddenly realizing my slip in manners, I ushered her toward the chess table, saying, "Forgive me, Doctor Stein. We need to give you a seat, so we can talk more comfortably. This is where I usually sit with my guests." I pulled out a chair for her to sit down. "Would you care for something to drink? Coffee, water, wine, umm ... beer?"

"No, please. I am quite fine." She was naturally cheerful, you could tell—or was it supernaturally cheerful? In any case, she made me feel at home in my own home. I'm always a bit nervous meeting the saints, but not so much the scoundrels. "You know, I was just now reading your autobiography."

"Ah, that is what put you into such a deep sleep!" she laughed.

"No, no, not at all. What put me to sleep was a certain dog of mine who doesn't like thunderstorms and insists I stay up with him at night to see him through the danger. That happened last night." I held up her book. "Your life is anything but boring! Let me see if I recall correctly; you were the youngest of eleven children, born on the Jewish holy day of Yom Kippur, the holiest of holy days on the Jewish calendar."

"Yes, I was the youngest of eleven, but four died in childhood. My father died when I was very young, and so I was the last child in the family." She smiled slightly. "I assume that there is much less pain in the death of a father you never knew. My dear mother was always so proud of the fact that I was born on Yom Kippur, the Day of Atonement, the day on which the High Priest used to enter the Holy of Holies to offer the sacrifice of atonement for himself and for the people. After this, the scapegoat, upon whose head, symbolically, the sins of all the people had been laid was driven out into the desert," she explained, pantomiming what she described. "We Jews fast and pray on this day every year. We refrain from taking any food or drink for twenty-four hours or more!"

"You say 'We Jews.' That's an interesting way to speak, given that you are a convert to Catholicism. I don't want to say that you are no longer a Jew, but ..."

"I am a Jew, always a Jew, even after my conversion to the Catholic Church," she said, sitting up proudly. "I am, in this, just like our Lord Himself, *God incarnate as a Jew*, always a Jew, forever a Jew!"

I confess here that I found this rather stunning, and at the same time I was amazed that I hadn't internalized what should be an obvious fact: Jesus Christ, God incarnate, did not become a generic man, even less a European-looking man, but a Jew. And He did not exchange His particular body for a generalized human nature in the Resurrection; He was and always will be a Jew!

She could see that something about what she had said hit me at just the right angle to startle me.

"You don't know what it means to me," she continued, "how much it means to me at the very heart of my vocation, to be a daughter of the Chosen People — to belong to Christ, not only spiritually, but according to the flesh."

She smiled even more broadly as she looked admiringly at the flesh of her hands, which she displayed for me, turning them over as evidence of her profound pedigree.

"I have to say, I never thought about it all that … that … exactly." That wasn't the right word, but I was unable to find any other. "Could you tell me a bit more about your conversion to Catholicism?" I asked.

"It is a very long story," she said, carefully smoothing her brown hair on both sides, "and in the deepest sense a very private one." She turned her large brown eyes away from me for a moment, as if in modesty. "Of course, in the most obvious sense, my Jewishness led me to Christ. Who could not see that Yom Kippur is a foreshadowing of the sacrifice of Christ Himself, our 'scapegoat,' who takes our sins upon Himself, who atones for all our sins? So, looking back, I might even say: How could I not convert? Judaism has its fulfillment in Christ, and so I had my fulfillment in Christianity!"

"So, you were a good and observant Jew?"

"I wish I could answer yes!" she replied as she looked down and brushed out a few wrinkles on her lap with her hands. "My mother was, very much so, very much a good Jew. She loved her faith deeply, practiced her faith. It was her heart, her mind, her soul, her breath — everything. We, her children?" she added, looking off into the distance. "When we were young, yes, as more docile children, more innocent. But then we drifted away from Judaism, as so many did at the time." She clasped her hands together and gave a grim, confessionary smile. "I myself lost any belief in a personal

God when I was about fifteen years old and did not come back to belief until years later, in my twenties."

"You were a complete atheist, then? You completely rejected God?"

She thought a moment. "Even when I did not believe, I loved my mother and hence my mother's faith, though I had none of my own. I thought I had *outgrown* it; I was too 'big' to believe in God, too smart! I became passionately dedicated to finding the truth with my reason, and so let go of my Jewish faith as something childish," she said, as she pretended to drop her faith from her hand like a handkerchief that fluttered away in the wind. "Little did I know that God, Who is Truth, would lead me to Himself, through my passion for truth. Whoever seeks the truth is seeking God, whether consciously or unconsciously."

"So, try as you might, you couldn't escape from God as long as you honestly sought the truth?"

She nodded.

"Could you tell me more about your conversion, the conversion to understanding that the Truth is a person, not a thing?"

"Well, I might give something of a sketch," she said, sitting back in the chair, and folding her arms thoughtfully. "My quest for the truth led me to enter the University of Göttingen for a degree in philosophy—under the great Edmund Husserl. You have heard of him, no?"

"Yes, certainly one of the philosophic giants of the time."

"True, very true. But wait, let me make things clearer. Actually, I had been at the University of Breslau from 1911 to 1913, studying psychology, philosophy, history, and philology, and *then*, after reading Husserl, I decided to go to where he was in Göttingen, where I was later to become his assistant. And what do you think? I was chasing philosophy for the truth, and while at Göttingen I found that many of my esteemed teachers, including Husserl, were Jews who had converted to Christianity! Husserl was a Lutheran. Another brilliant teacher of mine, Max Scheler, had just converted to Catholicism. So, I had to realize, studying with these brilliant men, that Christianity was no obstacle to reason. All the barriers set up by my atheistic, rationalist prejudices that had led me to reject belief in God as irrational — they just crumbled to the ground! A world of faith unfolded before me, a world that fulfills reason, not rejects it. Persons with whom I associated daily at the university, people whom I esteemed and admired, *lived* in it."

She laughed at the joke of a gently providential God. "But I was not there very long when the Great War intervened," she said, her brows furrowing. "I became a Red Cross nurse. I was very patriotic, a good German. I wanted to help, so I served in the lazaretto, a hospital for soldiers with infectious diseases."

"Your mother was still living at the time?"

"Yes, my mother did not want me to go. She told me, very sternly, 'You will not go with my permission.' And I had to reply, to my dear mother, whom I loved, 'Then I must go without your permission.'" She paused, lost in that poignant moment again. "And so I did. My poor mother! I had never dared to contradict her like that before. I served dutifully as a nurse, but I became sick and was sent back. I returned to the University of Göttingen to finish my degree."

"And then?"

"Well, much, much happened, too much to tell! But to focus on my conversion, one of my teachers, whom I greatly admired, Adolph Reinach, he and his wife had become Christians. He had volunteered for the war but was killed in 1917. By then I had moved with Husserl, as his assistant, to the University of Freiburg. That's where I finished my doctorate."

"And you wrote your doctoral dissertation on empathy, if I recall."

"Yes, completed in 1916. But to go forward, not long after this, I immediately went back to Göttingen to help Adolph's widow, Anna. I expected her to be crushed, ruined by her husband's death. Why would anyone expect otherwise? Instead, through her Christian faith, she was filled with hope, consolation, and peace."

A little emotion welled up in recalling this, and Stein cleared her throat. "She accepted his death, this horrible loss, *in union with Christ* as part of her redemptive suffering. This was my first encounter with the Cross and the divine power that it bestows on those who freely choose to pick it up and carry it. For the first time, I was seeing with my very own eyes the Church, the true Church, born from the Redeemer's sufferings and, through the grace of that birth, triumphant over the sting of death. Death was conquered for Anna in and through the Cross. That was the moment my unbelief collapsed and Jesus Christ shone forth in such, such luminosity, such power, *in* the mystery of the Cross."

"I guess God put an end to your 'rational' doubt, but what a difficult path to the truth."

"If Jesus is the Way, the Truth, and the Life, we should not be surprised that such a path must be taken."

"But here is the thing that fascinates me. You did not turn away from reason. You encountered a truth *with* your reason. Here is a woman, Anna … Anna …"

"Reinach, Anna Reinach."

"Yes, Anna Reinach. Here is Anna Reinach right before your eyes; you see her, and you see the truth about the way she reacts to her husband's death, but this truth is, somehow, if not against reason, certainly *beyond* reason, beyond human reason to grasp."

"A mystery, yes, mystery in the sense of stretching beyond reason but yet, as you say—she was right before my eyes! This was reality, not fantasy. My reason had to accept what could be explained only by faith, faith in the Cross. And so, as I said, my unbelief collapsed at that moment."

"Did you then seek to enter the Catholic Church?"

"No, this first encounter with the Cross made me a Christian, but not yet a Catholic." She looked down thoughtfully at her lap, as if gathering her memories there in front of us. "I was staying with friends and fellow philosophers, Theodor and Hedwig Conrad-Martius, likewise students of Husserl. This was, I believe, in the summer of 1921, yes, when I was almost thirty years old. They had gone out—Theodor and Hedwig—and I was at their home alone, browsing their bookshelves when I came upon St. Teresa of Avila's autobiography."

"Yes, yes, I've always meant to read that. My wife's name is Teresa, so I thought I should certainly read it."

"You need to get yourself a copy right away!" she scolded kindly. "I picked it up that night and could not put it down. I stayed up all night, *all night*, and read it. The next morning, when I finally finished it, I closed the covers and said, 'This is the truth.'"

"And not to tire out this point, but you were not any less of a philosopher seeking the truth. St. Teresa was speaking the truth, a truth truer than you sought, so to speak."

"I think we must put it just that way," she said approvingly. "You can see why I was already attending daily Mass at this point, even before I became a Catholic. And I do not think it will surprise you that I took the name Teresa as my baptismal name. I was baptized on the first of January in 1922. I knew, even then, that I would someday become a Carmelite, just like Teresa of Avila." And then she shook her head. "But I could not utter such a wish in front of my mother. It would have broken her heart—I knew that—if I had entered a convent so soon."

"She was such a devout Jew."

"Yes, she loved her faith, deeply, so deeply."

"How did she respond to your conversion?"

Edith Stein smiled grimly. "She wept. I had never seen her cry before, in all my life up to that point, I had never seen her cry. It was so painful; it tore out my very heart. I would rather have endured insults and abuse. There were none. Just her pain, welling to the surface. Those tears were most painful to me."

Though it was not particularly good timing, given Doctor Stein's emotional recounting, at this point there was a sharp rap at the door. Perhaps, providentially, it was a good time. From God's perspective, things must look quite different.

"Ah, if you'll excuse me, Doctor Stein. I believe that's our other guest for this evening. I'm sure you've not only heard of him," I said, getting up from my chair at the chess table, "but, being a student of philosophy, you've read his works. Friedrich Nietzsche. He's our other guest this evening."

"Indeed I have," she said, with great interest. "I know his works very well."

As I passed my desk on the way to the door, a sudden thought occurred to me, from I don't know where.

"Doctor Stein," I said, turning back toward her. "If you could trust me for a bit on this, I'd like not to reveal *everything* about you at once, especially that you are such an eminent philosopher who already knows Nietzsche's thought. Could I, may I have your permission, to refer to you as just *Fräulein* Stein in front of Herr Nietzsche, just for a little while?"

She thought this was a great joke and cheerfully nodded.

"And I know how you loved to write plays and other performances when you were a child, so could you just play along with me for a while, pretending that you are a quite ordinary woman — if I might put it that way?"

"You have me intrigued, Doctor Wiker, I must play along! Yes, I will be most happy to play along."

I nodded my thanks, walked over, and opened the door. Before I could say anything, the man himself entered, nearly bumping into me, squinting as he entered the room.

"Good evening. You are Herr Doctor Wiker, I assume?" he asked, pursing his eyes to try to get my face in focus.

"Yes, so I am, so I am. Welcome! Please come in, Herr Doctor Nietzsche," and I made way for him, gesturing for him to pass me in the small foyer.

Instead, he thrust out his hand rather nervously, and I shook it. "I am most grateful, Herr Doctor Wiker."

I ushered him inside once again, and this time he walked past me a few steps and then peered around, finally seeing—we might assume, rather dimly—another person across the room at the chess table, unsure about what he ought to do next.

I pause at this point because, for those who have read Friedrich Nietzsche's philosophy—with all its bluster about the need for cruelty, rejection of Christian charity, and going beyond good and evil to embrace the will to power—it is very surprising that in person the philosopher himself was quiet and unassuming, self-conscious, and somewhat clumsy. Indeed, he was intensely shy, exceedingly nearsighted, and quite sickly. Along with all that, he was quite gentlemanly and formal around women. Given the awful things that he said about women in his various works—including his loud assertions about their inability to understand philosophy—this gentle gentlemanliness was a most surprising thing.

Edith Stein had to be fully aware of his opinion of women, having read him, and so, I think, understood the game I was playing with Nietzsche.

So, rather than lash out loudly against a woman in the room, he said in a very courtly manner, "Ah, I see that you have a guest already. Please forgive me for interrupting."

Stein had gotten up at this point, and she began walking forward a bit to get more within the range of his eyesight. Even then, his squinting let us know how little his glasses helped.

"You're not interrupting; in fact, we were waiting for you. Well, I was anyway. Please allow me to introduce you," I said, gesturing for my guests to approach each other. "Herr Professor Nietzsche, this is Fräulein Stein. Fräulein Stein, Herr Professor Nietzsche."

Nietzsche took her hand in a most gracious, old-fashioned way —not in an American handshake—and bowed slightly.

"I am honored, Fräulein Stein."

She gave a slight curtsy. "Likewise, Herr Doctor."

There was an awkward pause from which I chose not to rescue him. He stood there, waiting for the next social step.

"Perhaps this is a bad time, or I have come too early?"

"No, indeed," I replied, "as with all my guests, you've come at exactly the right time." Having tortured him enough, I gestured toward the other side of the room. "Please come over to the chess table and have a seat with us. We were just having a chat."

Nietzsche walked over and politely pulled out a chair for Stein, and then took the other for himself. I rolled my desk chair closer so that I would be part of the conversation. Edith Stein and I then just sat there, smiling and looking at Nietzsche, who was getting more and more uncomfortable.

"So, Fräulein Stein," he said, turning his attention to her, "what brings you here?"

I interrupted, not wanting to put her on the spot in the charade I was composing on the spot: "She was just on her way through, to the convent, you might say."

This did nothing to increase his comfort. "I see. How ... nice for you," he said, offering a condescending smile. "Which order, if I might ask?"

"The Carmelite Order, Herr Doctor."

"How nice," he smiled again, smoothing out his pants. After a little more awkward silence, he said, "I was invited by Herr Doctor Wiker to talk about my philosophy. I do not know how much our conversation would interest you."

"You would be surprised, I think, Herr Doctor. But please, allow me to excuse myself. I am rather tired after my journey." She got up and walked over to the other side of the room, and this seemed to fill Nietzsche with a sense of relief. "I will not bother you, but just listen from afar, so to speak." I thought she would go to my comfy chair, but instead she sat down at the piano, making me wonder if she had a sudden dramatic inspiration.

"I do want to discuss your philosophy with you, Herr Doctor Nietzsche, very much so," I said turning toward him, "but I would like to find a bit more about you first, if you would. But first, would you like some coffee or tea? Or perhaps, wine—or, since you are German, a glass of beer?"

Now that Stein was out of his very restricted field of vision and we were about to discuss his philosophy, he perked up and became quite suddenly affable.

"Alcohol! No, no, no, no! I am afraid alcohol is very bad for me. If I have a single glass of wine or beer in a day, I can assure you, Doctor Wiker, that my life will be turned into a vale of misery—my head, my stomach!"

"Coffee or tea, then?"

"Coffee! I must tell you that coffee spreads darkness," he said dramatically, moving his outstretched hand slowly across the air in front of him. "Now tea is another matter, but one must be aware that it is wholesome and healthy only in the morning." And here he chuckled and leaned toward me, shaking his finger back and forth. "Tea is very *un*wholesome and gives one the sicklies the whole rest of the day *if* it is made too weak, even by one, single degree!" he said, pinching his index finger next to his thumb, to emphasize the needed precision to avoid such a fate.

His sudden bout of strange whimsy made him even more relaxed. All I could think to say was "I see," and then after a short pause to get my bearings, "and so, how about getting back to telling me about your life?"

"I was born in town of Röcken, near Leipzig," he began before immediately interrupting himself, "but I am so completely alien, in my very deepest instincts, to *everything* that is German, everything! If there is a German anywhere near me," he nodded, then patted his stomach, "it causes me indigestion!"

Out of the corner of my eye I caught Stein's stifled laugh and attempt to regain composure.

"You see, Herr Doctor Wiker, my ancestors were Polish noblemen, *not* Germans. From that noble source, I can assure you, my body is filled with racial instincts." He sat back and confided with a hint of braggadocio, "When I reflect on how often I am addressed *as a Pole* in my various journeys, and by contrast how very rarely anyone ever assumes that I am a German, it seems that I have merely been lightly dusted with 'German.' But, I must confess that my mother, Franziska Oehler, is very, very German, and the same must be said of my grandmother—that is, on my father's side. Her name was Erdmuthe Krause."

This was very peculiar, I thought, the pretense to Polish nobility. "And your father? Could you tell me about him?"

He replied abruptly, as if this were all the information he cared to offer. "My father was born in 1813 and died in 1849."

"And you were born in ..."

"On the fifteenth of October 1844."

Another curt answer. For some reason, this line of questioning had dampened his spirits. I was weighing whether I should pursue further or simply go on to another subject.

Nietzsche was gazing off to the left of me, thoughtfully stroking his astoundingly bushy, brown mustache. He then looked down at his lap and added, "My father died when he was only thirty-six. I remember him to be — to have been — delicate, and kind, and morbid. He was fated, destined it seems, merely to pass by me, pass through life. He was, how can I say it, more like a gracious memory of life, perhaps, than life itself."

He was obviously moved, so I let him have his thoughts to himself for a moment.

"I was not yet quite four years old when he started to have seizures," Nietzsche continued. "We were told that it was a softening of the brain." His eyes flicked to mine, then to his hands neatly folded on his lap. "He was a Lutheran pastor. Did I mention that? Of course, he had to give up his duties. It was in July of the following year that he lapsed into a coma, and three days later, my father was dead."

Nietzsche was not the only philosopher marred by some paternal tragedy — Hume, Camus, Sartre, Schopenhauer, and who knows how many others were as well. It seems that this great void all too often helps to nurture a bad philosophy, a philosophy born from a broken, fatherless heart.

"In the same year in which my father's life spiraled downward, so did mine."

The other philosopher, the philosopher of empathy, spoke up from her seat at the piano. "How very sad, Herr Doctor. I have for you the deepest compassion for your loss. I was not yet two when my father died. He was on a business trip; he owned a lumber mill, and often went on such trips. But on this trip, he died of a stroke. It was on a very hot day in July. He had gone to inspect a forest, and he had to walk a very long way." She was tearing up, and Nietzsche was listening intently. "From a distance, a postman walking his rounds happened to look up and notice my father lying down. But the first time he saw him, since it was a hot day, he just assumed he was resting, so he kept on his rounds. It was several hours later, when the postman was returning, that he saw my father, still in the same spot, the same position, and so he thought he had better take a look. He found him dead. He had been dead the whole day."

Nietzsche was genuinely moved—at least it appeared that way to me—but he didn't speak up.

"I have a photograph of my family," Stein said, recovering a loving smile. "It was taken two years after he died. I don't have it with me now, of course, but in it, my mother superimposed an old photograph of my father—a trick of the photographer's art—to make it seem as if he were still alive and watching over the family. I ... I cannot view it without a deep, sweet sadness, for that greatest of losses in my childhood. So, Herr Doctor Nietzsche, I am very sorry to hear about your father's early death too."

"Interesting," said Nietzsche, in a rather odd way. "I have no such welcome memories of my childhood."

Stein looked at him for a moment in both sympathy and incomprehension. "I am very sorry to hear that also. I have many wonderful memories, especially of my dear, very kind, and loving mother. Forced to be both mother and father to us after my father's death, she was a very strong and determined woman, strong as an oak but gentle as a willow—her love for us made her both. She took over the lumber business herself and not only paid off my father's debts, but built up a very prosperous business." She said this quite proudly, but then an embarrassed look crossed her face. "Oh, pardon me! I have interrupted. Please return to your conversation."

"As much as I'd like to hear more about your life, Herr Doctor Nietzsche," I said, "I have a feeling that a lot of our precious time is slipping away, and I really do want to discuss your philosophy."

Nietzsche gave a polite, formal nod.

"Now I would like to jump right to your *Jenseits von Gut und Böse*—forgive my pronunciation of the German—your *Beyond Good and Evil*, as it has been translated into English. This was the first work of yours I read, as an undergraduate. I think we should begin with your concept of the *will to power*."

"Yes! Yes!" His eyes immediately lit up. "Each living thing seeks, above everything else, to discharge, to expend, to manifest its natural strength," he said, curling his right fist. "Life itself, the very act of living, *is* the will to power." He drew out the last words, as if pounding each one into the floor like so many large spikes.

"To be clear, you mean something like this, I take it: that every living thing, including every human being, has a desire for self-preservation?"

"Here, the Darwinists are too flat, too brown, too unalive! Self-preservation is only one of the indirect and most frequent consequences of the desire of every living thing to live. What each thing really desires is to grow, to expand, to flourish, and to express the inner power of its life *for* life! All living things pursue this *for* themselves and *against* other things—at the *expense* of other things! *That* growing up and over, standing on others to reach the sky, that, Herr Doctor Wiker, is the will to power."

"And in human beings, is that a free will? Is it fundamentally different from other things, the human will?

He shook his head as if I had committed a foolish intellectual blunder. "Free and unfree? No, no, no, we are talking about *strong* wills and *weak* wills. In real life, it is not a matter of free or unfree, but of strong and weak."

"And what about reason in human beings? You are a philosopher. What about philosophy itself? Isn't that about *truth* rather than power—the will to power?"

He leaned forward. I could see his eyes twitching, not with nervousness, but a kind of strange, not-quite-human nervous energy.

He rocked back and forth slightly, as if that energy was rattling his whole body from within.

"Philosophy! The truth! Herr Doctor Wiker, philosophy *is* the most sublime and tyrannical of drives. It is the most *spiritual* will to power, the power *to be the creator* of worlds, to be the *first cause* as we used to believe a god was the first cause, to be the maker, the crafter, the artisan of reality for oneself, a reality that one imposes on those of weaker wills, those who are not creators but can only be created."

"Do you really mean to say that human beings are, like all other creatures, *entirely* driven by their will to power, the desire to 'discharge their natural strength,' as you put it? And that the notion that we human beings discover truth is a fiction? That philosophy itself, rather than being the search for truth, is really only ... what? ... an expression of each individual philosopher's own *irrational* will?"

Nietzsche laughed—not a mirthful laugh but a kind of promethean disdainful rumble. "Gradually it has become very, very clear to me," he said, squinting at me through his glasses, "what every great philosophy so far has been. Not a selfless search for truth, not a discovery of an underlying creation ordered by a god or nature. No, not at all. Each philosophy tells you about one thing and one thing only—the *will* of its creator. It is a *personal confession* of its author, a memoir, so to speak, that he himself takes to be the truth!"

"So, philosophy—even the most abstruse and seemingly impersonal philosophy—is really, what, a kind of autobiography, a mere expression of that particular person's will? Socrates isn't telling us about wisdom, but only about Socrates? Plato is telling you only about Plato? Kant about Kant?"

Nietzsche sat back in his chair smugly and rubbed his hands together rather gleefully at his revelation. "No, autobiography assumes that the philosopher *understands* what he is really doing.

He really *thinks* that he is making claims about the truth, grand metaphysical claims about reality," he declared, sweeping his hands in the air, "when what is *actually* happening is that he, quite *un-consciously*, is describing *as true* his own wants, his own desires, perhaps desires hidden even from him!"

"And that includes *moral* philosophy, philosophy concerned with human ethical life?"

"Most of all, most of all!" he fairly giggled. "The real moral—and perhaps immoral!—intentions in each and every philosophy, *these* constitute the real seed and root from which the whole philosophical plant grows and grows, conquers and overshadows, strangles and climbs to the sun!"

"We're back, then, to your *Beyond Good and Evil*, I think, because what you are saying—correct me, please, I wish I were wrong—is that at the very bottom, at the very heart of every philosophy is that particular philosopher's own beliefs, irrational beliefs, about good and evil. It is never good and evil in some real sense, existing in the real world, but the definition of good and evil that particular philosopher happens to want."

"Yes, but you do not understand the full profundity of what I preach, what I proclaim, what I declare as a prophet. I am not saying that someone's self-consciously constructed moral philosophy is the mere result of his moral preferences. I am saying something far more horrible and wonderful: that the most abstruse and technical metaphysical claims of any philosopher *and* his moral ruminations are *both* merely a reflection of his will to power. As a god, he creates his own universe and good and evil to go with it! So, you can see that Socrates, Plato, and all the rest of them entirely misunderstood the aim of philosophy. Philosophy as the desire for wisdom, the perfection of reason? No! Reason and philosophy are both *instruments* of will, the creative reflection of irrational passion to express our living strength!"

He now started rocking back and forth again, driven by some kind of manic passion, bubbling over with a kind of rebellious excitement that boys get from setting fires and breaking windows.

"Passion, yes, passion! Plato would have us suppress it—but that *was* his passion! Look at every basic drive inside men and ask yourself: Which of these has not, at one time or another, been the mischievous midwife of yet another philosophy? A spirit—or is it a demon?—driving the mind to create great webs of self-deceit, but such beautiful self-deceit! Each passion—name any one, I dare you—has at one time or another been the master architect of some philosopher's view of 'reason,' 'the cosmos,' even 'god.'"

Of course, I had read Nietzsche and knew where he was going, so I led him on, getting him to spell his whole view out. "So, philosophy is not the impersonal search for truth, but again, rather ... what? ... a kind of—"

Nietzsche interrupted, "In the philosopher there is nothing whatever that is impersonal. His philosophy tells you one thing, as I have so beautifully said: It reveals the inner order of his desires—which one is the master desire and which are its slaves, what his dominant and dominating lusts are, and where his creeping cowardice lies. His reason 'reports' this order, we might say, as if it were describing the world outside, when what is really happening is that he is creating the world outside in his own image!"

Nietzsche was really working himself up and was so absorbed in revealing to me the truth about philosophy and philosophers that he didn't at first hear that Edith Stein was playing the piano—and not just any piece, but one of Nietzsche's own compositions, "Enleitung."

I will not pretend that it was an amazingly beautiful piece. Nietzsche was an accomplished piano player, but he was not, by any means, a great composer. He worshiped Richard Wagner and became his good friend—or at least that's what Nietzsche thought.

As it turns out, behind Nietzsche's back Wagner laughed at the philosopher's compositions, however polite he was to his face. They had a great falling out, but I will not go into that here.

The important thing to point out here is that Nietzsche had a deep appreciation for beauty, especially in music, a great love of harmony and integrated complexity. Edith Stein had the same deep love of beautiful music, but she was a follower of St. Thomas—or, rather, *the truth*—and firmly held that beauty *and* truth were intimately, essentially connected. She understood that true beauty led to truth, just as the beauty of creation leads us to the existence of God.

So, Stein was more than rising to the occasion: She was baiting Nietzsche with beauty, the beautiful music that he himself had written and that now so evidently stirred his soul. After hearing several measures, he stopped talking as if struck by an arrow, slowly got up, and walked to the piano. He was drawn by the harmonious chords that Stein wrapped around his soul to reel him in, as if she were a fisher of men.

"You ... you are playing my music—my music ..." he said, as if he were a sleepwalker entering a delicious dream.

"Yes," she smiled at him and continued, "it's very beautiful, isn't it?"

"And you are playing it beautifully, with such feeling.... I ... I am very grateful. You somehow know how it sounds, within me, when I play it."

Stein acknowledged the compliment and stopped playing. "That was composed, if I'm not mistaken, by you, after Lou Salomé gave you one of her poems? No, I am mistaken—now I remember. I am thinking of 'Hymnus an das Leben,' 'Hymn to Life.' That is an even more beautiful piece. You put her poem to music, didn't you, because you loved her?"

"Wow!" I thought, she doesn't go for the little pricks and prods, but a spear and sword!

Nietzsche, who had been acting like some kind of thundering philosophical god, was now stammering as he tried to recover himself.

"This, this is all quite, quite personal, Fräulein Stein. I . . . I . . . I came here to speak about my philosophy. Yet, I am . . . so . . . moved by your playing, I would like to express my gratitude . . . but about Lou Salomé . . . if I may be excused from speaking about something so deeply personal . . ."

"But you just told us that all philosophy—including yours—was merely a *personal* memoir, a manifestation of a particular philosopher's inner drives, his passions, his deepest desires. I take you at your word, Herr Professor, and so I am just seeing if I can uncover what is driving *your* philosophy from within."

She said this all in apparent innocence, but she was being just as devious as Socrates ever was. Nietzsche still hadn't recovered, a sign that the philosopher Stein had played him correctly. He was having trouble moving beyond the stunned and stammering phase, so she helped coax him forward, at least to where she wanted him to go.

"You have a profound love of music, don't you, Herr Doctor Nietzsche, a deep, deep love of the beauty of music and poetry. And of Fräulein Salomé. She is still somehow in your heart, even now, along with the music that you wrote to her poetry?"

"She is a great woman . . . a beautiful woman, if I might say so. She deeply understands my philosophy."

"I wonder, did she read and approve of the rather awful things you said about women? That women were incapable of seeking truth, but merely sought ephemeral beauty? That women are wicked? That they are cats and cows, the weak and unintelligent half of mankind? That they are responsible, in their weak wickedness, for creating religion, so they can rule over men by using it as an instrument?"

"Well, I ... I ... you see, Fräulein ... you must understand that ..."

Needless to say, I had no desire to interrupt Stein's delicious inquisition. I thought she would continue to pound him on that point, but she instead began to play his song again, which did seem to soothe Nietzsche's somewhat savaged breast. He was, again, entranced.

She ended, folded her hands on her lap, and looked up at him with her very large, dark eyes. "Beauty and truth. Does it not seem that beauty leads to truth, real truth?"

Here, Nietzsche seemed to be able to shake himself out of her coils, and he struck somewhat a dismissive yet dramatic pose. "Truth! What is truth, says Pilate—and rightly so!"

"Well, Herr Doctor, I would say that truth is the conformity of the intellect to being—to what truly is—and that falsity is the lack of such conformity," she said matter-of-factly. "Philosophy got woefully off track, would you not agree, when René Descartes tried to found truth in the mere human intellect, as if the human intellect were the ultimate source of order in the world rather than nature, and the Creator of nature, God Himself. Of course, this error has its culmination in Kant, with his notion that we have no access to reality—the *noumenal* world, or 'things-in-themselves,' as he called it—but rather that it is our own mind that imposes order. But I believe that we would both agree that Kant's view of rationality was very thin—don't you think?—an undue restriction of reason rather than a healthy expansion of it to its proper perfection. This is too much indebted to the Enlightenment notion of a reality defined merely by numerical measurement. For what is Kant's understanding of reason but a reified notion of Newton's philosophical presuppositions? In any case, the attempt to place the source of truth in the human intellect has greatly misled us all philosophically for far too long. In particular, I believe that it is misleading *you*, and that you are really a great-grandson of

Descartes rather than an original philosopher. Please forgive me for being so blunt here, but these are the most important questions a human being can ask. So it is that you cry out that there is no truth but that which is fashioned by the human intellect, and that you are the first to realize this. But this all leads to a dead end, a very dead end, and you are trying to fashion a philosophy out of this dead end by declaring that God is dead and that we are the only creators left in the universe. That is a philosophical position — a position about life itself — that can lead only to insanity. Now, if you do not mind, Herr Doctor Nietzsche," she said, standing up, "I would like to join in the conversation, because I would like to ask you in more detail about your *Zarathustra*. But first, I would like to discuss your thesis in the *Genealogy of Morals*. Is that how it has been translated into English, Herr Doctor Wiker?" she asked, turning to me.

I nodded affirmatively, trying desperately not to laugh. Nietzsche looked as if he had been pinioned to the wall with a dozen sharp knives.

"Yes, that is what I thought," she continued. "I would especially like to focus on your notion of master and slave morality, Herr Doctor Nietzsche. Shall we go back over to the chess table?"

Nietzsche was gulping like a fish, trying to find some word, any word. But he had been pretty much stunned speechless by the rapid-fire display of Edith Stein's deep philosophical education, including her close reading of his works.

"I ... I didn't expect you to have such detailed knowledge of philosophy, Fräulein," he finally got out.

"That's Fräulein *Doctor* Stein. She has her doctorate in philosophy. Oh, did I forget to mention that?" I asked, lifting an eyebrow inquisitively.

"Doctor Stein?" he mumbled, as she walked past him and seated herself by the chess table.

And an interesting conversation it should be, I thought as Nietzsche walked slowly over. Two philosophers wrestling over the deepest questions: What is truth? How are we to live? Does God exist? I suspected Herr Nietzsche might very well have met his match.

Part 2

Edith Stein and Friedrich Nietzsche, a most unlikely pair, were sitting together passionately discussing philosophy at my humble chess table. Nietzsche had thought Edith Stein was merely a diminutive, uneducated woman on her way to the convent. Well, she *is* on her way to the convent—to enter the Carmelite order—but she is certainly no shrinking violet intellectually.

Nietzsche was quite fired up, fully engaged with Doctor Stein in setting forth his account of philosophy. His face had not only reddened, but the veins on his forehead stood out, as if his entire body was intent on pumping all its life to his brain for the effort.

"So you see, Doctor Stein, if we understand how moralities —and you would be so kind as to note I use the plural here, for they are only human creations, and quite diverse ones at that—how these morali*ties* come about historically and genealogically, then we find—we *always* find—that at their distinct beginnings there are always brave warriors, noble men, men who command!"

He sat upright, poking his right-hand index finger in the air, as if he were one of these commanding warriors, and declared, "And what *they* mean by good and evil, these noble ones, these ruthless ones, is simply this: 'Good' is a manifestation of their will to power. Good is what these men *will* as good. This is the first morality, *noble* morality, morality as defined by the nobles as opposed to the peasants and priests."

He spoke these last words as if spitting them out of his mouth with disdain. "Historically, this noble morality of the masters at first defines the entire society," and then he leaned forward, whispering to Stein, "including the gods," seemingly enjoying in advance the effect he thought it would have on her. "What is evil for these noble men? These masters? What is 'evil' is all that is *beneath* them! The poor and weak and pitiable and contemptible. The *slaves*!" He sat back and smiled, basking in his own illumination.

Rather than being shocked, Edith Stein seemed impatient to speak, as Nietzsche's string of declarations were coming in a dramatic torrent that was difficult to enter. "Yes, Herr Professor Nietzsche. I have read your *Genealogy of Morals*, and your *Zarathustra*. I therefore clearly understand your notion of master morality and slave morality—"

Before she could utter another syllable, Nietzsche literally jumped in again, leaping forward in his seat excitedly. "Slave morality! Yes, this is the morality created by the lowly, the natural slaves, the men without pride, the humble, groveling, sickly, weak sheep crawling along the earth," he said, walking his index and middle fingers across the chess table to illustrate. "And they, these natural slaves, create a god in their own miserable image. This god of the weak favors the weak and poor over the great and mighty, the real masters, the real wolves! I tell you, Fräulein Doctor Stein," and here he squinted at her, the better to see his effect on her, I assume, "I am here to liberate the wolves from sheepishness, from sheepery!"

He bobbed up and down in his chair now, barely able to contain himself. "What is good, Fräulein Stein, what is good? I will tell you! All that heightens the feeling of power, all that intensifies the will to power in the man who is a born master. What is bad? All that proceeds from weakness. So you see, that *is* master morality, the morality of the master, of the blond beast, of the lion that prowls and devours!" he shouted and then licked his lips. "The weak and ill-constituted shall perish, indeed must perish. Their extinction, their removal, that is the first principle of our *philanthropy*." He said the last word with evident relish. "And one shall have to help the weak to do so, to perish! Yes, because do you know what is far, far more harmful than any vice? Active sympathy, compassion, empathy for those who are ill-constituted and weak! *That* makes Christianity the greatest vice!"

"That last sentiment, it comes from the beginning of your book, *The Anti-Christ*, am I not right? I have read it, and would like to discuss it, but I see you squinting, Herr Nietzsche. You seem to have *weak* eyes."

"Yes, yes, I do," he admitted, almost in a way that seemed to be an invitation for sympathy from her. "It makes study very difficult, indeed excruciating."

She pressed him further on this rather interesting point. "And you mentioned previously your *weak* digestion. You didn't want coffee, so as not to upset your delicate stomach?"

"I must admit that it is delicate," he shook his head, oblivious to the deeper point she was making.

"And headaches, you tell us in your book *Ecce Homo* that you are plagued by migraines, thereby making your work even more difficult, I assume?"

"That is all too true. I believe the weakness of my eyes affects the weakness in my brain, in its proneness to headaches."

"A weak brain. Interesting, Herr Doctor Nietzsche, interesting."

She paused and looked at him quite directly, which made him rather uncomfortable, so that his eyes flicked off to the side. And then she continued, "But let me get to the main point, a very important point for me, to say the least. I know of your great contempt for Judaism, Herr Doctor. You regard it as a religion *of* the weak and lowly *for* the weak and lowly. In short, Judaism is slave morality." Her large brown eyes were piercing Nietzsche. "You should be aware that I am a Jew."

He fell back in his seat and laughed a bit strangely, I thought, as if he were expelling the notion with a burst of air. "I am not an anti-Semite, if that's what you mean! Indeed, I really do think it would be quite useful, not to mention fair, to expel all of those anti-Semitic screamers from Germany!" And he made a shooing motion, as if he were sweeping them away.

Stein was unconvinced. "But again, you do regard Judaism as the great corrupter, the religion of the weak that has corrupted master morality. Be straightforward with me, Herr Doctor. Do not consider me too weak to hear it from you in person, just because I am a Jew, for I have already read it in your books!"

"Very well then. You are a Christian now, and so I may speak to both," he said, smoothing out his mustache with his right hand and then rubbing both hands on his brown trousers, as if warming to the task. "Christianity is called the religion of pity, a religion of concern for the weak, the outcast, the lowly members of society. Fräulein Stein, you must understand that such pity, such compassion, *thwarts* the law of evolution. It throws a wrench into nature that hinders the law of natural selection, wherein nature *without pity* ceaselessly destroys the weak and elevates the strongest and the most fit. Such pity then is, as you can see, against nature — it denies life!"

He was twitching again, and his veins could be seen coursing the blood through his temples. "Christianity is therefore unnatural, for what is natural is the will of the strong over the weak, the strong dominating and eliminating the weeds. But what do we have with Christianity? It turns nature upside down! Christianity elevates the weak over the strong, and that is decadence itself!

It is the religion of the weakest, most pathetic sheep who think that they can dominate the beasts of prey by taming them, by pulling out their teeth and claws—and calling that holiness and humility!"

His voice had risen to a crescendo, but as he pronounced the last word, he suddenly grasped his temples and began rubbing them.

"Herr Doctor?"

"Yes," Nietzsche replied wearily, taking off his glasses and massaging his eyes.

"Your migraines, Herr Doctor? Could I get you some … wine perhaps? I am sure Herr Doctor Wiker would have some on hand."

"No, no, my weak stomach cannot take it!" He then paused, trying to gather his strength. "But I fight against my own sickness; that is my strength. What does not kill me makes me stronger!" He paused again, as if trying to drag his body uphill. "So I force myself to continue. As I was saying, Christianity is the religion of the weak slave. But Christianity came from Judaism."

"Christianity was and is the fulfillment of Judaism."

Nietzsche acted as if he hadn't heard. "The Jews! They started out well, you know. They began as a healthy, natural tribal religion, a religion defined by warfare and conquering. Yahweh was for them a conquering God, a God of war, a tribal deity, and the good king was a man of war." He smiled weakly. "That was master morality, morality defined by the noble warriors among the Jews—the warrior judges, not the whining prophets!"

Again, he gathered his strength, rubbing his temples. "But then the Jews were conquered, first by the Assyrians and then by the Babylonians. What then? The Jews then created a religion of losers, of defeat! Or, more precisely, the *priests* created it, a religion out of Jewish defeat, resignation, pitiful sheepery! Yahweh became the god of the conquered, the weak, the poor, the oppressed! A god created by slaves watching over slave morality!"

He put his glasses back on; his eyes were quite bloodshot. "The Jews, the Jews, the Jews—a people born for slavery, or borne into it by defeat. That marks the beginning of the slave rebellion in morality, the rebellion of the weak against the strong, against the natural masters, the conquerors! And we all know the next chapter, do we not? From Judaism grew Christianity, a sickly tree from a withered root. It gave us—as a deceitful and destructive 'gift'—the ultimate victory of slave morality!"

He then seemed to shrink in a kind of stupor, staring off to the left, worn out by his efforts.

"So, speaking as a Jew, would you like to see us eliminated?" asked Stein. "Would that not be *natural*? We who are responsible for bringing about Christianity, for the ultimate unnatural victory of the slaves over the masters, the masters of the master race, as it is called by so many today."

Nietzsche's attention returned as Stein continued: "I hear your words echoed all throughout Germany, Herr Doctor Nietzsche, and I feel the hand of Providence preparing a horrible sacrifice, a holocaust, for my people. I speak as a Jew and as a Christian."

This comment enlivened him; he gave a great snort and slapped his thigh. "Germany! Germany! I must tell you one of my little secrets, Fräulein Doctor Stein. It is one of my greatest ambitions to be considered a *despiser* of the Germans *par excellence*! Whenever I seek among the German people for some sign of tact, of taste, of delicacy of manners and subtle and strong intelligence in their assessment of *me* and *my* philosophy, I do so entirely in vain! But among the Jews? What a difference! Yes, in the Jews I find it all. They understand me! Germans? Never!"

"I thank you, as a Jew, for that small compliment," Stein said, deadpan. "But Herr Doctor, forgive me for pointing out that you were born in Germany. You are a German who writes his philosophy in German! You are angry because you believe that your fellow Germans have neglected your philosophy? Put aside your anger, Herr Doctor Nietzsche, because now I hear it reverberating throughout our land, creating a deafening din, something terrifying and terrible among the Germans!"

This very much pleased him and revived him further. He leaned forward and scowled menacingly, "Let the terror come! Fräulein, I am by far the most terrible human being who has existed so far!" He lifted an eyebrow and added, "This does not mean that I am not most beneficial as well! For I shall pull sunken humanity out of the swamp, the mire, the mud of Christianity that pulls it down, pulls it toward the lowest and weakest. And in pulling humanity out, I shall create a new greatness—new noble men, bold and pitiless, men driven by the will to conquer, and they will conquer weakness and the weak, and create the over-man!"

At the thought of this, he was giddy, rocking back and forth several times before he leaned toward Stein like a prowling lion. "I am no man, Fräulein Stein; I am dynamite! I am the Antichrist!"

At that moment, he looked the part. His eyes were dilated; his nostrils flared; and the veins on his temples were now visibly palpitating. He had also begun to twitch around his eyes.

"You mean you are the destroyer of Christianity, and, therefore, of its foundation, Judaism. You are the self-proclaimed destroyer of slave morality, of my people!"

He stood up abruptly and held his hands out wide, "Yes, *ecce homo*! Behold the man!" He then leaned down and looked Doctor Stein in the eye. "But I, Zarathustra, bring with me the call for the higher man—the over-man, the aristocratic man—a return to the natural and original foundation of 'morality,' and I do it for the *sake* of humanity."

He threw back his coattails and walked briskly past Stein to the bookcase behind her. "Do you not know—must you not agree—Fräulein Doctor Stein, that every advancement, every step of progress of mankind has been the work of an aristocratic society! All the greatest art, all the greatest literature, all the greatest music, all the most glorious temples, gods, and kings! Let us admit to ourselves, shall we, for once not even trying to be considerate to the feelings of the weak, how *every* higher culture on earth so far has begun."

He began strutting back and forth, gesturing to make his points. "Let us go back to the beginning, shall we? If we look at human beings whose nature was still natural, that is, when they were as yet unspoiled by Christianity and the rule of the weak, these men were still barbarians in *every terrible sense of the word*! They were men of prey, lions, wolves, eagle-men with the sharpest teeth, claws, and talons, men who were still in possession of the unbroken strength of the will to power and hence full of the natural and beautiful *lust* for power! These men *threw* themselves upon the weaker but far more 'civilized' and peaceful races, devoured them, digested them, and turned them into their slaves!"

He had come around to his seat again and flopped down in it as if exhausted but happy. "Ah, yes! These beautiful barbarians were more fully human beings, more natural—which also means, at every level, *more beastly*!"

Edith Stein looked at him intently for a moment, her hands folded calmly on her lap, her large brown eyes searching Nietzsche's face for I don't know what. Finally she said, "The barbarians you call for are at the gates—in fact, inside the gates. And they chant your song, Herr Doctor. It rings in my ears, as I have said. The Germans have embraced you. They have embraced your philosophy as the truth, and it has made them more beastly. So, as good philosophers, shall we examine what so many have accepted and test it to see if it is genuine? Let us get right to the heart of things. I sense there is not much time. At the very heart of your philosophy is the denial of the existence of God—more exactly, the Christian understanding of God. Instead, you believe that the universe is without a creator. The universe is unknowable and meaningless, even cruel—something you imbibed from the philosopher Schopenhauer, wasn't it? This is not a new idea, by any means."

"I have read him deeply, yes. But I have gone *beyond* him!"

"And precisely because, like Herr Schopenhauer, you believe that there is nothing left in this meaningless, godless universe but our naked will, you also believe that there is ultimately no truth, no beauty, no morality, no true goodness. And since there is none, then we human beings must *create* it all—as if we were gods, each creating our own universe? Or, to be more accurate, this is a task for the greatest master, the greatest philosopher. For not just anyone can be this creating 'god.' It must be someone quite *un*ordinary, not a man of the common herd as you might put it, but someone quite extraordinary—not a mere man!"

Nietzsche was bubbling with enthusiasm and blurted out, "Not, not a man, but an *over*-man!"

"So speaks your Zarathustra! I've read your ... 'Bible,' as you call it."

"My dear *Thus Spoke Zarathustra*! My dearest book. You've read it!" He sat back and sighed in self-satisfaction. "Nothing like this has ever been written, has ever even been felt or suffered, not in the history of the world. Oh, how I suffered to bring forth this book of life! Thus suffers a god, a Dionysius! I, Zarathustra. I, Dionysius!"

And here, believe it or not, he stood up and bowed and then reverently put his right hand over his chest.

Not amused by philosophical blasphemy, or philosophical foolishness, Stein said quite sharply, "You speak as if you were already deified, already a god yourself!"

"Oh, but I am, I am, I am! Yes, Zarathustra experiences himself as the supreme type of all beings, the supreme being!" he declared, speaking of himself in the third person.

"You are a god because there is no God?" she said, incensed. "Because God is 'dead,' as you say? God is dead? So you must take His place—step into His sandals, so to speak?"

"Yes, we are no longer believers in God, we modern men. But we *need* a god, a commanding god, a created and creating god, a source of meaning and value who can lift us out of the mud and mire created by the democratic herd, always mooing and grunting about equality! Without such a god, humanity will end in the most wretched state of mediocrity, where all have been equalized in the herd. This is the last man, the herd animal, barely a man at all—with no God to redeem him! No shepherd and one herd! Everybody is the same! And whoever feels different, whoever tries to stand upright in the midst of the bleating herd—well, he must go voluntarily into a madhouse!"

Stein paused and then said with a note of sarcasm tinged with sadness, "Or involuntarily." Knowing that Nietzsche had ultimately been driven insane and ended his life in a madhouse of his own making, she both saw his future and was determined to save him from his own mental damnation. "You reject the existence of God because ..." she said, waiting for him to fill in the blank.

He replied smugly. "Because, because, because," he almost sang, "because if there *were* indeed gods, how could I possibly endure *not* being a god? A mere mortal—that is more than I can bear! So, logic dictates, we might say, that there are no gods!"

In fact, Nietzsche seemed even now to be losing his capacity for logic.

"Jealousy of the divine! A very old disease, Herr Doctor! Old as the devil."

Nietzsche seemed not to mind the implication at all.

She continued, "But do you really think that you, a mere man, can take the place of God? Do you believe that you have the *strength* to face the Great Darkness, the Formlessness, the Chaos of a world without God, a chaos where there is no real meaning, no real order, no true moral goodness or beauty but only that which man himself creates out of nothingness? Or is this all a rebellious child's poetry and bluster?"

He stretched out his arms as if floating above the void. "I am a god brooding above that chaos, the meaningless nothingness of nature, mastering that chaos, giving form to ultimate formlessness, creating with my hammer after smashing with my hammer! I declare that all is chaos and darkness, yet out of my superabundant strength I squeeze that darkness and create light! I give light! I am light from the darkest abyss of the heavens! I create meaning out of nonmeaning, gods out of not-gods, and I make good and evil, *my* good and evil, all crafted out of pitiless and indifferent nature!" he shouted triumphantly.

"You are quite mad, Herr Doctor! Sanity is only had by truth, and truth is, as I have said, to grasp reality—what *really is*! But the universe has its own order; it has its own form; it has its own wisdom expressed in the intelligibility that makes science possible. We do not create order; we discover it."

Rather than bringing Nietzsche to his senses, Stein's rational philosophical scolding pushed Nietzsche further into his self-made universe, where he reigned as god; he now stood on his chair and struck a pose, as if a Greek statue of Zeus.

Stein stood up, lashing out at the mad philosopher, "You, Herr Doctor Nietzsche, seem to be jealous of that order precisely because you did not create it. You do not *want* God to exist! You want to believe that the heavens and earth are merely accidents so you can be the god of it all. Am I right?"

He stared off nobly into the distance and declared solemnly, "Truly, truly, it is a blessing, not blasphemy, when I teach, when I *reveal*, that over all things and at the root of all things is 'accident,' mere 'chance.' But no, no, my dear Fräulein. If there is one god who rules all—the deity that governs our universe, and it is actually the fickle and blind mother goddess, Chance! That is the goddess with whom we must wrestle!"

Stein snapped back, "You *want* to create truth. You *want* to create good and evil. You *want* to create meaning. You *want* to be the creator of gods made in your own image! You *want* all these things *and therefore* you embrace an entirely meaningless, purposeless cosmos! You wish to worship Chance; you wish her to be the idol before which you bow down so that you may become the god before whom all others bow down!"

Nietzsche struck another imperial pose. "By Chance! Yes, that is the most ancient nobility of the world, the cruelest and most noble truth that we have smothered under our layers of gods. But I, Zarathustra, have restored to all things this brutal and natural beginning point, a very sharp point indeed. I deliver all from the bondage of purpose, meaning, intelligibility, truth, good, and evil. I reveal the great mystery of nothingness and purposelessness!"

And here he was laughing almost maniacally, and then suddenly he crouched down and stared right into Stein's face from inches away. "In everything, everything, everything, everything, *one* thing is impossible. Rationality!"

He then did a little dance as he moved away from her, and he then began peering at my books on the shelf.

"So you embrace irrationality and madness? You embrace mere will without reason, and so reject the defining human capacity, the capacity rooted in our being made in the image of God as the only creature on earth capable of knowing truth?"

Nietzsche swung his hand as if it had a giant club in it. "I smash that image! I free humanity from that idol! A will to truth? You desire truth? Well, now, my dear Fräulein, let us will untruth instead!"

And again he began dancing, this time humming to himself the "Blue Danube Waltz," of all things. He then looked around for a partner, quickly deciding on an old coat that I had hung on my coatrack. Taking the coat in hand as if it were an elegant lady, he bowed before it quite graciously and began waltzing around the room as he hummed the tune louder and louder.

Poor Edith Stein now nearly had to shout to be heard. "To embrace falsehood as if it were true — that is the essence of insanity! You are courting insanity, Herr Doctor, as if it were health!"

Nietzsche was not strong, as I've noted, and he soon collapsed on the piano bench, smiling as his eyes looked off into some distance of his own imagination.

Doctor Stein walked slowly over, with a look of compassion. She glanced at me and then leaned on the piano, studying Nietzsche's faraway face.

"You are truly mad, yet I believe that you, above all, have understood what atheism truly means. The denial of God means embracing a universe as a meaningless ebb and flow of matter, a universe in which there is neither high nor low, good or evil, truth or falsehood. There is only the raw and ultimately pointless efforts of the human will as the source of order in a cold and purposeless cosmic ocean. You understand — as a Jew understands from Genesis — that without God, there is only the void. And you — I congratulate you on this, at least! — *you* feel the real terror of a world without God."

Her voice was so tender now, almost a whisper. "For Christians, this shapeless darkness is called the dark night of the soul, where one feels entirely abandoned by God, adrift in a formless sea, abandoned as Christ Himself felt abandoned on the Cross, as Christ Himself *suffered* on the Cross. I see what you have done, what you are trying to do, Friedrich. You try to embrace that dark night where there appears to be no God; you embrace it as an atheist, and you try, with all your strength, to rejoice in that darkness, to *create* in it, even though you know that these creations

251

are ultimately meaningless as well. You embrace that darkness as if it were Light? You want to be both Christ and Creator? Do you think you really have the strength of God? Won't that burden break you, crush you, destroy you? Isn't that a burden only Christ Himself, only a true God, could bear?"

She had tears in her eyes and her voice was trembling.

Nietzsche suddenly laughed, and looked straight into her eyes, "I am the crucified one! That is how I sign my letters now."

"I beg your pardon, Herr Doctor?" Stein said, confused.

"Yes, I must tell you, all of you, that I run crisscross on my Mount of Olives with warm feet," and he made little running motions with his index and middle fingers. "And in the sunny nook of my Mount of Olives, you will hear me sing and sing—and mock all pity!"

Edith Stein and I exchanged glances. Nietzsche was clearly losing his mind right in front of us. In fact, he was losing his mind in my office in much the same way that he lost it over the last few years of his life. Some have tried to blame the boiling down of his brains on the syphilis he had contracted when younger. But it was quite clear to both of us that the burden of being a true atheist, of pretending he could be a creator and redeemer in a godless cosmos, was crushing his soul.

He suddenly sat bolt upright and declared, "The old God has abdicated, and so I shall have to rule the world from now on!"

And he truly looked as if he was readying himself for the task, preparing to take that great weight upon his fragile shoulders. But then, oddly, he giggled.

I cleared my throat and walked closer to the piano. It was time to intervene. "Herr Doctor Nietzsche, I think we'd better—"

Before I could take his arm, he stood up, walked briskly past me, and began pacing in front of my desk.

"Take a letter to Franz Overbeck," he said as he breezed by Fräulein Stein, thinking she was his secretary. "I cannot see well enough to write." He stopped and looked off toward the window, folding his hands behind his back officiously. "Say this: 'Dear friend, please know that I myself am even now preparing a memorandum for all the courts of Europe, for the sake of creating an anti-German league.'"

He walked over to my bookcase by the window and picked up a small dagger I had displayed there. "'I mean to sew up the German Reich in an iron shirt, and thereby I shall elicit from them a war of desperation!'"

He then unsheathed the dagger, but instead of thrusting it at one of us—which was what I immediately feared—he held both arms out wide, as if being crucified himself. "'I shall not have my hands free, you know, until I have the emperor in my hands.'"

Before I could grab him or the knife, he came out of his cruciform position and said quite casually to Doctor Stein, "Sign that 'Nietzsche Caesar'—just sign it 'N.' Have you got all that, just as dictated?"

She was completely at a loss for words. I took the opportunity to remove the dagger carefully from Nietzsche's hands and then led him back to the piano bench. On the way there, he stopped again and said to Stein, "No, sign that, 'The Crucified.'"

She gently took his other arm and helped lead him the rest of the way to the piano bench. His head bobbled, rocking back and forth between his escorts, speaking with us as if we were confidants.

"This autumn—I was lightly dressed as I could be in such weather—I twice attended my funeral. The first time I attended as Count Robilant." He then stopped, trying to recollect the facts of his fantasy. "No, Count Robilant is my son, insofar as I am Carlo Alberto!"

We were both quite at a loss as to what we should do next. The good philosopher then suggested, "Perhaps, Herr Doctor Nietzsche, Friedrich, a little music would soothe your savaged breast?"

This seemed to delight him; he struck his thighs and then rubbed his hands, readying himself to play something that, we now hoped, would bring himself partly back to his senses. Before setting his hands to the keys, he abruptly sang, quite loudly and out of tune, "I am Dionysius, Dionysius I am! God of music, of poetry, of will, and chaos and creation!"

We had no idea what would come next, but he began playing very thoughtfully and slowly one of his own pieces—I cannot recall which, since I do not know his music. But then, when all seemed much better, he began to bang on the keys, first with his fists, and then with his elbows. As an accompaniment to this cacophonous offering to Dionysius, he began howling like an animal.

Before we could seize him to try to calm him down, he sat upright and announced, "I should tell you that I have had Caiaphas put in chains. Yes, I too was crucified, at great length mind you—last year. By the German doctors!" Then he made a dismissive sweeping motion with his right hand and added "Wilhelm Bismarck and all the anti-Semites—I shall do away with them!" As Stein leaned forward to hold his arm again, he leaned toward her and whispered in her ear as if confiding a conspiracy, "All the anti-Semites—I am just about to have them all shot!"

We got on either side of him again and helped him up. I motioned toward my blue plush chair. He was a bit difficult to guide, as he had relapsed into a kind of catatonic state.

"I think that it's time for a bit of a rest, Herr Doctor," I said as we set him in the chair.

He then intoned, mechanically, like a creature with a shattered soul, "I am dead because I am stupid. I am stupid because I am dead. I am dead because I am stupid. I am stupid because I am dead. I am dead because I am stupid. I am stupid because I am dead ..." He soon seemed to drift off to sleep, muttering the same thing over and over again.

I looked down at him, the great atheist philosopher. "So ends the quest to become a god, a Tower of Babel, falling into babble."

I continued to watch Nietzsche as he mouthed the horrible words he seemed doomed to repeat eternally. What I did not see, at first, was that Edith Stein was now dressed in the full habit of the Discalced Carmelites. How this happened, I cannot tell you.

"Yes, he thought he could be a god," she said, full of pity, "holding up the heavens and creating a new earth. So he ends, his music crumbling into noise, harmony into cacophony, rationality into irrational insanity, rebellion into utter self-destruction. He thought he could take the place of God as Creator and Redeemer. He thought he was strong enough."

She paused, and I turned around, quite astonished to see the philosopher transformed into St. Teresa Benedicta of the Cross.

Taking no notice of my perplexity, she continued, "So, God let him have what he thought he desired. The most merciful and wise and just God put the great burden of being God upon Nietzsche and, behold, it entirely crushed him. Yes, Nietzsche got what he wanted, but he really did not understand what he desired. He was crushed by the darkness that he willingly embraced."

"Fräulein Doctor Stein, I mean Teresa Benedicta of the Cross. Yes, yes, I believe that you are exactly right."

"I sometimes think, as I have indicated, that he was the only honest atheist, the only one who truly understood what the absence of God really meant — that it is the darkest night that the soul can experience. He did not understand, as Teresa of Avila understood, and as I myself know so very well, that no human being can withstand that dark night without the Grace of God won in Jesus Christ, who immersed Himself in that dark night on the Cross."

She then smiled peacefully, adding, "In a way, he was strangely in tune with Christianity — in wanting to become Christ-like, even to the point of crucifixion. He wanted to be the Antichrist, but he then had to define himself by Christ. In doing so, he believed he could become more than Christ."

She then walked slowly over to the great crucifix on my wall, which hung just above where Nietzsche now sat. She reached up and stroked it. "The dark night of the soul. All those who belong to Christ are destined to pass through all the stages of His life, leading to Gethsemane and Golgotha. When that terrible hour comes, external sufferings are nothing compared with the dark night of the soul—in that night when the divine light ceases to shine and the voice of God is silent."

She turned around to look at me as if I needed comfort—which, I must admit, I rather welcomed. "It isn't that God isn't there, but that he's concealed and silent." She glanced down at Nietzsche's head, slumped off to the side as he continued to mutter in his sleep. "Or, in Nietzsche's case, rejected and silenced."

I felt compelled to ask why God allowed such a thing, why He would embrace such a thing on the Cross, why He would ask it of us pitifully weak creatures, but all I could croak out was, "Why ..."

"Why the dark night of the soul? That is one of God's secrets, and no one can fully penetrate it. Each of us, in this life, is balanced perpetually on the razor's edge. On one side, there is absolute nothingness. On the other is the fullness of Divine Life. Nietzsche wished to leap into nothingness and create his own divine life, but that cannot be done."

She reached down over the top of the chair and, like a gentle mother, brushed Nietzsche's hair away from his closed eyes. "Herr Nietzsche wanted to become a god. The irony is that that is just what we are offered in Christ. He offers us divinity. Through Him —through the Cross—we are made divine. But Herr Nietzsche rejected that gift when he rejected God."

She stepped back from the chair and faced me, with her hands now tucked into the sleeves of her habit. "That's why I gave up on my career in philosophy ... well, that, and the fact that the Nazis prohibited all Jews from teaching! All my life I was on fire to discover truth, and after years of studying philosophy—which was quite wonderful, please understand—I realized by the grace of God and a great push from St. Teresa of Avila that the truth isn't a set of propositions, but a Person. And so, if I really loved Truth with all my heart, as every philosopher declares, then I must love that Person with all my heart. So, you see me now!" She lifted her arms, her habit fanning out as if she were a great bird, or a black and brown angel. "I have traded in my doctoral gown for the habit of the Carmelites. From Jew, to atheist, to a Discalced Carmelite—only God could bring about such a journey!"

"Given what you said about your awakening while reading St. Teresa of Avila, I understand why you chose the name Teresa, but tell me more about the 'of the Cross' part."

"The Cross is where we meet Truth. The Cross is both the heart and the mind of faith. It is the destiny of every Christian," she added.

I must admit that I know this to be the case, but I am continually trying to avoid giving it much thought—unlike the saint before me. This is an act of cowardice on my part, but of the greatest courage on hers.

She continued, "The Cross is my destiny in a very special way—a Jew like Christ who has embraced Christ and His Cross. By the Cross, Doctor Wiker, I understand the fate of the people of God, of the Jews, the fate now being prepared for the Jews in Germany. I embrace that crucifixion as my vocation." She smiled, adding, "After all, one cannot wish for a deliverance from the Cross when one bears the noble title 'of the Cross.'"

"And, Sister Teresa Benedicta, this man, this madman, helped prepare that cross for you by the influence of his philosophy among the Germans, whatever he may have uttered against anti-Semitism."

"Well, he may have personally hated both anti-Semites and his fellow Germans, but even in the Great War the German troops received copies of *Thus Spoke Zarathustra*. He had died in 1900, almost fifteen years before that horrible war broke out. And now again, his words are in their mouths. Whether the Nazis now truly understand him or not, they have welcomed his description of Judaism as the origin of slave morality—as a contagion—in order to give philosophical support to their anti-Semitism. The Germans believe they are, indeed, the master race, and we are parasites, to be exterminated once and for all."

"You are afraid, then?" I asked.

"I willingly go to the Cross, as both a Jew and a Christian. Nietzsche proclaimed himself to be the Antichrist. Well, the Antichrist now comes. Like Nietzsche, he hates the Cross. I can tell you, more than ever, the Cross is a sign of contradiction, and these followers of the Antichrist show it every dishonor. They desecrate images of the Cross; they make every effort to tear the Cross out of the hearts of Christians."

"Will you not try to escape to safety, out of Germany?"

I knew this was a foolish thing to ask, but also that I was not the only one to say it. I'm sure many had begged to escape. But what would it mean if she took my advice? Would she now be *Saint* Teresa Benedicta?

Smiling serenely, she said, "I have made a vow to my Mother Superior, and she accepted it. Such vows may not be broken. I asked her, please, to permit me to offer myself to the Heart of Jesus as a sacrifice of atonement for true peace—a holocaust. For what? I offered myself so that, if possible, the reign of Antichrist might be broken so that we could avoid another world war—and instead a new social order might be established, one built upon better foundations. And so you see, Herr Doctor Wiker, I joyfully accept in advance the death God has appointed for me to allow me to fulfill that vow, and I do so willingly, in peaceful submission to His most holy will, knowing that His Son went before me on His Cross. I pray, then, not to avoid the Cross, but rather that the Lord will accept my life and death for the honor and glory of His holy name and for the needs of His Holy Church—especially for our holy order of Carmelites. But even here I ask for more, for I offer myself in sacrifice for the Jewish people—my people, God's people. I ask that the Lord may be received by His own people, for He became one of them, and that they may know and love Jesus Christ as I have come to know and love Him as my Redeemer. I also ask for the deliverance of Germany from its self-inflicted madness, and for peace throughout the whole world. Yes, and I pray finally, for all my relatives, both alive and dead, that none of them may be lost to God's kingdom."

I nodded at Nietzsche. "And do you offer yourself for him, for the man who helped Germany prepare this sacrifice?"

She looked at him with almost painful tenderness. "I firmly believe that the Lord has accepted my life as a sacrificial offering for all, just as Christ died for all—for the Jews, for the Nazis, and, yes, even for Herr Doctor Nietzsche. If God is within us, as we profess He is, and if God is love, as we know He is, then we must love our brothers and sisters. So it cannot be otherwise than this: that our love of human beings, all human beings, is the measure of our love of God. For the Christian, the true follower of Christ, there is no such thing as a stranger, for even the enemy is to be loved. Our neighbor is always the one who needs us most; it does not matter whether he lives next to us or whether he is related to us, or whether we like him, or whether he is morally deserving of such love, or whether he is a friend or an enemy. He must be loved."

"And so you willingly go—to your death. You know that, don't you? They *will* kill you."

"It is my vocation, Herr Doctor. She lifted her hands again, gesturing to her habit. "All who want to be married to the Lamb, as members of a religious order, must allow themselves to be fastened to the Cross—with Him, the bridegroom."

"Thy will be done," I managed to say, taking out my handkerchief to wipe my eyes. When I looked again she was gone, and so was Nietzsche.

Reflections

Friedrich Nietzsche is one of the most influential *and* misunderstood modern philosophers. I remember in graduate school—and this was in a religion course, mind you—my far-left professors, especially the women, all crowed about Nietzsche. They believed that he was a great ally in getting beyond Christianity and modernity to something they called the post-Christian, postmodern world. They didn't understand what Nietzsche quite clearly grasped: that in a world without God, the only deity left is the raw human will, which meant the transfer of worship to our own unguided passions—especially the most powerful passions of the most powerful people. The Nazis were the awful political guides ushering us into a post-Christian, postmodern world, a world beyond good and evil.

On Sunday, August 2, 1942, at about 5 p.m., the Nazis knocked on the door of the Carmel convent where St. Teresa Benedicta of the Cross was staying. She and her sister Rosa were seized by the Gestapo. As with all those shipped off in cattle cars, St. Teresa was given a number: 44074. A week later she arrived at the notorious Auschwitz concentration camp, and along with her sister and who knows how many others, she was ushered into the gas chambers—fastened to the Cross with Christ, as a willing sacrifice.

St. Teresa understood, in the deepest sense, that the reign of the Nazis was part of the reign of the Antichrist: the satanic bid for power over the earth and all in it. Their cruelty was superhuman cruelty, relishing in blood and destruction, and especially in the destruction of God's Chosen People.

This fact, which St. Teresa Benedicta embraced in all its mysterious depth, we must never forget: Jesus Christ chose to be a Jew, and ascending into Heaven, body and soul, He did not shed His Jewish body to rise as a disembodied deity. Once a Jew, always a Jew. I think we can assume that the devil hates Jews even more than the Nazis did, or at least that the Nazis' hatred was a reflection of satanic hatred.

But this fact must not be forgotten either: The Crucifixion is the victory over Satan and death. In willingly embracing the Cross, St. Teresa Benedicta prevailed over those who tried to destroy her. St. John Paul II beatified her as a martyr in 1987 and canonized her in 1998.

I am often amazed at the ignorance and confusion of so many who call themselves philosophers but dismiss theology as irrational, pridefully proclaiming that they have chosen *reason* over blind faith. The modern philosophical attempt to affirm human reason as the highest authority ended in Nietzsche, who boldly announced that *all* human reason was based on irrational will. The modern rejection of God ended, appropriately, in the modern rejection of rationality.

By contrast, Edith Stein—every bit as intelligent as Nietzsche —searched diligently for truth, first as an atheist, but then as a convinced Christian. Reason led to a faith that was not a rejection of rationality and reality but rather the greatest affirmation of both. She found *more* truth through her reason transformed by grace; it was as if with her natural eyes she could see two miles, but with supernaturally transformed eyes, a thousand. As St. Thomas rightly taught, "Grace does not destroy nature but perfects it."

Edith Stein and Friedrich Nietzsche: Reflections

That is a good place to end my accounts of saints versus scoundrels. The saints are not out to destroy our enjoyment of this life but to usher us toward far *greater* joy and exaltation. The modern philosophers who rejected God all promised that, once freed from God, we could become as gods — the great definers of our own good and evil, of our own truth and falsity, of our own Heaven. This is the greatest act of idolatry ever perpetrated by mankind, and it culminated in the twentieth century with the creation of a man-made hell on earth — not only among the Nazis but among the communists as well.

This dual darkness caused more suffering than the world had ever witnessed, and precisely under the promise and pretense of replacing Christianity with something better. In doing so, these movements proved the central truths of Christianity more profoundly and practically than any debate ever could. Human beings are made in the image of God. If we reject God, we will always create false gods in *our own* image. In so doing, we destroy our identity, our humanity, and our very selves.

Let us end with one saint's praise of another: St. John Paul II's words about St. Teresa Benedicta of the Cross at her canonization.

> The depth of the divine mystery became perceptible to her in the silence of contemplation. Gradually, throughout her life, as she grew in the knowledge of God, worshiping him in spirit and truth, she experienced ever more clearly her specific vocation to ascend the Cross with Christ, to embrace it with serenity and trust, to love it by following in the footsteps of her beloved Spouse: St. Teresa Benedicta of the Cross is offered to us today as a model to inspire us and a protectress to call upon.
>
> We give thanks to God for this gift. May the new saint be an example to us in our commitment to serve freedom,

in our search for the truth. May her witness constantly strengthen the bridge of mutual understanding between Jews and Christians. St. Teresa Benedicta of the Cross, pray for us! Amen.[4]

What better way to conclude than in supplication to the great men and women whom we met in these pages. St. Augustine, St. Francis, St. Thomas More, and yes, Flannery O'Connor: Pray for us, so that we may become saints rather than scoundrels!

[4] "Homily for the Canonization of Edith Stein," October 11, 1998.

About the Author

Benjamin Wiker is, first of all, a husband and a father of seven children. He graduated from Furman University with a B.A. in political philosophy, and has an M.A. in religion and a Ph.D. in theological ethics, both from Vanderbilt University. He is also a Senior Fellow at the Veritas Center for Ethics and Public Life, Franciscan University.

Dr. Wiker has taught at Marquette University, St. Mary's University (Minnesota), and Thomas Aquinas College (California) and is now professor of political science and director of Human Life Studies at Franciscan University (Ohio). During these many years of teaching, he has offered a wide variety of courses in political philosophy, political science, philosophy, theology, history, the history and philosophy of science, the history of ethics, the Great Books, Latin, and even mathematics. He has published thirteen books and is the writer and host of EWTN's *Saints vs. Scoundrels*.